continued . . .

D1051771

"CWO Mike Durant's heroism should be read by every American. His riveting story epitomizes the courage and leadership of the members of our military forces, and the sacrifices they make for all of us—and the terrible impact these sacrifices have on their families. I was thrilled and moved by this book."

—Ross Perot

"Hats off to Mike Durant's gripping first-person account of his Somalian combat and captivity. He never lost hope, and like his Night Stalker comrades, this *Black Hawk Down* pilot never quit. His inspiring true story should be required reading for all Special Operators, and anyone who wants to understand this breed of courageous, devoted warrior."

—Major John Plaster, U.S. Army Special Forces (ret.),
author of *SOG: The Secret Wars of
America's Commandos in Vietnam*

"*In the Company of Heroes* is the heroic narrative of a brave and selfless soldier performing his duties the only way he knew how—with honor and respect for his country. This is a significant account of men at war, but more important, it is a personal account of duties performed in combat, of personal courage and an unbreakable will to survive. Mike Durant's story, told so well in these pages, is a must read for those who send troops to fight, those who lead them, and first and foremost, those who, like Durant, take the fight to the enemy."

—General Gordon R. Sullivan, U.S. Army (ret.)

THE NIGHT STALKERS

**Top Secret Missions of the U.S. Army's
Special Operations Aviation Regiment**

Michael J. Durant
and Steven Hartov

with Lt. Col. (Ret.) Robert L. Johnson

NAL
CALIBER

NAL Caliber
Published by New American Library, a division of
Penguin Group (USA) Inc., 375 Hudson Street,
New York, New York 10014, USA
Penguin Group (Canada), 90 Eglinton Avenue East, Suite 700, Toronto,
Ontario M4P 2Y3, Canada (a division of Pearson Penguin Canada Inc.)
Penguin Books Ltd., 80 Strand, London WC2R 0RL, England
Penguin Ireland, 25 St. Stephen's Green, Dublin 2,
Ireland (a division of Penguin Books Ltd.)
Penguin Group (Australia), 250 Camberwell Road, Camberwell, Victoria 3124,
Australia (a division of Pearson Australia Group Pty. Ltd.)
Penguin Books India Pvt. Ltd., 11 Community Centre, Panchsheel Park,
New Delhi - 110 017, India
Penguin Group (NZ), 67 Apollo Drive, Rosedale, North Shore 0632,
New Zealand (a division of Pearson New Zealand Ltd.)
Penguin Books (South Africa) (Pty.) Ltd., 24 Sturdee Avenue,
Rosebank, Johannesburg 2196, South Africa

Penguin Books Ltd., Registered Offices:
80 Strand, London WC2R 0RL, England

Published by NAL Caliber, an imprint of New American Library, a division of Penguin Group
(USA) Inc. Previously published in a G. P. Putnam's Sons edition.

First NAL Caliber Printing, January 2008
10 9 8 7 6 5 4 3 2 1

NAL Caliber Trade Paperback ISBN: 978-0-451-22291-6

Book Design by Lovedog Studio

Printed in the United States of America

ACKNOWLEDGMENTS

Many thanks to Al Zuckerman at Writers House, Mark Chait and all the staff at Putnam/New American Library for their assistance in making this project a reality. They recognized, as did we, the significance of these incredible stories of courage and sacrifice that otherwise would have remained untold.

There are scores of people who helped in the research, interviews, preparation, and completion of this book. Many will be found within these pages, while others participated in critical ways, yet due to time and space constraints, their stories must wait until a later date to be fully told. Several senior officers who serve in critical positions within the Department of Defense encouraged the publication of this work without seeking credit. We are grateful to all, and ask the indulgence of anyone whose contributions to the success of this project, and more importantly to the defense of this great Nation, remain inadvertently unmentioned.

Maj. Arlo Hurst, 160th RS5; Kim Laudano, 160th Public Affairs Officer; Kelly Tyler, 160th Public Affairs Officer; Carol Darby Jones, USASOC Public Affairs Officer; Walt Sokalski, USASOC Public Affairs

Officer; Charles H. Briscoe, Ph.D., USASOC History Office; MW4 (ret.) Carl Brown; Col. (ret.) Randy Cochran; Col. (ret.) Ben Couch; BG (ret.) John "the Coach" Dailey; CW5 Terry Frabott; MG (ret.) Lou Hennies; CW5 (ret.) Randy Jones; Kurt Muse; SSG Doug Wonacott; BG (ret.) Howard Yellen.

Like most things in life, this effort could not have been accomplished without the support of our families. We are forever indebted to them for their love, patience, courage, and understanding.

And, finally, to those who've served in this great organization. The incredible accomplishments and the contributions made by so few have helped provide stability and freedom for so many.

CONTENTS

FOREWORD

IN THE DEEPEST DARKNESS, at some hour between midnight and dawn, you believe you hear them coming.

At first it is merely a pulse, a disturbance in the ether, and as your ears prick up and you tilt your head to listen, a gust of wind obscures it, and for a moment you return to illusion. You are safe. They could not possibly reach you here, so far away, so high, so hidden. They may want your life for the things you have done in the name of your cause, but it will not happen here in this impregnable place. Your heart rate slows again. You smile thinly at your own fears. You nod slowly, and then you suddenly freeze as the sound returns. It is unmistakable now. Helicopters.

Long before they are upon you, which will happen very swiftly now, you see them in your mind's eye. Their black armored bodies gleam beneath the starlight, their engines thunder, their sharp blades dice the clouds to ribbons. Behind their soulless eyes you can see their pilots, their hard-set jaws, centurion-like helmets and the glowing tubes of their mechanical eyes. From the gills of those charging sharks, charcoal-colored gun barrels bristle. From their open flanks, the boots of many warriors whip in the wind. Their weapons gleam.

You can barely breathe now. Nothing you do to deter them will matter. They will still come. You can flee, but they will find you.

They own the night. . . .

TWENTY-FIVE YEARS AGO, on an October dawn at Fort Campbell, Kentucky, a new battle flag was unfurled. The pennant featured a starless night and a full yellow moon, the background to a white-winged Pegasus ridden by a grim reaper wielding a sword. Below the image in blazing red letters were the embroidered words "Night Stalkers," and above, "Death Waits in the Dark." The United States Army's first Special Operations Aviation element was born.

It would not be the first time that American helicopter pilots would volunteer for dangerous duty. Although rotary wing aircraft had been in existence only since the end of World War II, they had already flocked above the battlefields of Korea and had been so ubiquitously used in Vietnam that that conflict had become known as the "Helicopter War." Yet the Night Stalkers' mission would be something new, an endeavor previously untested. While conventional aviation units would still rule the daylight, only the 160th would crave the darkness. If a target was too far, the weather forbidding, the enemy skilled and cruel and the mission seemingly impossible, they would fly it. The men who rode with them would be only the very elite of the U.S. Armed Forces, and the successes or failures they endured together would probably never be told. They would pay dearly for their courage, and when they died, very few would know where, or how, or why.

For many years, the unit was hardly known to exist except within certain circles in the American military establishment. After all, special operations aviators are not prone to talk, at least not to anyone outside their small community of warriors. You may have encountered them in a bar somewhere, heads bent close and murmuring over their beer. They would have been dressed in jeans and sweatshirts, looking anything but military, and you wouldn't have imagined who they were. And if by chance you ventured too close, their aviators' eyes would have narrowed at you, and their conversation about a recent mission that was nearly their last would have turned to sports scores and bawdy remarks about cheerleaders.

That has always been the nature of these hawks that shun the light. And yet as their exploits accumulated, it became inevitable that some missions would be revealed and some credit duly given. In 1993, events in Somalia brought unwelcome attention to the U.S. Army's Special Operations Aviation Regiment (Airborne). Thereafter, the publication of *Black Hawk Down*, and later, *In the Company of Heroes*, was somewhat reluctantly blessed by the army. It was time to give the Night Stalkers their due. The proposal to write this book, the first of its kind about the 160th SOAR(A), received the army's and the unit's nods because its authors could be trusted to tell those stories that needed to be told, while keeping the secrets that should not.

It has not been an easy process for anyone involved. Men who had never spoken to a soul of these things were being asked to recount not only their victories, but many painful events as well. Almost without exception, each Night Stalker being interviewed was surprised to receive such an invitation, as if they were postal workers being asked to discuss their daily routes.

Colonel Kevin Mangum, the 160th regimental commander, graciously found the time to speak to us while managing helicopter warfare on multiple fronts. Despite his service record, he had virtually nothing to say about his own exploits as a helicopter pilot among the very best in the world. He could not be pressed to admit that only the finest of American officers and aviators would have been selected to command such a regiment, and his final words were telling: "The honor has been mine, to serve amongst this company of heroes."

Another high-ranking officer in the regiment volunteered to clear his schedule, yet barely mentioned a single personal adventure until begged to do so near the close of the interview. He then related briefly that he had only recently returned from Afghanistan. While flying as the air mission commander aboard an MH-47 Chinook, the aircraft's fuel line had ruptured and the helicopter crashed onto a mountain peak and burst into flames. The officer managed to escape the inferno along with his crew, then spent two full nights and a day on that frozen summit along with a team of U.S. special operators, during which a massive earthquake thundered out of Pakistan and brought them all to their knees. "Other than that," he said, "I haven't really done much lately."

Perhaps most significantly, General Bryan D. "Doug" Brown generously lent his support to this endeavor, while modestly declining to tell his own personal story. General Brown is the commander of U.S. Special Operations Command, as well as a founding Night Stalker and a legend in that close-knit community. A former Green Beret sergeant, he went on to become an unparalleled helicopter pilot and commanded at every level in the regiment. Beginning as flight lead for the second Iran rescue attempt, he held two company commands, battalion and regimental command, and then rose to the position of commanding general of the Army Special Operations Command. The position he currently holds at USSOCOM, at the pinnacle of special operations warfare, speaks to his qualities as the ultimate professional. General Brown has always "led from the front" and has inspired a generation of Night Stalkers. Without his support, we could not have told this story, yet he chose to let others speak of the events that he shaped and guided.

That is the nature of these men. They are not celebrities, nor do they wish to be.

Many books have been written about the intrepid combat pilots of America's wars, yet this is the first to recount some of the episodes in which the Night Stalker aviators and crews played the most pivotal roles. It is not so much a story about helicopters as it is about hearts. It is not the machines, the technological wonders or the weapons of war that make this story. It is the men, the quiet professionals, their wives and children, all of whom have dedicated themselves to an effort so perilous that their lives are certain to be torn by loss. There are scores of Night Stalker missions that will never be spoken of, yet at least some of what these men have done must not be allowed to fade into history, unheralded, for these few have done so much for so many. It is a story about sacrifice, sworn to secrecy; a grateful nod to those men in the corner of that bar.

These, then, are just some of the incredible true stories of the Night Stalkers' struggles, victories, heroism and losses. It is not by any means a comprehensive history, for that would require the spilling of too many treasured secrets during a time of war. But it is important for Americans, and those who care for America, to know some of these things. We enjoy our liberty because, as George Orwell once said, rough men stand ready in the night to visit violence on those who would do us harm.

—The Authors
Autumn 2006

Army helicopter pilots are God's lunatics.

—JOSEPH GALLOWAY,
VIETNAM WAR CORRESPONDENT

CHAPTER 1

URGENT FURY

IN THE EMERALD ISLANDS of the Caribbean Sea, dawn was a gentle thing.

The sun, rising in the east from the deep blues of the Atlantic, seemed to wade slowly through the shallower sapphire waters. The sands, though they had cooled and hardened in the darkness, softened in the early warmth, and the palm fronds waved in whispering breezes. Pelicans skimmed over crystal bays and the scent of bougainvillea rose up like a mist of perfume.

It was the kind of dawn longed for by most North Americans. Soon, they would be winter bound. Soon, they would daydream of respite in these sun-drenched islands. But for the helicopter pilots and crews of Task Force 160, the U.S. Army's fledgling Special Operations Aviation Battalion, the robin's-egg blue sky was an evil omen, and the brilliant sun a curse. To these men, this perfect tropical dawn was a vampire's nightmare.

They were late, and even though the delay in their launch was no fault of theirs, the only thing more unnerving than impending combat was arriving off schedule to a surprise attack. Operation Urgent Fury, the invasion of Grenada, had begun. Naval gun batteries were pounding their targets, the marines had come ashore, the Rangers were hurling themselves from the yawning doors of C-130 jump planes. The enemy was already wide-awake, heavily engaged and no doubt looking to the sky and at the ready. Yet there were no other options. Press on.

Fifty feet above the waters of lavender blue and iguana green, nine UH-60 Blackhawk helicopters charged toward the distant objective, a patchwork island of slim beaches and sharp hills, an orphan in the midst of nowhere. The Blackhawks' forms were thick and heavy, nine tons of metal each, yet there was something sleek in their sharp snouts and tubular tails, a prehistoric grace as they raced along in staggered formation, one behind the other. The spinning blades of their main rotors flashed back sunlight as they flew, and they bobbed in the turbulence of one another's turbine wash, like corks in a rippling pond. Their pilots squinted through the windshields, while navigators struggled to match their maps with the impending reality ahead. In their bellies, the Blackhawks carried the elite of the U.S. Armed Forces: members of the navy's SEAL Team Six and the army's Special Forces Operational Detachment—Delta. The helicopters were painted in dark flat green that was almost black, for they'd been adopted by an aviation unit whose every intention was to assault after sunset and be done before dawn.

Yet here, on this day, the dawn had passed. They would stand out in this sky like minks on snow.

In the cockpit of the seventh Blackhawk, Major Robert Lee Johnson shifted slightly in the right-hand seat, easing the tension in his long legs. It had been warm in Barbados, so his nylon flight jacket was folded up beneath his armored bucket seat, his Nomex coverall open near his throat. He was wearing a standard-issue Search and Rescue vest, as they were flying over open water, but other than his pilot's helmet he wore no personal protection gear of any kind. In the holster on his vest was tucked a brand-new Beretta 92-SB pistol he'd purchased at a gun shop. The Beretta held fifteen rounds. He wasn't going into combat with one of those six-shot, .38 revolvers that the army thought was good enough for helo jockeys.

On paper, Johnson was the commander of Charlie Company, 101st Aviation Battalion, 101st Airborne Division, though his outfit was secretly attached to the classified Task Force 160. And as the air mission commander for the entire flight of nine helos, his task was to ensure the proper coordination of all elements of the assault. So, for now, he had left most of the flying to the man in the left seat, Chief Warrant Officer-3 David "Rosey" Rosengrant. Johnson's brown eyes scanned the helo's instruments. Between his knees, his *cyclic*—the stick that controlled speed and direction—tilted from left to right like some disembodied cobra. Near his left thigh, his *collective*—the stick that controlled power and altitude—rose and fell in small increments. He didn't need to touch the cyclic to key its mike switch; he could use the floor switch, either talking "internal" to Rosey as he read out numbers from the radar altimeter, or transmitting "external" to the rest of the flight. Of course, at this juncture radio silence was mission-critical, so there wasn't much to say. He had to trust the men in the lead Blackhawk to take them all downtown.

Yet inside Johnson's helmet, his headset was far from silent. He and Rosengrant had tuned in to the Ranger frequency, and they could hear the urgent orders being spat out above the chatter of gunfire and the *whumps* of grenades on the tarmac at Point Salinas. The major's gloved hand rested on his kneeboard, where his rubber-banded maps fluttered in the rush of air through the open side window. For a moment, he pulled off his glove and smeared his palm on his thigh.

"Those Rangers are in some shit," Rosengrant's voice hissed in his ears.

Johnson reached for his mike switch. "Up to their asses," he replied.

Bob Johnson had been in the army for ten years, and today would be his first taste of combat. It was "John Wayne" time, the moment he'd dreamed about since he was a kid in Baltimore. At thirty-three years old, and like most of the soldiers of his rank and age, he had grown up in the late sixties and early seventies, out of step with the bulk of that generation of youth. At the height of the Vietnam conflict, when most high school kids were wearing bell-bottoms and love beads and protesting the war, he was in honors classes at Baltimore Polytechnic and taking weekend flying lessons. While most college freshmen were still dropping acid tabs and undulating to Jimi Hendrix, he was enrolling in ROTC at the University of Delaware and jumping out of airplanes at Fort Benning over the summer. His father and his uncles had been proud World War II veterans, and Johnson viewed all those ponytailed, antiestablishment types as cowards who just wanted to wallow in their simple, easy lifestyles. They were the antithesis of what John F. Kennedy had encouraged Americans to do.

"Ask not what *we* can do for our country. . . . We're too busy getting high."

Johnson had always pictured himself as an Airborne officer or a Green Beret, but after college the army had its own ideas about how to utilize his talents, and he'd been sent to the mechanized infantry at Fort Carson, Colorado. The post-Vietnam army was a mess. The United States had retreated from its fight in Southeast Asia and morale was at an all-time low. It wasn't unusual to find some soldier still in his rack long after morning formation, strung out on heroin, a syringe discarded nearby. Blacks and whites regularly engaged in all-out slugfests in the enlisted club. Johnson had joined the army as a young officer ready to make a difference, but if he didn't get the hell out of Fort Carson, the difference would be made in *him*. He applied to flight school and wound up at the top of his class in helicopter training at Fort Rucker, Alabama.

By 1979, when fifty-three American hostages were seized in Tehran, he'd already served a tour in Korea flying Bell UH-1 Hueys, spent three years at Fort Rucker as the personnel officer and then company commander of the post's Headquarters Company, and graduated from the Infantry Officer's Advanced Course. At last, he'd been assigned to the 101st Airborne Division (Air Assault) at Fort Campbell, Kentucky, where each infantry brigade had its own aviation platoon of four Hueys and six OH-58 light observation helicopters. By the summer of 1980, as the commander of First Brigade's platoon, he thought he was finally where the action would be. But it turned out that all the real action was happening "across the street," where the army was putting together a new, classified unit of special operations helicopter pilots.

In April 1980, the United States had launched Operation Eagle Claw, an effort to rescue the American hostages from the clutches of the Ayatollah's proxies in Iran. What happened there would change the nature of low-intensity conflict for decades to come, and ultimately deliver Bob Johnson to his fate in the dawn sky above Grenada. The rescue attempt was ambitious, multidimensional and highly complex, and involved elements of the U.S. Armed Forces that had never worked together before. At a remote location in the Iranian desert known as Desert One, air force pilots would maneuver their hulking MC-130 cargo planes to an ad hoc strip at night, ferrying an assault force of U.S. Army Special Forces, Rangers, Air Force Combat Controllers and the newly formed Delta Force. From an aircraft carrier in the Persian Gulf, Marine Corps helicopter pilots would fly eight RH-53D helos tasked with the assault on Tehran to that same Desert One strip, while further Air Force C-130 refueling tankers would set down with their highly volatile cargo. Without that fuel, the helos would not be able to make the next and most crucial leg to the target, nor would any of the aircraft be able to return from the mission.

From the get-go, fate plagued the hunters. A busload of Iranian civilians happened upon the secret assembly area and had to be stopped by force, with the terrified travelers rounded up and held at gunpoint, lest they disclose the operation before it could begin. Shortly thereafter, an

Iranian fuel truck barreled through a checkpoint at the clandestine airstrip and was stopped with a Light Antitank Weapon, but the ensuing fireball lit up the sky. The Marine Corps helo pilots, although certainly bold and game for the mission, had little experience in long-range night operations. Their night vision goggles were primitive and cumbersome, their Forward Looking Infrared systems had been discarded due to their weight, and the aviators were unprepared for the enormous sandstorm that smothered their squadron en route to Desert One. Only six of the eight helos finally arrived at the strip, and only five remained flyable after one more suffered a crippling hydraulic failure. There was no choice but to abort Eagle Claw. There simply weren't enough helicopters to deliver the rescue force to the target.

Then, frustration was quickly followed by tragedy as a helicopter refueling from the belly of a C-130 suddenly collided with the air force plane, dazzling the night in a horrible eruption of flame and cooked-off ammunition. Three marines and five air force crewmen died instantly in the inferno, and every one of the Marine Corps helicopters had to be abandoned to the triumphant Iranians, while the remainder of the assault force barely escaped aboard the remaining C-130s.

It could not have been worse for the already flagging morale of the U.S. Armed Forces. Yet nothing other than such a debacle could have catalyzed the formation of the army's Task Force 160. The Joint Chiefs of Staff realized that the United States was entering a new era of worldwide, small-scale warfare, and cobbling together quick reaction forces from all sorts of uncoordinated assets was just not going to work. The Ranger, SEAL and Delta "door kickers" would need a force of dedicated helicopter pilots who could work with them all the time. A fresh effort to rescue the hostages, Operation Honey Badger, was quickly put into the planning phase, and pilots from the 101st were secretly selected to come over to a remote compound at one corner of Fort Campbell to start training. When the hostages were suddenly released in January 1981, Honey Badger stood down, but Task Force 160 was already in the pipeline.

Bob Johnson knew that something *cool* was in the wind. As he put-
tered around Fort Campbell in his lumbering Huey, he would see
huge flights of modified Hughes OH-6 "Little Bird" helos, carrying elite
commandos and executing "nighthawk" training missions—without
night vision goggles in utter darkness. A company of twin-rotor Chinooks was also involved, and the secret unit had two companies of
brand-new Blackhawks that had just come online. It was clear to him
that if somebody was going on a real-world mission, it would be *those*
guys, and he wanted to be one of them.

Johnson had a reputation as a "good stick," and over a few beers in
the Officer's Club with Major Mike Grimm, the charismatic commander of the Little Bird outfit, he was quickly accepted into the classified organization. But his transfer was dependent upon his being
released from his position over at the 101st, and it took him nearly a
year to "find some sucker" to replace him. Yet at last, in the summer of
'81, he packed his gear and moved on to his new life as a special operations pilot of Task Force 160, whose very existence would be denied
for years to come.

It was all new. It was damned exciting. It was dangerous as hell.
They were flying very low and very fast and strictly after sundown, already calling themselves "the Night Stalkers" and eager to prove that
only *they* should be chosen as the pilots and crews for any upcoming
special operations venture. There were constant "VIP demo missions,"
where generals and Pentagon officials would swagger down to Fort
Campbell to see what TF 160 could do. The kind of flying they executed under training conditions was much riskier than anything army
pilots had ever undertaken, and their new motto, "Death Waits in the
Dark," would prove to be a double-edged sword.

In those early years, the Night Stalkers' growing pains were excruciating. One of the unit's best commanders was killed in a night operation when his Little Bird impacted with a high-tension power line
tower. His copilot was blown through the cockpit window and miracu-
lously survived after landing in a muddy riverbed. Five Night Stalkers

were killed when a Chinook lost an aft rotor, inverted and crashed into the Atlantic. Another six met their fates when their Chinook sped into a fog bank, which happened to be concealing a small island. A Blackhawk came apart in midair and its crew of three was lost, and during a low fast flight over water in Panama, another Blackhawk smacked into the sea, leaving two more dead and one bewildered survivor. By the time Bob Johnson took command after qualifying to fly Blackhawks in the summer of 1983, the Night Stalkers had already suffered a total of twenty-one men killed in training accidents. By October of that year, the unit was in grave danger of being disbanded by the army.

And then, Grenada.

It was the last small island in the curving chain of the West Indies, a beautiful strip of volcanic hills, lush tropical forests and white sand beaches, about twice the size of Washington, D.C. Yet not only had Grenada failed to appear on anyone's political or military radar screen, few Night Stalkers had ever even heard of it.

Back in 1979, Grenada had still been enjoying its independence from Great Britain, when its government was overthrown by a leftist junta known as the New Jewel Movement. The new Marxist prime minister, Maurice Bishop, made his affinity for the Soviet Union and Fidel Castro well known, but that was of no immediate concern to the United States, given the island's diminutive size and lack of a substantial military. Yet when Bishop invited the Cubans to build a ten-thousand-foot runway at Point Salinas, the picture changed. Castro's military advisers began arriving on the island, along with eight hundred armed Cuban construction workers and combat engineers. The airstrip, at the southern tip of the island, would be more than adequate to handle long-range fighter bombers, and the nearby capital of St. George's would make a fine naval base. Grenada was just a stone's throw from Venezuela and could serve as a convenient jumping-off point for ongoing Cuban adventurism in Central America and Africa. In March 1983, President Reagan warned Americans that a gateway to the Caribbean, festooned with Soviet-inspired military posts, was not to be taken lightly.

Apparently, Maurice Bishop saw the writing on the wall and began secret negotiations with the U.S. government. Consequently, on October 12, 1983, he was ejected by his own deputy prime minister, in collusion with the commander of Grenada's armed forces, and placed under house arrest. As the situation deteriorated, the American ambassador to Barbados warned his State Department superiors of its gravity, and that six hundred American students studying at Grenada's St. George's Medical College might soon be in danger.

By October 19, Maurice Bishop and his closest advisers had been executed at Grenada's central military barracks, Fort Rupert, and another fourteen citizens had been massacred while protesting the assassinations. The Grenadian Armed Forces commander, General Hudson Austin, had taken power and imposed a twenty-four-hour, shoot-on-sight curfew across the island. The next day, Prime Minister Tom Adams of Barbados sent a formal cable to the U.S. State Department requesting military intervention to restore a legitimate government on Grenada.

Back in Washington, the leviathan that was the U.S. Armed Forces began to stir. The Joint Chiefs of Staff initiated secret meetings with special situation groups and crisis intervention groups. Navy, marine, army and air force assets were quietly placed on alert, but the closely held planning sessions made access to proper intelligence difficult. Not even the National Security Agency or Defense Mapping Agency were informed, an error that would later thwart the ability to have real-time enemy radio intercepts and up-to-date maps and recon photos. And while special tactics units such as the Night Stalkers always had their antennae up for whispers of potential operations, they, like most Americans, were focused on Beirut, where the marines were trying to help stabilize a bloody showdown between a dozen warring factions. Down at Fort Campbell, the rumors about something brewing in Grenada didn't even take wing until the weekend right before the invasion.

In that small community of special operations aviators, Bob Johnson was at the top of his game. He had been promoted to major and was a company commander. He was married to an army nurse who was stationed right there at the Fort Campbell post hospital, so his domestic life was comfortable and essentially stress-free—he didn't have a civilian spouse who would wring her hands over his job or ask him questions about his missions. He was free to play "Secret Squirrel," and she "got it." The regular unit that Johnson's company worked with was SEAL Team Six, the superelite, counterterrorist operators he was proud to call his "customers." He wore his enthusiasm for special ops and helicopter flying on his sleeve, and because of his affinity for verbal displays of glee, they called him "Awesome" Johnson.

On Saturday, October 22, he was up at Norfolk, Virginia, having just wrapped up a training mission with the SEALs. Captain Robert A. Gormly was the hard-charging SEAL team commander, and Charlie Company's Night Stalkers enjoyed working with Gormly's coterie of some of the nation's finest warriors. On duty, the SEALs were courageous, cold-blooded, meticulous and professional. Off duty, they seemed to have the mentality of a biker gang. In turn, the navy's commandos had come to appreciate the aviator skills of "the Ghost Riders," as Johnson's company had dubbed themselves. They would fly anywhere, anytime, at night under "zero illum" (no moon) conditions or in heavy weather, low, fast and with a time-on-target plus or minus thirty seconds. It was a marriage made in heaven, with the intention of consummating it in hell. But training was one thing; they had yet to work together in combat.

One of Johnson's captains was getting married that night at Fort Campbell, so one of the battalion's operations officers drove him to Norfolk Airport for the flight home. As they were parting company, the ops officer's beeper went off, summoning him back to the SEALs' base. Neither man thought much of it, and Johnson continued on his way.

The wedding down at Campbell was a throwback to *Gone With the Wind.* The men wore their dress blues, almost raven-black, tailored uniforms gleaming with brass buttons. At the post chapel, they formed an arbor of crossed ceremonial swords for the bride and groom, and at the Officer's Club reception they looked like ghosts from the days of Custer as they twirled their satin-swathed wives across a parquet dance floor. By midnight, with the liquor flowing freely, bow ties had loosened and high heels had been discarded, when suddenly every Night Stalker beeper in the place went off. Half in the bag, Bob Johnson staggered to a pay phone and called headquarters, and a voice answered simply, "Come to work."

Twenty minutes later and still in his blues, Johnson drove into the Night Stalker compound and strode into headquarters, to find the unit's S-3 planners poring over tourist maps of the Caribbean and load-out diagrams for the helicopters. The men had just flown in from Fort Bragg, North Carolina, and something in their demeanor told him this wasn't going to be your typical ready-and-react drill.

"Where we goin'?" he asked with a whiskey-slurred smile.

"Grenada."

"Grenada?" He pushed his dress cap back and scratched his head. "Where the hell is that?"

"West Indies. Last island in the chain."

"What's the problem? Some bikini girls got mugged by a local?"

At that point, every planner stopped working and looked up at the major, and he knew this was going to be the real deal.

"Bad guys have taken over the island," one warrant officer said. "We're going to take it back."

Johnson was suddenly as sober as a judge.

"*Awesome.*"

Over the next four hours, the 160th's maintenance men struggled to prepare nine Blackhawks—five from Charlie 101 and four from Charlie 158, the other attached Blackhawk company—for "self-deployment" (i.e., flown by their pilots) to Fort Bragg, where they'd link up with their respective customers for the next leg of the mission. The precise operational plans had not yet firmed up, but a rough sketch of the proposed targets gave the Night Stalkers an idea of how many customers they would have to deliver. The 160th AMCO—Air Movement Control Officer—had determined that the helos would first have to be loaded up with all of their reserve fuel tanks. These were pie-shaped "blivets" of rubberized fabric, supported by wooden cruciforms requiring careful assembly in the cargo holds of each bird.

While the maintenance men hauled blivets and wrenched the cruciforms together, Colonel Terry Henry, commander of the 160th, informed Johnson that he would be the air mission commander of the Blackhawk force. It was a heavy responsibility, but he welcomed it. The only thing that bothered him was that Henry himself would be riding along in one of the birds, which would be sort of like taking the SATs with your math tutor frowning over your shoulder. But once the shooting started, it would be Johnson's show.

At four o'clock in the morning, the maintenance platoon started cursing and kicking the tarmac. An order had come down to remove all the fuel blivets from the aircraft. The Blackhawks were now going to deploy to Fort Bragg aboard C-5A transport jets. Their main rotors had to be folded, as well as their stabilators, the small wings below the tail rotors. Loading ramps would have to be deployed and the Blackhawks hauled aboard the huge jets. It was going to take hours. Johnson went home to get some sleep.

Early Sunday morning, he awoke to the grim news that 241 U.S. marines had just been killed in Beirut by an Islamic suicide bomber driving a massive truck bomb into their Battalion Landing Team HQ. His wife, who actually outranked him, was already watching the news on TV. She looked up at him as he quickly dressed in his flight gear.

"I assume that's where you're going," she said, without expecting much enlightenment.

"Can't tell ya, hon." He shrugged and grinned. "See ya . . ."

By Sunday evening, a constant train of lumbering C-5As from Fort Campbell was landing at Pope Air Force Base, adjacent to Bragg. While all the helicopters, ammunition and ancillary equipment remained aboard the jets, Night Stalker company commanders Johnson and Major Larry Sloan were hustled over to the headquarters of Joint Special Operations Command—the as yet untested body that was born in the wake of the Desert One debacle and would coordinate all special missions units from the various elite services. The JSOC building bustled with intelligence officers and other staff officers coming and going, while inside a large planning room, Johnson and Sloan joined an intense powwow of special ops pilots and ground commandos from Delta Force and Gormly's SEALs. It turned out that Major Neil Judd, the 160th S-3 operations and planning officer, had already been up at Bragg for two days, along with his team of warrant officer flight leads, working out the various target details and exactly who was going to go where. Rumors would later circulate that the invading Americans were so unprepared for Grenada that they didn't even have maps of the island. That might have been true for some larger units such as the 82nd Airborne, but not so at JSOC. There were so many maps that most of them had to be left behind.

It was decided that the nine helos from the two 160th Blackhawk companies were going to handle three targets. The first was Richmond Hill Prison, where hostages from the legitimate Grenadian government were reportedly being held, although no real-time intelligence was available, as the Americans didn't have a single reliable human asset on the ground. But it was a sprawling facility and would require six Blackhawks to deliver all of Delta Force's B-Squadron. The second target was the mansion of the governor-general. Sir Paul Godwin Scoon, the veteran diplomat appointed by the British Commonwealth to oversee its protectorate, was in imminent danger of abduction by the coup leaders and might well befall the same fate as Maurice Bishop. Sir Paul, via the U.S. ambassador in Barbados, had urgently submitted a formal "invitation" to the U.S. government to intervene. His rescue would require two helos of SEALs. The third target was the radio station at Beaujolais, to which the governor-general would be brought to address his fellow Grenadians and urge their compliance with the American effort. One load of SEALs would be sufficient for that.

JSOC also had plenty of other objectives to worry about. The 75th Rangers would have to seize the airfield at Point Salinas, and would be followed up by the army's 82nd Airborne. The navy also wanted a piece of the action, and the marines were going to take the northern airfield at Pearls. At that juncture, it hadn't yet been decided exactly who was going to rescue the American medical students.

But Bob Johnson could only focus on the Night Stalker mission at hand. He quickly decided that he was going to take every pilot he could muster along for the operation. A couple of them were Vietnam vets who'd already seen plenty of action, but most of them had never been shot at, and he knew that that experience was vital for future performance. Eighteen pilots and copilots would do the actual flying; nine more would function as navigators; nine more would serve as M-60 door gunners on one flank of the birds; nine crew chiefs would handle the remaining door guns. A total of forty-five Night Stalker Blackhawk crew members would be earning their combat ribbons—if the whole damn thing wasn't canceled at the last minute.

Larry Sloan was technically senior to Johnson and would lead the Delta assault on Richmond Hill. Johnson decided that the single bird assault on the radio station wasn't very "sexy," but that rescuing the governor-general would be something to tell his kids about—if he survived to have any. As the planning meeting broke up, more than one hundred SEALs and Delta operators began to hustle their gear over to Pope and the waiting C-5As, and they had plenty of it: load-bearing equipment packed with ammunition, fragmentation grenades, flash bangs, smoke grenades, signal strobes, commando blades, Satcom radios, first-aid kits. They carried weapons so meticulously cleaned they looked like they'd just arrived from the factory: CAR-15s (short-barreled versions of the M-16), Remington 700 sniper rifles, M-60 light machine guns, and pistols of various types and calibers per the preferences of each shooter. The men sorted themselves into assault elements called "chalks" and began boarding the enormous jets, each chalk making double sure it would be traveling along with its designated Blackhawk and crew. You didn't want to fly aboard the wrong C-5A and discover that your "taxi" had set down somewhere else.

As for Johnson and his men, they had little to prepare in the way of gear. It would be some years before the pilots and crews of the 160th would be regarded as commandos who fly, or be issued all sorts of "swoopy shit" when they signed into the unit. Their survival vests had been slightly modified with additional leg straps, so in the event of required extraction by air they could snap carabiners onto them and be winched up, but they contained the standard pilot's stuff: signal flares, signal mirror, space blanket, penknife, first-aid kit and a tourniquet. None of them were issued Kevlar flak vests. Only one man, Maintenance Captain Kurt Heine, managed to scrounge up a set of "chicken plates" from a buddy at Fort Bragg. These were ceramic plates tucked into a flak vest and would stop a heavy-caliber bullet. Heine and one other crewman would be the only Night Stalkers wearing such protection that day, and Heine's would save his life.

It wasn't until Monday night that the C-5As began to rumble off the tarmac at Pope. Operational plans for the invasion had been changed, discarded and modified again. There were new orders, fresh intelligence, then a hold due to heavy weather over the target. It was a shoot-from-the-hip operation from the start, but at last they were airborne. For a while, Bob Johnson made his way around the steel grid floor of the jet, weaving between SEALs and gear as he checked over his locked-down Blackhawk No. 725. Man for man, the jungle-camouflaged SEALs were formidable, muscled warriors, breaking down weapons and scrubbing parts that were already pristine. They had lanyards of parachute cord draped around their necks, with small windowed pouches containing the photos of "friendlies"—they didn't want to shoot the governor-general, his wife or any of his staff by mistake. These men were going to "fast-rope" down to the mansion lawn from Johnson's helicopters, sliding to the ground from pairs of thick green hawsers that would be deployed during the assault at an altitude of about sixty feet.

However, also aboard Johnson's bird would be a pair of civilian "strap hangers"—one State Department officer and a CIA officer—tasked with personally handing Sir Paul a formal letter from the U.S. government. These young men were also wearing combat fatigues, but they were easy to spot, with their wide-eyed expressions of green paratroopers just before their first jump. Their participation would greatly complicate Johnson's mission, as they had no idea how to fast-rope. That meant that his helo, rather than just dropping its customers, would also have to land. Yet overhead recon photos showed a pair of large trees smack in the middle of the landing zone. So, first both birds would fast-rope their SEALs, two of whom would be carrying *chain saws*. Presumably, under fire, the SEALs were going to cut down the trees, and then Johnson's bird would touch down so the civilians could step off like film stars at a Hollywood premiere.

Johnson approached Bob Gormly and gestured at two naval commandos working over their "forestry" gear.

"They're actually going to fast-rope with those saws?" he asked.

"Sure. They're not heavy. Maybe twenty-five pounds."

Johnson shook his head. The SEALs were already hefting sixty pounds of combat gear apiece, plus radios and weapons and even light antitank tubes.

"You know, Gormly? You people are friggin' animals."

"Thanks." The SEAL captain grinned. "First compliment of the day."

Johnson decided to get some sleep. The flight to Barbados was nearly two thousand miles from North Carolina, so he figured he'd wake up when the big jet set down at about 0230. They would need

about an hour to off-load and then "build up" each Blackhawk, and
then they'd launch for the one-hour-and-twenty-minute flight to the
objective. The Grenadians and Cubans wouldn't even know they were
there until the helos suddenly roared out of the night sky and the
SEALs started dropping on them. He climbed up to the passenger
deck of the C-5 and curled up in a seat.

When he woke up at 0500, they were still in the air. Something
wasn't right. He splashed water from a canteen onto his face and
cleared his eyes, then looked over at Gormly, who was riding in the
seat next to him.

"What the hell's going on?" Johnson demanded. "Dawn's gonna
break before we're even ready to launch."

"They changed H-hour." Gormly shrugged. "The buzz is, the marines can't go ashore without air support, and their Cobras can't fly at
night."

Johnson couldn't believe it. The Night Stalkers had just become
the *Day Stalkers*.

"This is definitely ominous," he said. "Not to mention fucked up."

From there on out, nothing went according to schedule. The airport at Barbados looked like a convention of the aerospace industry,
with C-5As landing at regular intervals, helicopters being built up and
equipment-laden commandos streaming over the strip. With all the alleged attention to super secrecy, Johnson wondered how the Grenadians could possibly *not* know they were coming. It would take nothing
more than a phone call from Barbados to St. George's to tip off the
enemy. And he had further problems, as the blade-folding pins on his
helicopter wouldn't cooperate, and it took the combined muscle of all
his SEALs to get the helo assembled and up and running.

Yet now, at last, they were airborne. The sky had paled to a silver
blue, the sun exploding on the eastern horizon. His frustration with all
the delays had receded and he was focused, en route, and that always
felt better than just waiting and letting your imagination run rampant.
Gormly and his SEALs were in back, jammed together like hard-

boiled eggs in a mixing bowl, their knees tucked up to their chests. The State and CIA guy were back there, too, probably pissing in their pants. That image made him smile. Maybe those SEALs weren't intellectual giants, but they could have delivered a letter to Sir Paul just as easily as some shit-scared civilians. *Leave it to the government.*

He keyed his mike switch and spoke to his crew as Rosey flew the bird.

"Okay, boys, listen up," he said. "Time for the Ghost Rider prayer."

Only a few months back, just before a major training mission, Johnson had surprised his men when he asked them to bow their heads. After all, he didn't appear to be very religious, especially since he and the Catholic chaplain, Father Pat, regularly got drunk together. Now it was the SEALs' turn to think the Night Stalkers loony, as they all intoned together:

"Dear God . . . Don't let us fuck up!"

It was Johnson's last laugh of the day. "All right," he ordered. "Weapons test."

It was standard operating procedure to test the door guns prior to an assault. But on the right-hand door, Johnson's crew chief made the mistake of opening the M-60's feed tray cover in the rushing slipstream as he prepared to load the ammunition. *Poom.* The feed tray cover flew off and twirled down into the sea below, rendering the weapon inoperable.

"I screwed up, Major," the crew chief reported grimly.

"All right." Johnson stayed cool as he spoke to his other door gunner, Captain Heine. "Kurt?"

Heine successfully loaded his M-60, cocked it, but fired only two rounds before it jammed. There was a long moment of silence until he reported back to his commander.

"The assholes gave me minigun ammo, sir. The links are too heavy. They're not gonna feed."

"Shit," Johnson hissed. All right, well, he had plenty of fine-shooting SEALs in the back and their guns should be sufficient to give them all cover, at least on the approach. He turned to Rosengrant. "Guess we better use the armor plates." The pilots' armored bucket seats also had side-armor plates that could be slid forward to protect the aviators' flanks. Johnson reached around to grip his, and was absolutely *stunned* to find it missing.

"Where's the fucking armored side panels?" he spat into his mike.

"Uhhh, we took 'em off, sir," his crew chief answered sheepishly. "For saving weight."

"Whenja do that?"

"Oh, about a week ago."

"*Damn.*"

Johnson blew out a long sigh as Rosey just shook his head. So now, they had no door guns, no side armor, no Kevlar. He looked down at the thin material of his coverall. *This is all I've got to stop a bullet?*

There was nothing to do but shrug it off. Like all army pilots, he believed in that "Big Sky, Little Bullet" philosophy; it would take one very lucky enemy gunner to pluck him out of the sky. He had the optimism of every soldier who has never been in combat. The worst might happen to somebody else, but it couldn't happen to him. Besides, back at Bragg, Neil Judd had come up to him after a session with the intel guys and said in his thick Kentucky drawl, "Don't worry about it. The United States coming in is gonna scare the shit out of those militia amateurs. When they see you comin', they're gonna throw down their arms and give up." Well, part of Johnson hoped that was true, and part of him didn't. How could you be John Wayne if nobody shot at you?

Judd's assessment was widely assumed to be accurate throughout all branches of the services that day. But what Johnson didn't know was that at that very moment, Fidel Castro was broadcasting messages to his combat engineer crews all over Grenada.

"You *will* fight to the last man," Cuba's dictator harangued. "Because if the Americans don't kill you, *I* will."

The formation had been flying due west from Barbados, and now as they turned to come at Grenada from the north, the sun streamed into the cockpit. Johnson took the controls from Rosengrant and flexed his fingers into position. The visibility was at about five miles, perfect for a weekend aviator, with every palm tree and primitive hill hut as clear and defined as a Kodachrome wall mural. The line of black helos curved like a scythe and then straightened, the lead bird flashing from above the waves to over land, going "feet dry" above a narrow beach. They were at the Release Point Inbound, closing fast on the target, where they were likely to be spotted and could expect enemy action. Like a small school of sharks, the Blackhawks rose together over a slim range of hills, then dropped again into a deep green valley. Thundering along at just above treetop level, images rushed by the cockpit windows: navy ships dotting the sea, marines already crawling over the strip at Pearls, Miami-colored cars on the winding roads.

The capital of St. George's came into view, tucked into the palm of a hand of high hills, like a mini version of Rome. Its red-tiled roofs and low stucco buildings spilled all over the hillsides, arching palm trees fluttering in the breeze. All the flight element's targets were right there in town; there was no way to skirt the suburban sprawl. As the small city loomed larger, Johnson spoke to his navigator.

"Make sure we hit the circle."

"Roger that."

The six lead birds would be heading right down the enemy's throat for Richmond Hill Prison. At a predetermined point, a large traffic circle in the center of town, Johnson and his two helos would break away for the governor's mansion, while the last bird peeled off for the radio station. He gripped the cyclic and hunched forward, and he could feel his heart in his chest, the adrenaline waking him up like no cup of black coffee ever had.

And then all hell broke loose. From the hills overlooking St. George's, *hundreds* of Grenadian and Cuban guns opened fire. Johnson had heard that tracer fire was hard to discern in broad daylight, but that wasn't the case here. Red and green and orange tracers suddenly lanced up from positions all over the city. Black puffs of flak began to explode in the sky dead-on. And they weren't just shooting *up* at the Blackhawks. They were shooting *down* at them from the peaks as the helicopters nearly scraped their bulbous black tires across the rooftops.

"Holy *Christ*," Johnson spat into his mike, though he hadn't keyed the switch. He had never imagined anything like this. Not here, not today. And the phenomenon that overtook his body and his mind wasn't something he could ever have prepared for. It was total sensory overload, and with a flood of adrenaline surging through his blood, his fine motor skills went all to hell. He had thought that at this juncture, he'd be the ultimate air mission commander, issuing calm orders, encouraging his fellow pilots to stay the course, suggesting slight changes in approach and attack as he swaggered through the gunfire, ignoring the bullets that kicked up dust at his feet. But this was no schoolboy hero fantasy. This was the OK Corral, times ten.

The lead birds were taking hits all over. He knew it, he could see it, those goddamn ground gunners couldn't possibly miss. *Throw down their arms, my ass!* And yet they stayed on course, noses down and barreling toward the prison. He could hear his navigator's voice, a tremble in it, asking him if they were nearing the traffic circle. But the ground was nothing but a rush of roofs and scattering civilians, and the only image that was absolutely clear was the fierce, multicolored quilt of tracer fire they were flying into. The Blackhawk seemed suddenly heavier than it had ever been, the controls sluggish, the pair of powerful turbines unresponsive. But Johnson knew it wasn't the machine. It was *him*, and he was flying the damned thing with all the control of a six-year-old on a roller coaster.

He had missed his turn point. He was sure of it. His navigator was tucked back behind the console separating the pilots and could probably see nothing more now than jinking Blackhawks out ahead and shock waves as bullets smacked through the air. Johnson glanced at the city map on his kneeboard, then down through the Plexiglas chin bubble near his right foot, but nothing on the ground was discernible as they screamed along at a hundred knots through a sky full of lead.

In that split second, he decided to follow Larry Sloan's element to the prison. Relative to *that* target, he knew for sure how to get to the governor-general's mansion.

Unbelievably, the fire intensified as the six lead Blackhawks swooped in on the prison compound. On the hilltops surrounding the crumbling structure, Cubans were firing Russian ZSU 23mm antiaircraft cannons in flat trajectories, at nearly point-blank range, while Grenadian irregulars joined in the crossfire with AK-47s. Johnson could actually see metal chunks of the helos before him being ripped away, the impacts of bullets shuddering the bucking machines. Inside those six helos, the Night Stalkers and the men of Delta's B-Squadron were already being wounded by the score.

Larry Sloan was sitting in the navigator's position in Chalk Four. Exactly three weeks before, he had been the only survivor of a Blackhawk crash at sea in Panama; still shaken up from that episode, he'd decided to forgo flying today and coach his company with his hands free and his head in the game. A bullet tore through his left shoulder, furrowed through his back and exited near his neck, spraying the Delta men behind him with his blood as he slumped over. Within seconds, nearly every one of his customers was wounded as well, with some suffering multiple impacts.

In the fifth helicopter, a 23mm round exploded through the cockpit window, instantly killing the pilot, Captain Keith Lucas, while further antiaircraft shells sliced through the main rotor and hammered through the tail. The aircraft commander, Paul Price, struggled to break off and fly the shattered bird toward the beach, but with its controls destroyed it rolled over and disappeared behind a hill, with a jagged section of its main rotor pinwheeling into the air as it impacted. By the time they were above the prison, the remaining five helos were nothing more than flying ambulances full of smoking, ragged holes.

The Delta commanders crawled over comrades slick with blood to stick their heads out the cargo doors and check the landing zones, only to find the prison compound utterly *abandoned*. Cell doors were flung open, and garbage and dust wheeled across the empty facility under the rotor wash. No one was home, and they called to the surviving 160th pilots to break it off and head for the navy hospital ships.

Johnson knew that his two birds were flying into a "shit storm," but he was *not* breaking it off. He spoke to Rosey in a voice that seemed to come from somewhere in his bowels.

"You have the controls," he ordered. Rosey had been one of the original Blackhawk test pilots and had more hours in the bird than anyone else in the army. No one could fly a fast-rope approach like Rosengrant.

"Roger that. I have the controls."

"Ninety degrees right turn *here*."

Rosengrant skidded the big helo around to the right, and the second Blackhawk followed, while the third wheeled away toward Beaujolais. Johnson leaned to the window, gritting his teeth and determined to find their target. Almost instantly he spotted it, about a half-mile dead ahead. The governor-general's mansion was hard to miss now, a three-story, ornate colonial palace stretching over nearly a full city block. The lawns in front were as reported, large enough to set a helo down, if it weren't for that damned pair of banana trees. Johnson clicked the mike switch to talk to the pilot of the second bird.

"Chalk Eight, keep it tight."

That bird had the SEALs on board with the chain saws, so they *had* to get on the ground fast and start working.

"Roger, Seven. We're on your ass."

As the pair approached, they swung slightly to the right, then back again to the left, presenting their right flanks to the mansion's face as they began to flare and hover over the front lawns just above the treetops. It looked okay. It looked like they were going to make it. And then every AK-47, submachine gun, shotgun and pistol in the neighborhood opened up on them. Johnson could feel his bird quaking; he could hear its metal skin echoing like a tin bucket on a firing range as bullets *whanged* through the fuselage. And there was nothing he could do about it. For those endless seconds, he wasn't even flying, he was just a passenger. He had no door gunners. He didn't even think to pull out his Beretta, stick it out the window and return fire. He twisted his neck and could see the ropes uncoiling from the cargo doors of Chalk Eight and the SEALs sliding to the ground so fast they seemed to be barely gripping the hemp. And behind him, Gormly's men in the doors were furiously firing their weapons, the spent shells pinging all over the cargo bay as they tried to provide some cover for their comrades. But they had to stop and sling their guns as Rosey pushed the Blackhawk forward for their turn to assault.

"Ropes!" Johnson called over the intercom.

Kurt Heine and the crew chief kicked the ninety-pound coils over the door sills, where they dangled and twisted below their armatures. There were no quick-releases for the ropes. After the SEALs descended, they would have to be pulled back in.

"Go! Go! Go!" Gormly was shouting in the back as nine of his SEALs dove out the doors like circus acrobats.

Johnson heard the AK-47 that raked his helo from directly below. It was so close that he actually saw the yellow-white muzzle flashes. Two rounds sliced through the floor behind his back and cracked past his helmet. Another six chunked into the bottom of his bucket seat and were stopped by the armor. A round pierced up through the console and shattered the instruments, showering him with glass. And then his left leg just flipped up off the floor as if it had been sledgehammered under the thigh. The 7.62mm bullet ripped through his sciatic nerve and tore off a hunk of flesh the size of a softball, which exploded all over the cockpit. He and Rosengrant were suddenly covered with blood and meat—*his* meat.

It didn't hurt. Not at first. Johnson was in shock, and he just looked at the gaping wound. It wasn't spurting, but the hole in his torn coveralls was steadily oozing bright red blood. Small-arms rounds were still punching into the helo, but he didn't really hear them. Rosengrant looked at him, his eyes wide and alarmed. He immediately picked up twenty feet of altitude and got on the intercom.

"Major's hit bad. Get those ropes aboard!"

Heine and the crew chief dove for the fat coils, using every ounce of strength they had to haul the ropes back up through the rotor wash. The navigator crawled forward on the console to reach the manual switch for the stabilator, which had failed to engage automatically as a bullet severed a control wire. The State Department and CIA officers were still curled up in the passenger compartment, praying for their lives. But Bob Gormly hadn't had the time to fast-rope down with his men, and he flung himself between the two pilots.

"Where the hell are you going?"

"We're breaking it off," Rosey yelled. "Major's wounded bad."

"But I've got to get down there with my guys!"

"They'll *wait* for you."

"Ropes aboard!" Kurt Heine yelled.

Rosey dropped the nose and hauled on the collective, effectively stomping on the accelerator. The Blackhawk roared away from the mansion as multiple gun barrels followed it, still blazing away.

Johnson pulled off his gloves. His hands were trembling. The navigator's fist appeared over his left shoulder, holding out a tourniquet. Johnson wrapped it around his upper thigh, but he couldn't get it tight enough, and the wound kept on pumping blood over his knee and onto the slick floor. He looked up at the shattered instrument console and the cockpit glass. They were covered with pieces of his leg, and thick crimson gobs seemed to be everywhere.

"Hold on, Bob," Rosey's voice said in his helmet.

Johnson looked at the map on his kneeboard and smeared some blood away. They had been briefed before the mission on where to go for medical contingencies. There were three options: Point Salinas, but that was no-go, as the Rangers were still heavily engaged on the tarmac. Back to Barbados was an option, but it was more than an hour away. The third choice was the USS *Guam*, which had medical facilities aboard, sitting somewhere out in the bay. Johnson's twitching fingers reached for the mike switch.

"Guess we'd better head for the *Guam*."

"That's where I'm going," Rosey answered as he rolled the helo to the right and headed out to sea.

They tried to make radio contact with Colonel Henry, to give him a situation report, but their radios were all shot up and wouldn't work. They decided that they'd come in close to the small carrier and just flash their landing lights, and if no one flashed back, they'd land the damned thing anyway. En route, Kurt Heine discovered that he'd been shot square in the chest, but that set of chicken plates had luckily saved his skin.

For about five minutes more, Bob Johnson tried to help with the navigation. He flipped through some maps, looked at the coastline, tried to spot the navy ships through a gathering haze. He didn't think about very much, he was just stunned that he'd been shot, and that nothing he had ever imagined about combat was even close to what had happened that morning.

And then, the adrenaline in his body began to ebb, and his shorn nerve endings began to awaken. And for the rest of the short flight, he screamed. . . .

THE SICK BAYS of numerous U.S. Navy ships filled with wounded that day. Major Robert Lee Johnson was just one of them. In the first few hours of Operation Urgent Fury, nineteen Americans would be killed in action and more than one hundred wounded, most of them special operations troops. Out of forty-five Night Stalkers flying the Blackhawk missions, eleven had been wounded and one pilot killed in action. For twenty minutes of work, the unit had suffered a 25 percent casualty rate.

When Johnson's Blackhawk landed aboard the *Guam*, he was quickly dragged from the shattered cockpit and hustled into surgery on a stretcher. The helo had forty-eight bullet holes in it and the power control levers were so shot up that Rosey couldn't shut the engines down. The navy deck crews had to use fire hoses and pump seawater into the engine inlets, flooding the big turbines into submission. Having no use for the crippled bird, the navy boys wanted to push it over the side.

"Over my fucking dead body," Kurt Heine said as he stood on the deck, protecting his helo like a grizzly mother defending her cub. Later that day, a CH-53 helicopter was summoned to heavy-lift the Blackhawk over to Point Salinas.

Back at the governor-general's mansion, Gormly's SEALs held off wave after wave of Grenadian and Cuban assaults, often accompanied by Soviet-built armored personnel carriers. Having no workable Satcom, the commandos used a mansion telephone to call the civilian air terminal at Point Salinas and got ahold of Gormly, who had hitched a helo ride to the strip from the *Guam*. Gormly quickly summoned air support, and a pair of Cobras did their best to suppress the enemy under withering antiaircraft fire, but essentially the SEALs were on their own, and would not be relieved for twenty-four hours. In his memoirs, Sir Paul Scoon would recall that the most thrilling and terrifying hours of his career were spent on the floor of his living room with his wife, while bullets smashed the windows and hammered through the walls as the SEALs fought back like raging tigers.

The SEALs at Beaujolais took the radio station with relative ease, but they, too, were quickly assaulted en masse. Realizing that the governor-general would not be arriving anytime soon to make his radio address, and in danger of being overrun, the SEALs blew up the radio transmitter. They fought until dark, then withdrew to the beach and swam out to sea, where they were picked up by a navy patrol craft.

The surviving Night Stalker Blackhawks went right back into action, regrouping at Point Salinas to deliver Delta to its next objectives.

Although many of the Delta boys already had wounds from the aborted assault at Richmond Hill—wounds that would have put most other troops out of action—they joined the Rangers in close-quarters battles at the airfield and went on to participate in the rescue of the American medical students, who it turned out had been separated into three different locations.

After a long night of continuous operations, by Wednesday afternoon, most of Urgent Fury's major objectives had been attained. The 82nd Airborne had landed and were pushing deep inland from the south, soon to link up with the Marine Corps maneuvering from up north. JSOC's elements—the Rangers, SEALs, Delta and the Night Stalkers—were essentially done and would soon depart for home.

The officers and men of JSOC's elite began to assemble at Point Salinas to regroup, refresh their gear and await further orders. They were filthy, exhausted, bloodied and bandaged. Back at Barbados, the air force's C-130 jump planes already sat in perfect assembly, looking good as new as ground crews pored over them, finding nary a bullet hole in any of the big birds. But on the airfield at Point Salinas, the 160th's Blackhawks sat like bloodied boxers after a fifteen-round bout. Their rotors drooped, their tail booms and fuselages showed streams of sunlight through multiple bullet holes, and hydraulic fuel leaked from shrapnel gashes.

In short order, as the Rangers, SEALs and Delta men began to talk, and the operators swapped stories, that was when murmurs turned to lore. Pointing out the absence of the pristine air force planes, a Ranger officer recounted how in the first jump wave over Salinas, nearly all the C-130s had been forced to abort due to the intensity of enemy antiaircraft fire. On that first pass, only one aircraft had successfully dropped its Rangers.

The elite commandos now turned their gazes to the decimated Blackhawks, nodding in deference to the courage of the army's special ops pilots and crews.

"*Those* guys ain't gonna bail out on you when the fuckin' shootin' starts," someone said.

The legend of the Night Stalkers was born. *No one* was going to disband Task Force 160.

Within ninety-six hours, Bob Johnson was in a ward at Walter Reed Army hospital in Washington, D.C. He'd already undergone two surgical procedures: one on the *Guam* and another at Roosevelt Roads in Puerto Rico. The bullet had taken out some major nerves and muscle groups, and his road to recovery would be long and painful. He would never again be able to lift his leg properly, and he would always wear a leg brace. But you didn't need to lift your foot to fly, you only had to be able to push down on the rotor pedals. In his mind, there was no question that he would fly again. For the time being, his pain was ebbing and receding in dull throbs, because he was high on morphine. He picked up a hospital phone and called his wife at her office on Fort Campbell.

"Hiya, hon," he slurred.

"Hi! Whatcha doing?"

"Oh, nothing much. Just lying around."

"Okay. . . . See you soon?"

"Gotta go," he said rather abruptly and hung up, still playing "Secret Squirrel." It would take a visit from one of the officers at Fort Campbell to inform Mrs. Johnson that her husband had been severely wounded in action.

Along with all the other soldiers wounded and killed in Urgent Fury, Major Robert Lee Johnson's name was printed in the *Washington Post*. He began to receive hundreds of letters from proud American well-wishers, strangers who blessed him and prayed for his recovery. An entire class of schoolchildren sent him individual greeting cards and cartoons that made him laugh and brought him to tears. He spent hours in physical therapy, days on end in the whirlpool baths. The army chief of staff appeared at his bedside to award him the Purple Heart. Every night after work, his father and mother would make the ninety-minute drive from their home in Maryland to spend a couple of hours with their son until visiting hours were over at 10:00 P.M. And then they would drive home. They did that for sixty days straight.

Just after Christmas, Major Doug Brown, a founding member of the Night Stalkers, sent a C-12 transport plane to pick up Johnson and his wife and fly them down to Fort Campbell. By that time, Johnson was in excruciating pain from dawn to midnight and battling an addiction to morphine. The aircraft encountered terrible headwinds, and when at last it set down at the post, the temperature was fifteen degrees and the ground was covered with a foot and a half of snow. Johnson hobbled down the ramp on his crutches.

One hundred and fifty officers, men and wives were waiting for him. They had a huge sign that said, "Welcome Home Awesome." They cheered and gathered around and hugged him, and they handed him back his flight jacket. His favorite expression, "Totally fuckin' awesome," had spurred an idea to replace his name tag. Instead of JOHNSON, it now read TF AWESOME. He cried.

His struggle had only just begun. He was back with the 160th, but there would be many days when he simply could not function, and only the love and support of his men ensured his position as company commander. Eventually, he and his wife divorced. Curiously, his wounding seemed to have shocked his mate with the reality that he was not remotely invincible, and that soon enough she would lose him on some foreign field. Many years later, he would marry again, this time another army helicopter pilot, and have a son. But in the meantime, he was going to fly.

He had to prove to the army medical board that he was capable of it, and he did so. He got back in the cockpit, often biting his lip in pain and barely managing to extricate himself from his seat after a mission. He flew in classified counterterror operations overseas, went to the Command and General Staff College at Fort Leavenworth, and held a 160th staff position at the Pentagon, along with Bob Gormly, who was serving on the navy staff. Together, the two veterans of Urgent Fury would make a pilgrimage to the Test Pilot School at Pax River, where Blackhawk No. 725 had been relegated to schoolhouse duties, with all its bullet holes patched but still apparent. They had their pictures taken in front of their trusty old bird.

During Operation Desert Storm in 1991, Johnson would fly as a battalion commander in Iraq, earning further combat decorations. After the war, he would hold two staff positions at Fort Rucker until he retired from the army in 1996. Yet he had to come home, and returned to Fort Campbell as a civilian contractor, running the 160th's flight training program for another five years. No matter what he did, no matter where he lived, he would forever be a Night Stalker.

His leg wound had healed, yet he would have to wear that brace until they buried him. It was fine in the summer months, when the crickets clicked in the trees around his home in Clarksville, Tennessee, and the sky was hot and the lake waters inviting. But each October, when the leaves would change from their lush green to autumn hues of red and gold, and the cold winds began to blow across from Kentucky, that chunk of riddled muscle and nerve would awaken in his leg. . . .

And he would always return to Grenada.

CHAPTER 2

SIGN WILL

SUMMER 1976

CAPTAIN MIKE GRIMM could have been a comic book hero.

He was not an exceptionally large young man, but he had the trim and powerful build of a college quarterback. His solid jaw was square, his nose sharply Nordic, and his hazel eyes smiled beneath rakish eyebrows. Where his short brown hair curled into a thick comma over his angular brow, it held the permanent streaks of years spent under hard Pacific suns. Grimm had seen more than any youth's share of bloody combat, yet none of that had tainted his gung-ho, can-do, balls-to-the-walls, let's-get-this-done attitude. He laughed often and easily. He shouted when he was passionate. He was a stickler for operational details, cool as ice water at a helo's controls, and loose as a goose at the officers' bar.

He was Smilin' Jack and Flash Gordon. He was Sergeant Rock and the Silver Surfer.

In January 1968, Grimm had arrived in Vietnam as a nineteen-year-old second lieutenant, a new platoon leader in Company B, Fourth Battalion of the Forty-seventh Infantry, Ninth Infantry Division. Less than a month later he was leading one of his first patrols along a well-worn jungle path when his sharp eyes spotted a tripwire. Grimm's instincts screamed *ambush*, and just as he sent his men to ground, a command-detonated mine exploded nearby, shredding the leaves above their heads with shrapnel. The Vietcong opened up at close range. Grimm's men answered with a furious barrage, and throughout those mad minutes the young lieutenant was seen sprinting through the firefight to find and destroy three more booby traps that would have decimated his patrol. He was cited for his first of many decorations, the Bronze Star with Valor device.

Barely another month had passed when, on March 8, elements of the Fourth Battalion, including Company B and Grimm's platoon, conducted an air assault into a sprawling rice paddy near the village of My Tho. Once again "Charlie" was waiting, and as the Hueys swept into the landing zone murderous ground fire sliced across the sodden fields, bringing one chopper down and forcing five others to break off their approach. Only Grimm's platoon and the company command element made it onto the exposed paddy, and in those first bursts of enemy gunfire ten men were wounded, including Grimm. His platoon sergeant and medic were already dead. The young lieutenant watched as the surviving birds wheeled away to safety, leaving them all alone.

Enemy rounds were chunking through the crashed Huey and splashing across the paddy as Grimm crawled to his company commander for guidance. His captain, although still unharmed, was wild-eyed and disoriented, issuing conflicting orders that were going to result in disaster. If any of them were going to survive, they *had* to get out of that killing field.

"You just stay right here and shut up, sir," Grimm yelled in his commander's ear above the racket of exploding mortar rounds and rockets, "or I'll have to shoot you."

He got up and sprinted to his right flank through a storm of gunfire, overrunning three enemy positions, killing Cong after Cong with his M-16. Then he ran back to the landing zone to shepherd his men out of the clearing. Still bleeding from his own wounds, he returned again to the kill zone to drag two of his fallen men to safety.

Single-handedly, Lieutenant Grimm was infuriating the enemy. They tried to flank him, so he called in artillery support, directing the thundering 105mm rounds to within fifty meters of his new perimeter while he regrouped his men behind a more substantial dike. As darkness fell, the Cong continued to hammer away, but they weren't going to make any headway against the "mad lieutenant." He coached his men, encouraged them, patched them up and kept them fighting. He gathered volunteers and stole back into the blood-soaked LZ to gather up the remaining wounded and pull them inside his perimeter. And when the Cong tried to move on the downed Huey to capture its armaments, Grimm got there first with another intrepid band of volunteers, stripping the smashed helicopter of all its weapons, radios and medical gear before at last it was overrun and completely empty.

Sometime before dawn, the enemy gave up on him and disappeared back into the jungle. That morning, when rescue elements of the battalion finally arrived to relieve their exhausted comrades, they were stunned to discover that Grimm and his platoon had fought off two full companies of Vietcong.

In addition to his Purple Heart, he was awarded the Distinguished Service Cross and submitted for the Congressional Medal of Honor.

Mike Grimm finished that yearlong tour in Vietnam—a year of skirmishes, ambushes, full-blown air assaults and the brutal Tet Offensive. And when it was over, he signed on for another tour. He was not a war lover but a natural warrior. He had gone from high school to the army, from Basic Training to Officers Candidate School and straight into combat. It was what he knew well, did best, seemed to have been born for, and he desired nothing else. Yet his time in Vietnam had shown him that the tactics of modern warfare were changing. Helicopters were the new steeds of America's modern cavalry, and there was still nothing more seductive to a young officer than leading a cavalry charge. In 1970, he went to flight school and ranked in the top of his class at Fort Rucker, Alabama. Before long he was a first lieutenant, an aircraft commander, and by the mid-1970s he had become a captain and the executive officer of A Company, Twenty-fifth Aviation Battalion, Twenty-fifth Infantry Division—stationed in Hawaii and waiting for another war. . . .

WHEN RANDY COCHRAN literally ran into Grimm for the very first time, the comic book hero was still smiling. Lieutenant Cochran, dressed in his summer khakis and about to present himself at his new assignment, yanked on the entrance door to the Twenty-fifth's HQ at Schofield Barracks to find Captain Grimm yanking on the other side. Salutes were exchanged.

"I'm Grimm." The captain grinned.

"I'm Cochran, Randy."

They shook hands, and an apprentice had found a mentor.

Randy Cochran's military experience had, thus far, been the antithesis of Grimm's. He had been raised in a factory town in southeast Ohio, working alongside his struggling father. The family was poor. Randy's dad had been a navy veteran of World War II who rarely spoke about his hell in the Pacific, but what did emerge were horrific stories about being torpedoed on the high seas and trapped belowdecks, and the nightmares of waves of kamikaze attacks. It was perhaps those rarely uttered accounts that made Randy want the army, but his father's mantra was "College first. College first," and Randy respected him and listened.

And so, he worked full-time at the factory, taking college classes at night until he finally earned his degree in 1973. Yet when at last he proudly joined up, he encountered the same disillusioned army that had almost sullied Bob Johnson's dreams. The ranks of green seemed tattered and desultory, as if no one was really home. The war in Vietnam was winding down, soldiers were leaving in droves, and it was a struggle just to maintain an active duty slot as an infantry officer at Fort Benning. When orders came down deactivating Cochran's battalion, he knew there'd be nowhere left for him to go. It was like working again at a failing factory as they shut down the assembly lines and turned off the lights.

"You're going to flight school."

Cochran's battalion commander had summoned the frustrated young lieutenant to his office, even as the barracks were being stripped and the soldiers were turning in their gear. Cochran stood at full "brace," his eyebrows raised.

"Uhh, I don't think so, sir. I don't want to be an aviator."

The colonel ignored him as he signed and stamped orders. Not only had the commander been a Huey pilot in Vietnam, but so had his second in command, and the battalion executive officer, operations officer and master sergeant were all decorated Special Forces veterans. Cochran respected these veteran warriors and had learned much under their tutelage. In turn, they were not about so see the army squander a young man determined to serve, so they had plotted his future together.

"You're going to flight school," the colonel said again. "You're going to take the Flight Aptitude Selection Test today and your flight physical tomorrow. You're going to do well. Are we clear, Lieutenant Cochran?"

"Yes, sir."

The colonel had a comrade who was the chief aviator at the Infantry Assignment Branch at the Pentagon. Two days later, he had all of Cochran's paperwork driven straight from Fort Benning to Washington and hand delivered. Less than a month later, Cochran was in flight school at Fort Rucker, scratching his head. He had no idea that someday he would be a full colonel and a veteran of an elite army aviation unit called the Night Stalkers. At the time, nobody in the army had even conceived of such an outfit—except perhaps for Mike Grimm.

Grimm and Cochran became fast friends. Nearly all the other officers in Hawaii were already married, some had kids, and as the only bachelors around, they spent many off hours at the "O" Club talking about tactics, techniques, procedures and girls until the wee hours. Grimm, approaching his twenty-seventh year in 1975, was a few years older, slightly larger, a combat veteran and an experienced pilot. Cochran, who had only just gotten his wings, was like a sponge eager to soak up every drop of knowledge from a man he came to regard as the older brother he'd never had.

Yet while Hawaii was certainly not a bad place to put in some time, after a year or so it was downright boring. Budgets for serious training and exercises were nonexistent, and the most serious decision to be made on a flight day was whether to circle Oahu clockwise or counterclockwise. Grimm was itching to *do something*. Cochran was anxious to be forged in fire.

On July 4, 1976, America celebrated two hundred years of independence. The tall ships sailed majestically into Boston Harbor. Orchestras across the nation played Tchaikovsky's 1812 Overture to the thunder of cannons. The fireworks displays were magnificent and unprecedented. For the army outfits stationed in Hawaii, it was another glorious summer day, replete with hula girls, barbecues and beer. Yet what really reverberated for Mike Grimm was an event taking place half a world away.

At a primitive airport terminal in Entebbe, Uganda, a combined team of Palestinian and German terrorists was holding 103 Israeli nationals hostage. They had hijacked an Air France jet and forced it to land at the remote African airstrip, knowing they would fall under the protective cloak of Uganda's mad dictator, Idi Amin. Once there, the terrorists had performed a chilling, Nazi-style *"selektion,"* separating the Jewish passengers from the non-Jews; tormenting the former, free-ing the latter. The demands they made to the Israeli government were nearly impossible to fulfill—and of course the results of noncompli-ance would be summary execution of the hostages.

For nearly a week the Israeli government, under Prime Minister Yitzhak Rabin, had negotiated, stalled and apparently prepared itself to surrender to the outrageous demands of freeing scores of incarcer-ated terrorists and paying a hefty ransom. Yet even as it appeared to the world that the terrorists' gambit would win out, Israeli commandos and pilots were planning, preparing and rehearsing. In the early hours of America's Independence Day, four Israeli Air Force C-130s set down by night on the tarmac at Entebbe. A Mercedes limousine, identical to the one in use by Idi Amin, raced from the belly of one air-craft, accompanied by Land Rovers full of Israeli commandos in "blackface" and wearing Ugandan lizard camouflage.

Within ninety seconds it was all over. All the terrorists were dead. Two of the hostages had been killed in the crossfire, and Yonatan Net-anyahu, the commando leader, had been mortally wounded, but all the remaining hostages were being hustled aboard cargo planes. The airport's control tower, antiaircraft batteries and every Russian MiG fighter on the tarmac had been destroyed by satchel charges or anti-tank rockets. In less than an hour, all four C-130s were heading home to Tel Aviv.

The entire world was stunned. Nothing like the Entebbe Raid had ever been attempted, let alone executed at a range of a thousand kilo-meters, at night, over hostile territory and with such precision and suc-cess. Terrorism as a global tactic had not yet touched the West, and only a handful of visionary thinkers knew that it soon would.

That night in the "O" Club at Schofield, Grimm and Cochran perched on their usual stools, downing beers as Grimm shook his head.

"I'm telling you, Randy," Grimm said. "Our nation does not have the capability to do what the Israelis just did."

"That's a fact," Cochran agreed as he waited for his mentor to expound further. Grimm was not, as he himself would readily admit, a great strategic thinker. The shifting sands of national policy didn't interest him, but he desperately wanted his country to have every possible operational option. He had that warrior's ethos: improvise, adapt, overcome.

"We have *got* as a nation to *form* this."

"Okay, Mike." Cochran almost laughed. "But you're a captain and I'm a lieutenant. How're you gonna convince Division leadership, when the biggest threat around here's a rowdy *luau*?"

Grimm raised his eyes and stared at Cochran. And then he just winked. . . .

MIKE GRIMM moved fast, onward and upward. His battlefield reputation preceded him, and Division had clearly identified him early on as a rising star. It wasn't long before he left Cochran's A Company and moved across the hall to command the Headquarters Company. The two friends still saw each other every day, until Grimm was tasked to the 118th Assault Helicopter Company. Shortly thereafter, and not surprisingly, Cochran received orders to do the same. And then Grimm rose to Division Staff and a top spot in the G-3 (Operations) shop, where he could really make things happen.

In the autumn of 1977, Mike Grimm took the Division's entire annual training budget and literally "blew it" on a single exercise. It was, of course, a hostage rescue scenario, to be conducted at long range and requiring every asset the Division had.

Grimm's Emergency Deployment Readiness Exercise (EDRE) involved the rescue and recovery of a building full of "hostages" being held by a select group of infantrymen playing the "terrorists" more than two hundred miles away on the Big Island of Hawaii. The raid was extremely complex, and the new terms and tactics developed by Grimm would remain as the boilerplate for future U.S. special operations of the type.

First, the alert and planning were conducted at Schofield Barracks on Oahu, where the First of the Fifth Infantry were selected as the raiders, along with their helicopter element of ten UH-1H Hueys and two AH-1G Cobra gunships from A Company, Twenty-fifth Aviation Battalion. From there, they self-deployed to the departure airfield at Hickam Air Force Base near Honolulu. To simulate a strategic deployment, the Hueys were prepared and loaded aboard Air Force C-141s for the "long" trip to Hilo on the Big Island, which Grimm coined the ISB—Intermediate Staging Base.

Arriving in Hilo on November 14, the helicopters were off-loaded and reassembled, and the next day the raiders proceeded to Grimm's FSB—Forward Staging Base—at Bradshaw Army Airfield in Pohaku-loa Training Area in the center of Hawaii. Further mission planning and rehearsals were conducted there, and then it was game time.

The target building was the fire station at the Waimea-Kohala Airport, thirty miles north of Bradshaw Army Airfield. Major George Anderson, A Company's commander, would be the operation's air mission commander, leading the assault in the first bird. Randy Cochran would be flying Chalk 3, a Vietnam-era Huey that had so many bullet hole repairs he had nicknamed it "Patches." First Lieutenant Frank Atkins was Grimm's transportation planner for the raid, the battalion executive officer was Major Ben Couch and Lieutenant Colonel Terry Henry was their battalion commander. Someday soon, all these men would reconvene to develop the most technologically advanced army aviation capabilities on earth, but at the time the Huey pilots did not even have night vision equipment. The raiders launched at dawn on November 16.

The thunderous *thwopping* of a dozen Hueys and Cobras rising as one could most probably be heard at Waimea almost as soon as they took off from Bradshaw. By the time they were visually spotted by the "terrorists" at the fire station—no less than ten miles away in that beautiful blue sky—all the hostages had been "executed." When the raiders finally landed at Waimea, they were wiped out to the last man.

To all but Grimm, the EDRE was a debacle. To him, it was merely a lesson learned. But the army didn't see it that way.

The next day, back at a World War II–era Quonset hut at Pohakuloa Training Area, the After Action Review was a funereal affair. With all the various element leaders assembled there weren't many positive things to say. Everything had gone wrong; nothing had gone right. The only ones who had properly executed their mission were the "terrorists." And then, bad turned to worse as the men snapped to attention to receive the Division commander, two-star general Willard Scott. The general did not mince words.

"Gentlemen," he began with a hard sigh, "this sort of thing is a really bad idea."

Randy Cochran winced, grateful that he had been promoted to captain just *prior* to the Waimea fiasco. He glanced over at Grimm, who was squinting at General Scott from his seat. Mike had also recently been promoted and Randy wondered if the general would somehow bust Major Grimm back to a "butter bar."

General Scott expounded for some minutes on the "inappropriate" idea that heliborne infantry would ever engage in such high-risk counterterror operations.

"Our army will never enter into this area," he concluded. "This is *not* our role."

Unbelievably, Mike Grimm rose from his seat. Jaws dropped as the brand-new major went toe-to-toe with a two-star.

"Respectfully, sir," Grimm said, "that is not correct."

Cochran was dumbfounded. *Sit down and shut the hell up, Mike!* he railed inside his head. But Grimm pressed on.

"Not only do we need to create this capability, sir, but if we don't, we are going to find ourselves at some point in our history embarrassed as a nation."

Nothing moved in that room but the ceiling fans. Grimm resumed his seat. General Scott raised an eyebrow, but being essentially a gentleman, he chose not to take the young major to task in open forum. Randy Cochran sat there and stifled a grin. You could be smart, or you could be right, but rarely both. Grimm might have had more balls than brains, but he was definitely *right*. And very soon, his words would be echoed in the gloomy halls of the Pentagon. . . .

THE MORNING of April 25, 1980, heralded a cold cruel dawn in the Iranian desert.

Spirals of smoke still billowed from the blackened hulks of five U.S. Marine Corps helicopters and one Air Force C-130 cargo plane. Charred leaves of classified documents fluttered like tumbleweeds through tufts of singed brush. The horribly burned corpses of eight U.S. servicemen lay buried inside their twisted metal tombs, while gleeful Iranian Revolutionary Guards fired their rifles into the air and flashed Vs for victory before incredulous news photographers.

The Americans had come to perform a rescue mission, and instead had retreated for home with their tails between their legs.

Back in Washington, general officers at the Pentagon shook their heads in defeat and disbelief. How had this happened? A ragtag bunch of Islamic fundamentalist revolutionaries had taken fifty-three Americans hostage, and a rescue was impossible? The Israelis had pulled it off at Entebbe with their Operation Thunderbolt, and just one year later, German commandos had mirrored that success by liberating a hijacked Lufthansa jet on the tarmac at Mogadishu. But the vaunted United States Armed Forces couldn't do the same? America had assembled a raiding force from the combined services, all of whom wanted a piece of the glory. But in the end, Operation Eagle Claw had proved to be an ill-coordinated effort of technologically unprepared resources. A disaster.

It was not going to happen again. Never again.

President Jimmy Carter had always been regarded as risk-averse by his Joint Chiefs, yet he had certainly shown moxy in green-lighting Eagle Claw. Now he would reap the bitter fruits of that public humiliation, and it would cost him the presidency in the coming election, yet he was still going to try to repair the stuttering machine that was America's special operations capability. As a former naval officer, Carter trusted the clear cold eyes of ships' captains and appointed former chief of naval operations Admiral James L. Holloway III to perform the autopsy on the failed mission. The Holloway Commission would discover many anomalies in the harebrained idea of throwing elite units from highly competitive services together for a crucial national mission, but in the short term, its members emphasized the immediacy of the problem: The hostages were still being held and the American military did not have a force of specially trained pilots and crews who could deliver and extract its most elite raiders.

Eagle Claw had failed, and ironically, all eyes now turned to "the Screaming Eagles."

The U.S. Army's 101st Airborne Division had nothing left to prove. It had been activated in the summer of 1942, when America was engaged in foreign fields and multiple theaters of war, and the concept of infantry assault from the sky was considered daring by all and foolish by many. Helicopters had not yet been developed past the prototype stage, and the division's newly trained paratroopers would be hurling themselves from the bellies of C-47 cargo planes, or thumping onto enemy fields aboard gliders made of steel tubing, wood and canvas. The men who volunteered for these missions did not need to be asked twice. On August 19, 1942, the division's first commander, Major General William C. Lee, stood before his new recruits and offered an oath: "The 101st has no history, but it has a rendezvous with destiny."

The division had parachuted into Normandy on D-Day, survived its near decimation at the Bulge and emerged victorious, parachuted again into Holland and then thundered on across the Rhine, earning four campaign streamers and two Presidential Unit Citations. In the two decades following that war, it had been activated four times, until at last the entire division was deployed to Vietnam in 1967. By that time the army understood that the only means by which to quickly deploy infantry over jutting peaks and into multiple-canopied jungles was by helicopter, and the division became Air Mobile. In nearly seven years of Vietnam combat, the men and machines of the 101st participated in fifteen campaigns, leaving their blood and their legacy in places like Dak To and the A Shau Valley.

The 101st had its home at Fort Campbell, Kentucky, an enormous plot of 105,000 acres straddling the Tennessee and Kentucky state lines. By 1980, while most of the army's surviving Vietnam-era helicopter pilots had long gone home to their families, some of the very best—and some would say those of questionable sanity—had remained with the division. If they were ever going to fly again in combat, the 101st was the place to be. Their skills and experience were unmatched, and as younger pilots found their way to the division, the mix of gnarled mentors and green enthusiasts had proved to be the ideal incubator for perfecting the newest techniques in air assault.

The division's air component, the 101st Aviation Group, had the men and the machines to serve as the embryo of a new plan to rescue the hostages, but someone was going to have to point that out. In Washington, sullen officers were shredding the ill-begotten plans for Eagle Claw while brainstorming new ideas that might possibly work. It was going to be doubly difficult now, like a surprise party blown by the birthday cake having burst into flames.

IN A MASSIVE and bureaucratic military organization like the U.S. Army, courage is not always measured in combat, although Major Ken Jacobs had certainly seen his share in Southeast Asia. In 1968, as the Distinguished Military Graduate of Norwich University in Vermont, he went straight from his college commencement to the army, and by late 1969 he was a young lieutenant and CH-47 Chinook pilot serving in Vietnam with the "Hill Climbers" of the First Cavalry Division. After two back-to-back tours, Jacobs seemed to follow the pattern of many other pilots who wanted to stay in, while most everyone else was trying to get out. He served five years in Hawaii as both an air operations officer and a rifle company commander, and eventually wound his way back to the 101st Aviation Battalion at Fort Campbell.

But what most impressed Jacobs's superiors were his analytical capabilities and his willingness to express the convictions born of years of aviation experience. Ten years after he had first landed in the steam of Saigon, he found himself about to engage in mortal combat in the most dangerous minefield of any officer's career—DCSOPS, the army's office of the deputy chief of staff for operations at the Pentagon. Without ceremony, he had been tasked to DCSOPS from his position as executive officer to the commander of the 101st Aviation Group down at Campbell. When the hostage crisis boiled over into the most public of failures, Jacobs was already serving as a force integration officer at DCSOPS.

Major Jacobs was summoned by his boss, Colonel Maddox, to the Army Operations Center deep below the Pentagon's main floors. There, he was introduced to a man he'd never met, Major General James Vaught, who as overall mission commander of the recently failed Eagle Claw—which he was about to be given one more shot at—did not have time for pleasantries.

"Jacobs, we're going to give you the mission of forming an aviation task force to go back in again," Vaught said. "Because you've just come in from the field, what I want you to do is to look at the operational plans and tell us what capabilities we have."

In addition to having a reputation as a good pilot, Jacobs had already gone through the Armed Forces Staff College. He had learned the martial arts of the consummate staff officer: knowing when to hold his peace, choosing his words carefully when he spoke, yet never letting his own career ambitions obstruct the goals of the mission. As orders of battle and unit records were shuffled across the conference table like résumés at a Broadway audition, Jacobs didn't need to think it over, and he uttered the words that would prove to be prescient.

"You've got to give it to the 101st, sir," he said with flat conviction, especially for a major treading water in a sea of colonels and generals. "They're the only ones who have the new Blackhawks and the only outfit that can handle this."

Colonel Maddox raised an eyebrow. The young major didn't back down.

Jacobs was challenged to back up his suggestion, and of course he was prepared, presenting a pilot's case full of available aircraft types, capabilities, aviators' records and crew manifests. There were few arguments opposing; the navy and Marine Corps pilots and machines had already shown a lack of capability, and the air force had a tendency to tack on eighteen-wheelers full of support equipment whenever operating at long range—that wouldn't do when infiltrating "door-kickers" like Delta into a hot landing zone. Ken Jacobs could have retired that very day and he would have made his mark on U.S. Army special operations history. But he did not retire; he was already plotting how to "steal" aviation assets and crews for the new mission. It was Army's turn to take the field. Operation Honey Badger was in play.

The mission would center around the Screaming Eagles' 158th Aviation Battalion, under the command of Lieutenant Colonel Ben Couch, whose Companies C and D had recently acquired brand-new UH-60A Blackhawk helicopters to replace the aging Hueys. With its main rotor blades folded up, the Blackhawk's airframe was only one hundred inches longer than the Huey's, and they were nearly identical in size across the beam, making the sleek helo eminently deployable. The UH-60 weighed in at more than eighteen thousand pounds, as opposed to the UH-1's slim five thousand, but the Blackhawk's powerful twin turbines could haul nearly a ton and half of cargo, or an entire squad of fully equipped combat troops. It was a "screamer," capable of racing along just above the deck at 140 knots, then skidding into a tight turn like an acrobatic biplane and setting down its assaulters in a patch the size of a preschool playground.

In addition to the Blackhawks, the developing rescue plan would also require a heavy lift element—aircraft capable of hauling even larger numbers of personnel and heavier payloads than the UH-60s. The C-130 cargo planes that had been packed with fuel blivets and used at Desert One—the site of Eagle Claw's debacle—did have Short Takeoff and Landing (STOL) capabilities, but they still required a carefully reconnoitered and substantial landing strip. The 159th Assault Support Helicopter Battalion was chosen to provide its CH-47C Chinooks for the mission. The twin-rotor, sixty-foot-long, twenty-five-thousand-pound monsters would not be easy to conceal, and packing them up and moving them to a Forward Staging Base would prove a logistical challenge. Still, the big birds could handle almost any type of weather, and with their ability to haul nearly their own weight in cargo they would provide the ideal Forward Area Refuel/Rearm Points (FARPs) in the distant desert.

But something else was also envisioned, something new. The Honey Badger planners realized that their Iranian adversaries anticipated another rescue attempt, so the hostages had certainly been relocated and split into smaller, less accessible groups. The insertion of fast-moving ground vehicles was not an option, so the raiders would need a highly flexible force of fast attack and light assault helos. During the Vietnam War, a very small, light observation and command helicopter, the OH-6A, had been used in a similar role. The "Loaches" had proven extremely effective when combined with AH-1G Cobra gunships in formations called Pink Teams. They swooped and darted like little birds above the jungle, trolling for enemy positions and drawing ground fire, then calling in the "snakes" to take on the Cong.

The OH-6s were only twenty-five feet long and weighed in at a mere two thousand pounds, but with a speed of more than 120 knots and the turning radius of a motorcycle, they would be perfect for maneuvering through the clusters of buildings and narrow streets of urban Tehran. Mounted with miniguns and rockets, they could substitute for the much larger Cobras, and when flown by a single pilot perhaps four or five raiders could huddle inside their egglike fuselages. As it turned out, the Screaming Eagles had no such airplanes in their inventory, but the Mississippi National Guard had plenty of them sitting in the sun at Gulfport. Pilots from the 229th Attack Helicopter Battalion of the 101st would be selected to man those Little Birds—once they learned how to fly them.

Major Ken Jacobs was not a very popular man in army aviation circles during those early days of Operation Honey Badger, but he had no time for smoothing ruffled feathers. It was already May of 1980 and he was determined to have a new raiding element ready by midsummer, a nearly impossible task. With the backing of Colonel Maddox and General Vaught, a "tasking" from Jacobs was an order from on high. Blackhawks and Chinooks, along with their pilots and crews, would be "borrowed" from the 101st for open-book periods of unspecified training. Given that the mission would require extremely long-range operations, fuel would be a problem. Jacobs issued orders to enraged quartermasters all across Europe to have army medevac helicopters stripped of their internal fuel tanks and the tanks shipped Stateside. He would not take no for an answer, and he became known as "the Iron Major."

Jacobs assembled a team of capable and innovative officers and men, who understood the mission's requirements and would do anything and everything to squeeze the equipment and personnel into the Honey Badger mold. Stu Gerald and Wimpy Pybus were Jacobs's "scroungers," finding the equipment he needed and making sure he got it. At Fort Rucker, Dave Funk took over the training elements, laying out timetables and benchmarks that the Blackhawks and Chinooks would have to meet. Mike Hoffman modified tools and techniques that would be crucial in the success of long-range, nighttime desert flying, such as night vision goggles that had never before been used in such a mission as was being planned. Being the flight release officer for Honey Badger, Hoffman was also, conveniently, the man who signed off on and approved of such equipment. A brand-new technology called FLIR (Forward Looking Infrared) was still in the experimental stage, but Jacobs and his crew managed to have the heat-sensing devices installed on helicopters for testing, evaluation and implementation. It would soon be discovered that the OH-6s did not have enough interior room to host the Delta snipers who wanted to be able to "perch" and shoot from the small platforms; Jacobs and Hoffman had fifty-five-gallon fuel drums cut in half and welded to the skids to serve as sniper platforms. Yet now, with all the additional weight of special operators, weapons and equipment on board those Little Birds, the small helicopters could barely struggle off the ground. Hoffman went to a drag race in St. Louis and observed the modified stock cars screaming off the line with an explosive burst of mixed water and alcohol. They tried it on the Little Birds and it worked. It was slowly coming together: Task Force 158.

It wasn't the way the army did things. It was "doctrine on the fly," but the Iron Major and his team were breaking ground and bullying their way through the bureaucracy. If army aviators had heretofore been thought of as "taxi drivers," now they would be commando pilots on a par with the customers they carried.

The Blackhawk and Chinook crews began to train hard for an "unspecified" mission. No one in their chains of command actually mentioned Iran, the failure at Desert One or the hostage crisis, but it didn't take a genius to guess where all this was heading. At the time, if you were a young, ambitious aviation officer hoping to perhaps someday wear general's stars on your epaulettes, this was definitely *not* the way to go. In the post-Vietnam army, supporting the Cold War in Europe was the priority. Funding was very tight and everything had to be done by the book and according to regulations, or not done at all. Most of army aviation focused on multiple, short-distance missions based on no more than two hours of fuel. The army and most certainly army aviation were regarded as daylight fighting forces. There was no Internet, no secure telephones, no cell phones. The definition of a high-speed, secure communication was sending a note by runner across the post in a jeep.

It was under these conditions, and with little hope of advancement or acknowledgment for the type of mission disdained by most of the conventional army, that officers and aviators dedicated themselves to Honey Badger, and to hell with the consequences. Major General Jack Mackmull, the commanding general of the 101st Airborne Division, gave his blessing to those leaders of his Aviation Group who would be risking their lives and their careers. Major Bryan "Doug" Brown, who would many years later come to lead all United States Special Operations Command during the Global War on Terror, was the dedicated young aviator commanding Honey Badger's Blackhawk element. Colonel Teddy Allen was heading up the 101st Aviation Group; Lieutenant Colonel Joe Drew was commanding the 229th Aviation Battalion; Lieutenant Colonel Ben Couch commanded the 158th Aviation Battalion and would become the very first commander of Task Force 160.

The pilots and crews of the 158th and 159th relocated to western American deserts for weeks at a time, flying longer and longer nighttime missions. They were introduced to the new technologies of night vision goggles, in particular the AN/PVS-5, a device that looked like an opaque diving mask with a pair of binocular-like tubes. The PVS-5 could intensify starlight or moonlight into a grainy green version of daylight, yet it was exhausting to fly with and provided for no peripheral view. Soon enough, Hoffman and his wonder boys would cut out the plastic skirts of the NVGs so that pilots could glance down at their instruments, and the interior lighting and instruments of the helicopters would be modified to keep the mission "dark." Within a few short weeks, the Blackhawk and Chinook pilots were flying "the black route," a complex, dangerous, nap-of-the-earth course of more than a thousand miles, and arriving on target "plus or minus thirty seconds," a feat that would become the Night Stalker calling card and claim to professional fame.

By late July, General Vaught and the Joint Chiefs demanded a progress report. What exactly had the Iron Major been doing? Ken Jacobs mounted a demonstration of Honey Badger, and all the various raiding elements began from the starting line—loading aboard CH-47s and C5-As, arriving at their ISB, moving to their FSB, flying more than a thousand miles at night and executing their mock rescue. Jacobs flew that mission himself, and then it was time to put his money where his mouth was. He privately regarded it as "letting the fox run the henhouse," but he declared, "We're good to go." In barely three months of round-the-clock, high-risk, never-see-home training, Task Force 158 was ready. Now they would wait for the green light.

Meanwhile, those companies tasked to Honey Badger were still informally "borrowed" from the 101st and always subject to returning there in support of the division's conventional requirements. Yet simultaneously, another element of the new rescue effort was being put together, one that would remain independent, permanent and outside the chain of command. It was a "renegade" element and it was called the Special Helicopter Operations Company, or SHOC.

There was a section of Fort Campbell far removed from the main runways and hangars, deep in the woods, past streams and over rolling hills. It was called the Old Clarksville Navy Base and not just anyone could go there. There were subterranean bunkers in that forbidden enclave, where nuclear weapons had once been stored for the unthinkable and where concrete guard emplacements had been manned by steely-eyed marines with .50 caliber machine guns. Far back in the forest behind those bunkers, a series of anonymous garages would house the SHOC helicopters, and due to incessant Soviet satellite flyovers, those aircraft would be rolled out only at night.

SHOC was to become a new breeding ground for special operations aviators, and of course Mike Grimm suddenly appeared there, as if he had sensed it in the wind, as if the "bat signal" had appeared in the clouds and he'd been summoned. Major Grimm, until that time, had never flown a Loach, nor had most of the other pilots who would be selected to quietly pack their gear and slither away from their parent units. Grimm and these other men would learn quickly, until no one could touch them at the controls of those Little Birds.

One of those men was Robert Fladry, who was about to take a turn that would veer him sharply away from his conventional path as an army helicopter pilot and lead him into the secret and seminal world of special operations aviation. Born in 1950 in Erie, Pennsylvania, "Flapper" didn't really hail from a military family, although both his parents had participated in World War II. His father had been in the Army Air Corps, serving at Howard Field in Panama, and his mother had joined the U.S. Navy as a Wave. After suffering a ruptured eardrum during a CH-47 flight, she had become a "Rosie the Riveter," working on P-38 Lightnings at a defense factory. Yet Flapper really had no idea what life choices he would make, until November 23, 1967. On that day, his older brother was killed in action at Dak To, Vietnam, while serving as a paratrooper with the 173rd Airborne Brigade. Three months later, on his eighteenth birthday, Flapper signed his own induction papers and volunteered for the army, just as his brother had done. Mrs. Fladry, divorced and struggling as a single mother, was still barely managing her grief after the death of her eldest son. She was less than pleased with Bob's decision to join up, but there would be no stopping him. The Fladrys weren't flag-wavers, but duty was a call to which they answered.

Flapper graduated that spring and went "from high school to flight school." One year later, in April 1969, he was a nineteen-year-old warrant officer-1 flying Hueys in Vietnam for "Killer Spade," the 229th Battalion of the First Cavalry Division. On Flapper's very first mission, he flew for eleven hours straight, and most of his first tour in Vietnam was no different. These incredibly young Huey pilots would get up in the morning and immediately be assigned to lift battalion-sized infantry elements into hot landing zones. Those infantrymen would commonly be spending two or three weeks in the jungle on combat operations, so the "slick" pilots would be making ammunition runs, delivering C-rations and mail, inserting replacements and bringing out the wounded and the dead. Flapper was shot at regularly, but it was his accidental run-in with a tent stake that took him out of action. He was medevaced to Japan with a festering leg wound, spent eighteen months Stateside as an instructor pilot at Hunter Army Airfield in Georgia, then retrained as a Cobra gun pilot and went back for more.

Serving in Delta Company of the 229th, the "Smiling Tigers" of the First Cav, for his second Vietnam tour, Fladry flew both Cobras and OH-6s—sometimes drawing enemy fire in the minuscule egg-shaped bird, and sometimes giving it back to the enemy in spades while flying the long and ugly killer "snake." When at last he left Vietnam on Easter Sunday 1972, he was already considered an "old pilot" in the aviation culture of that war. His dog-eared logbook held more flight hours than he would have amassed in ten years of peacetime aviation; and they were all combat hours.

While most of the veteran Vietnam pilots chose to pursue their civilian lives and try to forget about Vietnam, Fladry stayed on at Fort Campbell for four more years, then spent another three flying in Hawaii. When he rotated back to Kentucky once more, he was again assigned to Bravo Company of the 229th, 101st Airborne Division, where the new commander, Major Mike Grimm, informed him that he would be flying Cobras in support of the division. But Flapper didn't much care for the ungainly gunships.

"Don't really want to do that, sir," he announced bluntly to Grimm. "I'm much better in the Loaches."

If Grimm respected anyone, it was Vietnam combat veterans who had earned their professional preferences in heavy action. Fladry was assigned to the company's Scout platoon.

It was April 1980 when Fladry settled into his new home under Mike Grimm's command. On a break between training cycles, he read about the tragedy at Desert One in the newspaper, shook his head sadly and returned to work for a major division exercise. Like most of the other pilots at Fort Campbell, he had no idea that a major named Ken Jacobs was brewing up an interesting turn of fate for those who had the talent and the nerve. As May turned to June, Honey Badger's Blackhawks and Chinooks were shaping up their portion of the secret mission, yet the very tip of that spear needed a razor-sharp point. Fladry noticed that Major Grimm suddenly seemed to disappear from his position as company commander, while the executive officer took over command. Randy Cochran, who was by then flying for the 101st, also noted that his mentor from Hawaii was no longer showing up for their late-night beer chats at the "O" Club.

One Saturday late in June, Flapper was relaxing at home on post when the phone rang. An unfamiliar voice spoke to him.

"Mr. Fladry, be at G-1 at ten hundred hours. Wear civilian clothes, bring your ID and your dog tags, and don't mention this to anyone."

Flapper was, for want of a better word, "unflappable," but this certainly piqued his curiosity. When he arrived at G-1 (the division personnel office), there were twenty other pilots wearing blue jeans and bemused expressions. From the 229th, companies Alpha, Bravo and Charlie had each "donated" a captain and five warrant officers. Two more warrants had been selected from the Cav.

"We can't tell you where you're going," said a stranger who looked uncomfortable in his civilian suit. "Go home and pack your bags. You're leaving from here on a Chinook tomorrow at noon."

The next morning the twenty "volunteers" were flown down to the Mississippi Army National Guard Aviation Support Facility at Gulfport, where they ensconced themselves and took over the Guard's entire fleet of OH-6s to begin aircraft qualifications. The Mississippi National Guard commander was furious, but he had no defense against the manipulations of some "Iron Major" who was working out of the Pentagon. Fladry and one other pilot, Dave Spoor, had both flown Loaches in Vietnam. The rest of the men barely had a few previous hours at the controls of the OH-6s, while Fladry and Spoor already had hundreds of hours of experience and soon became instructor pilots. After a couple of weeks of familiarization, the secret team moved out to Fort Huachuca, Arizona, and began flying formations at night in the desert, with lights off. Flying "nighthawk" this way without any illumination or visual aids was risky business. It was all right on moonlit nights, but when the moon was down and clouds obscured the stars, just staying alive became the focus of the missions. That wouldn't do in the Iranian desert, where a "haboob" could spring up without warning, so NVGs started appearing in the equipment roster and the men were soon able to fly their Little Birds like bats in a blackened cave. The Little Bird component of Honey Badger, which was quickly developing into a small but formidable force, was designated as "Grizzly Fur."

As the summer of 1980 drifted into autumn, all the elements of Task Force 158—which still did not officially exist on any of the army's books—honed their skills and cross-trained with their customers until they far exceeded the requirements of what everyone hoped would be Eagle Claw II. Adding another item to the Grizzly Fur menu, Bob Fladry, Charlie Weigandt and Frank Whitehead flew out to Eglin Air Force Base to develop a Little Bird attack component. When they returned, Major Grimm had six of his OH-6s mounted with 7.62mm miniguns on one side of the fuselage, and rocket pods on the other. His SHOC organization now had a Little Bird assault element (MH-6s) and an attack element (AH-6s). Grimm, charismatic as ever and always leading by example, was relentless in his preparation for the hostage rescue. The hard lessons learned during the EDRE exercise in Hawaii had not been forgotten. He had known all along that this was coming, and he was going to be prepared when the balloon went up. During the daylight hours, his men maintained the helos, developed new tactics, techniques and procedures, and refined their plans. Every night, the birds were pulled from their lairs, and they flew.

They all waited for the green light, but still nothing happened.

They were like racehorses stamping in their starting gates, waiting for the bell. Autumn waned, Jimmy Carter lost the election to Ronald Reagan, and the cold winds began to blow at Fort Campbell. It didn't seem very likely that Carter's last political gasp would be a risky repeat of Eagle Claw, yet everyone associated with Honey Badger eagerly assumed that when Reagan took office, their beepers would go off and they'd be on their way. But the Iranians deduced that as well, and on January 20, 1981, Ronald Reagan's inauguration day, the hostages were suddenly released.

Mike Grimm held his breath. Honey Badger and SHOC had been stripped of their mission, but he had faith that at last, army leadership would no longer be claiming, "This is not our role." He was right, and Ken Jacobs was called once again before General Vaught and given his orders.

"Keep it in play, Jacobs. We're going to need it."

As Honey Badger stood down, the Blackhawks and Chinooks were returned to service their parent battalions, yet Grimm's Little Bird task force remained in place deep in the Clarksville Base woods. Rumors abounded about what exactly they were doing over there, but it was clearly something very special. Bob Johnson was serving as a platoon leader in the First Brigade's aviation platoon, commanding four Hueys and six OH-58 Scouts. Each night he would enviously observe flights of fifteen Little Birds racing around the post, overloaded with special tactics troops and delivering them to mock targets in what were essentially controlled crashes. He wanted to be part of that, and he cornered Major Grimm one night in the "O" Club. Grimm agreed that Johnson had the right stuff, and after battling the bureaucracy for many months Captain Johnson was finally released from his 101st duties to serve as the S-1 personnel officer of Grimm's organization. In the beginning, Johnson didn't get to fly very much, but he was thrilled to be part of a special operations aviation element that would soon be officially designated as Task Force 160.

Randy Cochran, by then also a captain and serving as a platoon leader over at Third Brigade, desperately wanted to come over to SHOC and work once again with Mike Grimm. Yet the jealousies of the conventional commanders regarding this "renegade" task force made it very difficult for pilots to be transferred from their units. Cochran's wife, Sharon, an army nurse, was about to be posted to Germany, and Cochran's staying behind to wait for an open slot didn't seem like the wisest idea for marital harmony. An aviation position could easily be found for him in Germany, and he would be allowed to accompany his wife if he wished.

"Go with her, Randy," Mike Grimm told him over one of their late-night discussions. "When you get back from Germany, I promise I'll get you in."

There was no reason for Cochran not to believe Grimm. The man had never broken his word in his life.

Bob Fladry, clearly one of the most experienced and talented pilots in Grimm's organization, flew with his commander on a regular basis throughout the spring and early fall of 1981. Grimm was pushing the operational envelope and Fladry pushed it right alongside him. The major and his chief warrant officer were similar in nature: both were decorated combat veterans; both loved to fly low, hard and fast with the doors off and the wind rushing through the cockpit. If the training mission was long, dark and circuitous, they made it harder because that was what they knew to expect in action. As October approached, the date for the official uncasing of Task Force 160's "colors" was set for the sixteenth. The unit would be on the army's roster as the 160th Aviation Battalion and comprised three companies of Little Birds: A Company would consist of the assault MH-6s, B Company the attack AH-6s, and HSC (Headquarters and Service Company) would be maintenance. It was widely assumed that Major Mike Grimm, now "promotable" to lieutenant colonel, was going to be the first commander of the Army Special Operations Aviation Battalion. But before that happened, there would be one final dog and pony show for army brass, just to prove that this "special operations thing" was worth the funding.

On the night of October 7, Mike Grimm and Bob Fladry climbed into their Little Bird to lead a twenty-two-ship mission through a twisting route along the Cumberland River in Tennessee. On the previous night they had flown a rehearsal for that demonstration, but had not tracked along every curve of the wide surging river below. On this night, with movers and shakers in the back of the flight, Grimm wanted to "make it look good." Bob Johnson was slated to fly in the back of Grimm's helo that night, because as a personnel officer who spent most of his days taking care of the numerous administrative demands of the task force, he needed the air time. Johnson happened to have a head-busting cold and with the open canopy of the Little Bird and a late night flight in the October wind looming, Grimm told him to sit it out in the "O" Club.

"Believe me, you'll get plenty of opportunities to freeze your ass off."

Johnson was grateful to skip it.

It was indeed cold that night. High clouds obscured the moon and stars and the tall thick trees bracing the wide black river reminded Flapper of many such jungles in Southeast Asia. Yet he was not focused on the lush landscape of Tennessee. In the left seat of the Little Bird, Flapper was wearing PVS-5s, his head down and concentrating on the course route, a map and the helo's dimmed instruments. Grimm was at the controls, leading the large formation at a very low altitude through sharp twists and turns. The lead echelon consisted of his bird, then three more to his left in a very tight formation, with the rest of the element spread out in flights behind. It was Flapper's job to tell his commander when to turn, how much, what heading to take, and to report their airspeed and altitude. The objective of special operations aviation was precision, and making every move exactly as planned was what gave you the proper time on target.

The helo was coming up on a way point in the mission course, a large bend in the wide, shimmering river just below. Fladry pressed his mike switch.

"Sir, we need to turn left now."

Grimm nodded, easing the Little Bird into a turn as he flew just above the right bank of the Cumberland. Through Fladry's doorless cockpit frame, the other three birds were so tight and close he felt that he could reach out and touch them.

"Okay, sir," he said. "We're coming through two hundred twenty degrees to a heading of one-seven-five. Altitude is one-three-niner. We need eighty knots."

"Roger," Grimm said. Mike worked the collective to make the airspeed needle pierce that number precisely.

Flapper lifted his head, relaxing his shoulders a bit. They were on course and on time.

"Okay, we're at eighty knots," he reported.

It was the last thing Fladry said on that mission. There was something out there in the night, something that none of the pilots could see through their primitive PVS-5s. Arching up from the tall trees on the right bank of the river was a high-tension steel girder tower laced with power lines. Those lines drooped dramatically down toward the water and were strung out above the river at only forty feet across double wooden poles. Grimm's three wingmen, flying at the same altitude of 140 feet, skipped easily across those black lines and never even saw them. But where the lines swooped upward toward the tower, Grimm's and Fladry's helo skids suddenly curled into the heavy cables and were instantly trapped. The lightweight helo skidded to the right, lanced up and smashed into the tower in an explosion of sparks and splitting metal.

Fladry instantly became a flying missile. His safety harness ripped from his seat and his body burst through the thick bubble canopy as he was launched into the night, spinning through the air and splashing onto his back in the dark waters below. The momentum of his impact shot him straight down to the river bottom, then he popped to the surface for a moment and sank again. Yet even as he submerged he didn't panic. He was a qualified scuba diver and had faith that he'd rise again. His helmet was still on; it had a foam core and would help him float. When he breached the surface once more he lay back in the freezing water and his first thought was, *Well, I guess I'm alive.*

He was certainly still in the world of the living, but inexplicably. He had two compressed vertebrae, three cracked ribs, four broken ribs and his liver had been punctured. His left leg was mangled and his foot broken. His left thumb was hanging from the joint by a thread of bloody sinew. His non-life-threatening lacerations would require more than a hundred stitches.

He had no idea what had happened, but assumed they had impacted with another helo in the flight. As he lay back in the surging water and tried to breathe, he could hear nothing but the panicky quacks of shocked ducks and geese. He twisted his neck around and spotted the shore, and with one arm he began to paddle. He made it to the muddy embankment, but it was so steep that he was only able to drag himself partway out of the water. He reached down for his strobe light and discovered that he must have hit the helo's console on the way out, because every pocket of his flight vest had been shorn away, stripping him of all his emergency gear, but he remembered still having some chemlights tucked inside the vest. He popped two of them and threw them in the river, and he grimaced in silent agony as he waved another one above his head.

Less than five minutes later another Little Bird landed on the muddy bank. Dan Satterfield jumped from the cockpit and raced over to Flapper, who raised a hand to stop him.

"Dan, let me tell you what my injuries are first," Fladry said, "before I pass out."

Satterfield bent to him. "Tell me."

"My back is really messed up and my leg really hurts."

"Okay."

"What happened to the other aircraft that ran into us?" Fladry asked.

"You didn't hit another aircraft. You ran into wires."

Satterfield reached down for Fladry's flight vest and started to haul him up out of the water.

"Okay, that's far enough," Fladry winced. "Hurts too much. Where's Grimm?"

Satterfield looked out across the dark waters of the river and squinted into the darkness. He cupped his hands and called out, "Mike?" There was no answer. Other Little Birds began to float down onto the accident scene. The pilots didn't dare move Fladry in his condition, so they waited for a medevac helo from the brigade. They walked along the muddy shore, calling out for Mike Grimm. If Fladry had survived that incredible crash, then maybe Grimm had, too. But Mike Grimm's luck had run out that night. His side of the Little Bird had impacted directly with the steel tower. He had been instantly killed and hurled into the forest, and it would take days to recover his body.

It was nothing less than a miracle that Fladry survived not only that impact but the hours that ensued. As it turned out, the brigade's only medevac helo on call that night was forced to land elsewhere due to a mechanical malfunction. Fladry lay in the mud for two hours until another medevac aircraft out on a training mission heard the Mayday call. The pilot was Cliff McGee, who had flown with Fladry during his second tour in Vietnam. He flew out to Tennessee and picked up his shattered comrade from the banks of the river.

While this drama was unfolding, Bob Johnson, whose head cold was keeping him up, decided to have a drink at the "O" Club with his first wife, Mary Beth, who was serving as the intensive care nurse at the Fort Campbell base hospital and had just come off shift. With a whiskey and soda halfway to his lips, Johnson suddenly felt the Reaper's chill course through his spine. He knew something very bad had happened out there, but he didn't know what.

Early the next morning Johnson showed up at the hospital to bring Mary Beth some breakfast. He spotted the task force flight surgeon, who had a look on his face that said it all. And there, lying alone in an ICU cubicle, was Bob Fladry. Half of his body was bandaged up like a mummy, black stitches were everywhere and tubes were running in and out of his bruised flesh. The two pilots looked at each other. Fladry realized that he was the only patient in the ward and had already drawn his conclusions about Mike Grimm. Johnson's spine chill had done the same for him.

"We lost a guy last night," Fladry whispered.

"It was Mike, wasn't it?" Johnson managed.

"Yeah. It was Mike."

If not for his head cold, Johnson would have been riding in the back of that Little Bird. Grimm's decision to let him skip the exercise had spared his life.

Bob Fladry would endure numerous surgeries, painful rehabilitation and the near loss of his left leg. But it never crossed his mind that he would not fly again. Having lost his left thumb, he had to request a special waiver from the army, which generally frowned upon pilots flying without all of their digits. On April 7, 1982, exactly six months to the day from his accident, he would be back in the cockpit.

Bob Johnson received a phone call at the S-1 shop that day from Colonel Ben Couch, who was now going to leave his command at the 158th and become the first commander of the 160th Aviation Battalion.

"Bob," the colonel said, "I need a Survivor's Assistance Officer for Karin Grimm."

"Yes, sir," Johnson said.

It was one of the worst assignments any officer could draw. You had to mourn with the family, comfort the children and help the widow with the reams of paperwork and the myriad details that followed such a death. The army as a whole wasn't very good at these things, but over the years the Night Stalkers would learn to be exceptionally good at it, and Johnson was about to begin that sad but ironclad tradition. As he donned his Class A's and prepared himself mentally, he recalled his very first task force interview with Mike Grimm. Reporting to Grimm's office, he had found the major changing into his Class A's, about to go off and perform the sad task of notifying the wife of a Chinook pilot who had been killed during a training mission for Honey Badger. Grimm had smiled sadly and excused himself. Now it was Johnson's turn to perform a similar duty, for a war hero, pilot and superb commander who had left an indelible mark, and had departed much too early.

One of Johnson's first tasks was to gather up Grimm's records and personal effects. As a pilot and commander, Grimm's professional paperwork was in perfect order, while his own personal matters had wound up at the bottom of the pile. Johnson found a "to do" list, and the first matter listed in Grimm's handwriting was a note to himself.

"Sign will."

A few days later and far away in Germany, Randy Cochran was sitting at the kitchen table with his wife as he opened up a copy of the *Army Times*. The death notice was small, and it mentioned nothing about the task force or the nature of special operations aviation flying that had taken a war hero's life. But the name, rank and list of decorations left no question.

"Mike Grimm got killed," was all he could manage to say.

Randy's wife looked at him and tears filled her eyes. Sharon knew exactly how Randy felt about the man who had been a legend and her husband's mentor. She also knew that any hopes of a mundane and conventional aviation career for Randy were gone now. He would not be getting out early, or considering the well-paid life of a civilian airline pilot. He would no longer entertain the idea of both of them shedding their uniforms for a quiet farm life somewhere. He would be doing everything in his power to make his way back to that task force.

On October 16, 1981, under a slate gray sky at the Fort Campbell Division Parade Field, the new 160th Aviation Battalion uncased its colors. Colonel Couch assumed command, and the soldiers passed proudly in review, yet already there were ghosts among their ranks. The Night Stalkers were born, but it was a quiet and inauspicious birth. They would appear on the army's formal order of battle, yet their mission would remain hidden from public view.

It was a different time back then. The Cold War between the Soviet Bear and the American Eagle still simmered across the globe, the struggle between Leninist communism and Jeffersonian democracy being played out in places like Afghanistan, El Salvador and Nicaragua. Russian spies and American agents engaged in dangerous games from Peshawar to Beirut, seducing proxies and supplying them with weapons in order to bleed each other's masters. Nuclear submarines slithered close to shorelines, and heavy rockets launched tons of surveillance satellites to peer down and steal secrets. Terrorism was just starting to be used by America's enemies as a weapon in the war of ideals. Intelligence agents just in from the cold and special operators just returned from bloody missions did not retire and immediately appear as pundits on television talk shows. Secrets were highly treasured assets.

On the heels of the debacle at Desert One, when American hostages were still being held by Iranian revolutionaries, the army's special operations aviation element had been more concept than concrete, an aggressive solution to an immediate problem. The idea had been to assemble select pilots, crews and aircraft from the best army aviation units already in existence, then secretly task them for a second rescue attempt. Unless and until the task force proved itself, those assets would remain on the manifests of their parent units, an arrangement that would cause more than one general to spew venom at those nameless powers hijacking his men and machines.

For the time being, and for many years thereafter, the unit that became the Night Stalkers would be as secretive as Charlie Beckwith's Delta Force and as risk-embracing as Dick Marcinko's SEALs. Members wore no colorful unit patches. There were no pickup trucks sporting bumper stickers that said "I'm a Stalker." Cameras were forbidden anywhere near the crews or aircraft—there would be scant memorabilia. Pilots traveling to remote training areas did so in civilian clothes, trying hard not to be noticed. In public places, crews discussed business in low whispers, and when barmaids approached, they heard only chitchat about babes and baseball.

Eventually, there would be a unit logo: a cloaked Grim Reaper wielding a sword and riding a winged white horse. There would also be a unit motto: "Death Waits in the Dark," yet that motto would hold a double meaning, for there would be many casualties in nighttime training, and more in secret combat. Soon, unit members would greet and take leave of one another saying, "NSDQ"—Night Stalkers Don't Quit. But back then, on that cold October day when the unit's first flags were unfurled, once the time-honored parade ground ritual had finished, the Night Stalkers quietly receded from view.

The division's band had played for them. But after that, and for a very long time, there would be no trumpets, no drums. . . .

CHAPTER 3

INBOUND HOT

BOB "WILD MAN" CODNEY was the kind of helo pilot who pushed his luck. It didn't matter that he had been shot at, shot down, wounded on six different occasions and then crashed once again. He was always going back for more.

Born in 1944, Codney was raised in Detroit in a tough environment that would mold his character. At the age of four, he lost his father to cancer, and his mother soon remarried a man who would regularly drink and then beat young Bob and his sister with a garden hoe. At Mumford High, he was one of the only white kids around, and his black schoolmates called him "Pale Face." Nobody messed with him much, because he was nearly six feet three inches tall, and his wry sense of humor and broad smile could easily turn to thunder when challenged, but between the horrors at home and the trials of a down-trodden neighborhood, he was ready to get out of there. One of Bob's uncles had been killed on Iwo Jima and another badly wounded on Guadalcanal, so he knew early on that the Marine Corps was what he wanted. He went to summer school, graduated three months before his seventeenth birthday, and joined up in 1962, as soon as he was eighteen. When he came home on leave from his first tour, he found his stepfather beating up his mother in the basement. Bob was no longer the cowering teenager in the corner; the strapping and battle-hardened marine threw his stepfather up against a wall and told him that if he ever laid a hand on anyone in the family again, he would kill him. From that day on, they were good friends until the old man died.

Codney had smarts, and after getting an associate's degree while in the service, he was accepted into the Marine Corps Aviation Cadet Program, but he never got there. The program became so overloaded with college grad applicants that it was canceled and Codney was in Vietnam as an infantryman, slogging through the jungles, hauling a machine gun and literally up to his ass in alligators. That was just fine with him, but he never forgot about flying. One day while in I Corps, he was making a "grab ass" run to Da Nang, rounding up candy bars and soft drinks for his men. One of the new Huey gunships landed, piloted by an army captain and a lieutenant colonel, and Codney went over and ogled the machine like it was a Corvette at a car show.

"Boy, I'd love to fly one of these," he said.

"Well, Sarge," the captain said to him, "why don't you come over to our side? Army's got a warrant officer flight program. Its called High School to Flight School."

"You can do that?"

The "light" colonel grinned. "If you're smarter than the average marine, you can."

In November 1965, Codney graduated from the army's warrant officer flight program at Fort Rucker along with eighty other candidates. He and three other men already had orders for Vietnam, while the rest of the class was going to remain Stateside. Codney was married by then and had a little girl, but his wife was used to seeing him pack his duffel bag. The other guys had all bought themselves boats and cars, ready to enjoy the good life as CONUS aviators. Three days before graduation, the commandant informed the class that *everyone* was going to Vietnam. Codney laughed his ass off.

By late 1966, Codney was flying Huey Slicks for the 128th Assault Helicopter Company out of Phu Loi in III Corps, supporting elements of the First Infantry Division out in the bush. Early one day in May, he was on final approach to an infantry battalion base camp and could already see the grateful grunts waving him into their clearing when the Vietcong opened up from the dense jungle perimeter. An RPG lanced up toward the cockpit, but due to the Huey's forward speed it blew off the tail rotor instead. Small arms started peppering the Slick and something sliced through Codney's arm, but what really scared him was his own trajectory. The Huey was out of control, and if he didn't act fast he was going to kill half the men who were still out there waving him in.

Codney pulled power with the collective, yanked the cyclic over and smashed the spinning Huey into the jungle, slicing off treetops as it crashed. The windshield wiper motor ripped loose and hit him in the head, knocking him out. As he fell forward, a compensating bar from the rotor head snapped and shot into the cockpit, spearing through his seat, right behind his spine. He woke up, shook it off, then ran around the cockpit to help his copilot out. Together they dragged their wounded crew chief from behind his smashed M-60, and the three of them hobbled into the base camp and fell into the clearing. The Huey was totaled. Codney was laughing. He was twenty-two years old and nothing could kill him. Within two weeks, he was flying again.

A few months later, he had transitioned to Huey gunship with the "Gun Slingers." Flying the assault Slicks had been fun, but giving the enemy hell with machine guns and rockets was more his style. One night a call came down from III Corps, where a Special Forces camp was under intense assault at An Loc. Typically, the Green Berets were way out in the boonies with a twelve-man A-Team, with their camp set up adjacent to the South Vietnamese regulars they were advising. They had a short runway for resupply and a modest artillery position at the end of the strip, but the NVA were massing nearby for another attack and the A-Team needed some air support.

Codney, as fire team lead, took off with his two wingmen and headed for An Loc. Night vision goggles had not yet been invented, so the gunships were equipped with a landing light and a searchlight that could be controlled from the collective. As he and his wingmen approached the camp, Codney could see muzzle flashes in the jungle. The Special Forces team leader called him on the radio.

"Check out the north side of the runway. See if there's anybody over there and bust 'em up."

"Roger."

Codney sent his wingmen up a bit higher and out of the way, while he armed his guns and rockets and swooped in low over the far end of the primitive strip. He squinted hard through the Plexiglas, but he couldn't see anything moving down there, so he told his copilot to turn on the lights. From the very center of that sudden pool of oval light, more than a hundred Vietcong raised their pith-helmeted heads, their expressions asking, "What kind of fool is this?" as they immediately brought their weapons up and opened fire.

"Turn out the goddamn lights!" Codney yelled as rounds hammered through the gunship from just meters away. "Turn them out!" A bullet pierced his knee and jerked his foot off the tail rotor pedal, and so many were striking the Huey that they sounded like handfuls of ball bearings. He managed to slew the gunship around as its rotor blades and control cables all came apart, and he smashed it down onto the strip in a running landing. He didn't even feel the pain in his knee as he and his partner sprinted for the A-camp; he was *not* going to be captured. His wingmen, still flying above and pumping out streams of machine-gun bullets, managed to keep the Viet Cong at bay and the camp survived the assault. In the morning, Codney was medevaced to a hospital.

General DePew, commander of the First Infantry Division, came across Codney while the pilot was lying on a cot in the area MASH hospital. His knee had required some surgery and he wasn't going to be flying for about a month, but his reputation preceded him. As the general's aide pinned another Purple Heart on "Wild Man," DePew asked him if he had ever thought about becoming a commissioned officer.

"Sure, sir. I'd like to be a commissioned officer."

"My aide here will come back in the morning. Just tell him what branch you want to be in."

"You bet, General." Ceremonial courtesy wasn't Codney's strong suit.

It wasn't the wisest choice to make, but Codney chose the infantry as his branch. Indeed he was promoted to second lieutenant, but his previous experience in the Marine Corps didn't seem to matter. The army wanted it their way, so he departed from his second tour in 'Nam and was sent to the infantry basic and advanced courses back in the States. When that was over, he returned to Fort Rucker as a gunnery instructor and was promoted to captain. He could have stayed home after that, but there was still a war on and he didn't want to miss the rest of it.

The Cobra gunships were the hot thing now. Codney had always been a World War II buff and those sleek and fast machines were the closest thing to a P-51 Mustang a helo pilot could fly. "Why drive a Ford when you can drive a Ferrari?" he reasoned, so he volunteered for a Cobra transition.

In 1970, he was back in Vietnam for his third tour, commanding a Cobra unit operating in support of troops in the infamous "delta" IV Corps region and close to the Cambodian border. The unit was full of wild men just like Codney, who flew mostly at night, without any visual aids, and were thick in combat every time they did so. Codney amassed more than 750 hours of nighttime combat without night vision goggles, a feat that the next generation of helo pilots would regard as insane. He was wounded twice more, but it wasn't enough to keep him out of the cockpit. When he and his "snakes" weren't out killing the enemy, they were swinging through the saloon doors of the Vinh Long Officers' Club, where bottles of Chivas were slugged down like water and the pretty Vietnamese bar girls never knew what to expect next from the crazy Americans. The girls were very superstitious and would cower in the corner when the pilots screened horror and monster movies in the club. One night, Codney's men shredded some bedsheets and wrapped their captain up like the Mummy. When he burst through the flapping doors with a roar, the girls leaped out the windows. It was a coterie of young pilots difficult to join. You could have a great reputation as a combat pilot, but if you wanted to fly with Codney's Wild Men, you first had to spend an entire night in your bunk with "Greg." Greg was a very large, ornery boa constrictor.

When his third tour was over, with nearly two thousand hours of combat time, Codney was happy to be back in the States—for about a week. He adored his wife and their young daughter and those first few days of reunion were ecstatic, but soon he would start to feel guilty about not being back there with his men. Secretly, it was even more than that; his drug of choice had become adrenaline, and very soon he was ornery and itching to get back in action. But this time, the army wouldn't hear of it.

"You're not going back, Codney." Colonel Robert Adams was the aviation personnel officer up at the Pentagon and Codney was nearly begging him for another tour.

"But why not send me back? I already know what I'm doing over there, and you're just gonna send some young kid who'll get himself killed."

"Tell you what," Adams said. "You're a commissioned officer, but you don't have a degree. We're going to send you to any school you want to go to, pay your tuition, your books, give you flight pay and everything else. But unless you go to college and get your degree, you're getting out of the army. You are *not* going back to Vietnam."

"That's bullshit," Codney said.

"Try me," Adams said.

Having no other choice, Codney embraced the rewards he'd earned and started looking at schools in Hawaii and Tampa. "No way," said his wife, Cathy. She knew her husband too well, and if he went to one of those big schools with so many beaches and bikinis around he'd just get himself into trouble. At the age of twenty-five, he needed to knuckle down and get serious, so she chose a small, private school for him in Iowa called Fairfield College. Codney selected physics as his major and nearly failed early on, until a Ph.D. candidate in the psychology department signed him up for a research program on a new drug called Ritalin. Through a battery of tests, the scientist discovered that Codney's brain waves fired at nineteen milliseconds faster than average. His reflexes were superb, but his ability to absorb and retain knowledge was compromised and he was easily distracted or bored. Codney received an army flight surgeon's permission to start taking a low dose of the experimental drug.

Within a few short weeks the results were amazing. Codney retook a statistical exam that he had failed and maxed it out. He had taken up bowling with his wife and his score went from 120 to 200. She barely recognized her husband, and she was thrilled. His temper had cooled, he didn't argue with her anymore, and he no longer had fidgety bouts of anxiety. By the time he left college, his grade point average had gone from a 2.1 to a 3.8. Eventually, he had to give up the drug in order to go back on flying status, but many of the benefits were permanent. He was now only "half" a wild man.

By 1984, Codney had nearly twenty-three years in the army. He and Cathy had proudly raised two great kids, Christine and Jim, and he had a fine career behind him. He had completed college, three combat tours, commanded a rifle company in Germany and gone to the Command and General Staff College. He had served as an S-3 (operations officer) at both battalion and brigade levels in the mechanized infantry, and had even spent two years as an exchange pilot with the navy, commanding a flight detachment. He had "punched all his tickets"

and been promoted to a lieutenant colonel at Fort Rucker, where
he managed the Training and Doctrine Command's missile system
program—flying Hueys, testing the new Hellfires and Stingers and
generally doing a fine job under Major General Don Parker, Rucker's
commandant. One day Parker called him into his office and told him
to prepare a brief on his systems for a helo unit up at Fort Campbell.

"What unit is that, sir?"

"Special unit."

"What makes them so special?"

"Just go give 'em the brief, Bob."

Codney had never heard of Task Force 160, but he did as he was
told. He flew up to Campbell and gave a detailed briefing on Hellfire
and Stinger missile systems to a group of anonymous pilots who had
unusually long hair and no patches on their flight suits. They thanked
him, he thanked them, and he went off to the "O" Club for a drink.
Standing at the bar was one of the officers he'd just briefed, a major
who introduced himself as Bob Johnson. Codney noticed Johnson's
walking cane hanging on the bar.

"Battle, or basketball?" Codney asked as he glanced at Johnson's leg
brace.

"The former, as I recall." Johnson grinned.

Codney leaned on the bar and sipped his scotch.

"So what's this special unit you've got here?"

"Can't really tell you much about it," Johnson said, "but it's a
good unit."

"You don't say." Codney wasn't finding out very much. On the other
hand, Johnson and many of the other Night Stalker officers had already seen his personnel records.

"Think you might like to come up here and join us?" Johnson asked.

"I don't know."

"It's a *really* good unit." That's about all the major would say about
the Night Stalkers.

Codney returned to Fort Rucker and was soon summoned to General Parker's office.

"Those guys up at Campbell want to talk to you again," Parker said. Bob Codney was one of his favorite officers and he'd been "mentoring" his career for years.

"What for?"

"Don't know. I think they liked you."

"Guess they're not as smart as they seemed."

"I agree."

Codney flew back up to Campbell and was escorted over to the highly secure Night Stalker compound, where he was ushered into the office of Colonel Clyde "Lou" Hennies, who had recently taken over command from Terry Henry. After so many years in the army, Codney could tell almost immediately what an officer was made of. Hennies, as physically compact as Codney was large, had arctic blue eyes, a razor-sharp wit and the burbling intensity of a small volcano. There was no way to tell that the colonel was already pushing fifty, and he didn't talk about his multiple tours in Vietnam, or that he was qualified in Hueys, Blackhawks, Cobras and OH-58s, but Codney could tell that Hennies had "been there, done that, got the T-shirt." Hennies was unabashedly profane as he interrogated Codney for more than an hour, without telling him a single thing about the 160th, and then he offered him a job.

"How'd you like to be my executive officer?"

"Well, doing *what*, sir?"

"You'll find out when you get up here." Hennies grinned like an imp. "You know how it is with us special ops types: Burn Before Reading."

Codney's laugh boomed. Secrecy was obviously sacred to these guys, but their CO could still make fun of it. He shook Hennies's hand and the deal was done.

With the exception of Vietnam, Codney's service with the Night Stalkers would prove to be the most intense and rewarding experience of his career. The pilots and crews were the kind of men he liked to be around: hard-charging, fearless, innovative and constantly on the move. They believed, as he did, that only the most intense training, under conditions that most closely simulated real-world operations, would mean success under fire. Hennies often had four or five Night Stalker elements deployed simultaneously in different parts of the globe, either training with the customers or just waiting for that green light from Washington to take down some bad guys. During those first few years after Grenada, when international terrorists were testing America's patience, there were a number of frustrations—the hijackers of the cruise ship *Achille Lauro*, who had murdered wheelchair-bound American Leon Klinghoffer and dumped him over the side, were ultimately allowed to escape; the bloodthirsty Hezbollah fundamentalists who had taken TWA Flight 847 and executed navy diver Robert Dean Stethem just narrowly avoided the fate that the 160th and their special tactics customers wanted so badly to deliver. In between, there were some missions executed in faraway places where even the Peeping Toms of the media dared not go, and these operations would always remain classified. But when the whole world was watching, higher authorities in Washington were very reluctant to let the Night Stalkers and their customers loose; once you unleashed those hounds, it would be very hard to call them back.

Still, Codney enjoyed himself and felt almost as good as when he'd been flying with his Snakes in 'Nam. He kept his flight status up and made the transition into Little Birds, the airplane you had to fly as a staff officer at the 160th. Hennies gave him the task of starting up a dedicated element to coordinate and standardize all research, development and new technology for the various types of helos and equipment used by the unit. Codney's ad hoc "skunk works" would later be developed by Colonel John Dailey into the Systems Integrations and Maintenance Office, or SIMO, which with its generous budget and access to all sorts of "toys" would have been the envy of Ian Fleming's Q. But between 1984 and 1987 there wasn't a lot of hard-core action, until the Iranians started attacking commercial shipping vessels in the Persian Gulf.

Between Saddam Hussein and the Ayatollah Khomeini, there had never been much love lost. In fact, the kingdoms of Mesopotamia and Persia had been at each other's throats for many centuries, yet none of their intermittent conflicts would compare to the bloody slugfest that took place between 1980 and 1988. The dispute began over rights to the Shatt al Arab waterway, which divides the two countries at the apex of the Persian Gulf and is crucial for the export of oil shipments. Iraq launched an invasion of Iran's western Khuzestan Province, the Iranians counterattacked, and soon the border area between the two countries was the scene of massive ground assaults that would rival the slaughter once seen on the western front of World War I. Over the course of the decade, well over a million Iraqi and Iranian men would fall in battle without a decisive victory or significant change in the status quo. The rest of the international community witnessed the war without shedding many tears, until the flow of oil became seriously threatened.

Early on in the conflict, both Iraq and Iran began attacking oil tankers in the Gulf, hoping to deprive each other of commercial revenues. More than 550 commercial tankers would be severely damaged and more than four hundred civilian mariners killed, but when the "Tanker War" reached its peak in late 1986, the Iranians began laying mines in the Gulf and using Silkworm missiles to assault Kuwaiti vessels. The government of Kuwait begged foreign powers to protect its shipping, yet United States law prohibited a forceful response from the American military unless U.S. property was attacked. In short order, eleven Kuwaiti oil tankers were re-flagged under the Stars and Stripes and the U.S. Navy began an escort program dubbed Operation Earnest Will.

On the very first escort mission in July 1987, the reflagged tanker *Bridgeton* encountered an Iranian mine and was seriously damaged. Soon after, the Iranians fired a Silkworm at the U.S. tanker *Sea Isle City*, wounding eighteen men. The U.S. Navy responded by destroying two Iranian oil platforms, but it was clear that a much more aggressive, preemptive response was in order. An air element needed to be added to Earnest Will, one that could not only provide reconnaissance duties but execute attack missions, as well. It had already been determined that Iranian mine-laying vessels were doing their deeds under cover of darkness, so whoever flew these missions would have to be very adept at low-altitude, over-water, pitch-black flying. The navy had some ship-borne LAMPS (Light Airborne Multi-Purpose Systems) helicopters, which could use a suite of surveillance technologies to spot suspicious targets, but they were not trained to make closer inspections of suspicious activities at sea and were unarmed. And nearly eight years after the fiasco at Desert One, Marine Corps Cobra pilots were still novices at night vision flying. It wasn't long before someone in a meeting at the Pentagon raised a finger and said, "What about Task Force 160?"

Bob Codney was sent up to Pope Air Force Base and a meeting at JSOC, to discover that the navy had "reluctantly" agreed to host army helicopters aboard its Persian Gulf escort vessels. *This is gonna be fun,* he thought as he returned to Campbell and preparations began immediately. Major Bryan "Doug" Brown, the 160th operations officer, assembled a planning team including Bob Fladry, who was certainly one of the unit's most experienced Little Bird pilots. The Little Birds were ideally suited for this offspring mission of Earnest Will, now dubbed Operation Prime Chance; they were fast and flexible, relatively quiet, had a flying radius of one hundred nautical miles, were difficult to detect on radar and light enough so that virtually any ship could accommodate their small mass. The Night Stalker element that would proceed to the Gulf would be called the Detachment 160 Aviation Group (DET 160 AVGP), and would consist of two MH-6s, four AH-6s, their pilots, crew chiefs, armorers and maintenance personnel. But first, there were a lot of kinks to be ironed out with the navy.

Paul DeMilia had been flying AH-6s with the 160th for two years and was suddenly summoned back from leave in Minnesota. He had just walked into the house, anxious to spend some quality time with his wife and six-month-old baby, when the telephone rang and he had to turn right around. DeMilia had started out in the army as a Ranger, then quickly saw the benefits of flying as opposed to crawling in the mud. By 1987, he was an experienced Scout, Huey and Little Bird gun pilot, but had yet to see action. He had seen plenty of high alerts turn to stand-downs, though, and figured this one would turn out the same way.

Back at Fort Campbell, DeMilia was ordered to take a fully armed AH-6 and a crew chief and fly up to Dalgren, Virginia, where the navy tested all of its shipboard electronic warfare and communications systems. Major Chuck Gant, the former commander of A Company's attack helos, now working in the S-3 shop, rendezvoused with De-Milia at Dalgren to supervise a process of having the navy subject a 160th AH to every conceivable emission that might be found aboard a Prime Chance vessel. The navy used a different set of frequencies, radars and even armament types from the army, and the concern was that one of these devices might shut down the Little Bird's navigation systems, or even inadvertently detonate a rocket warhead. DeMilia sat in his helo on the test bed for two days, feeling like an egg in a microwave as he and his machine were bombarded with every frequency the navy could throw at them. In the end, a few adjustments were made and some operational limitations defined. The chief of naval operations showed up and handed Chuck Gant a "memorandum of agreement," stating that the army would officially authorize its aircraft to operate from the specified U.S. Navy vessels. Gant signed, while DeMilia observed the "cover your ass" formalities with some amusement. Exactly who was going to sue whom if they all accidentally blew themselves up?

When DeMilia returned to the Night Stalker compound everyone was already packing up for Prime Chance, but he was going to have to stay behind. He had been in the middle of training "Green Platoon," the process whereby new aviators were initiated into the tactics, techniques and procedures of the 160th, and would have to complete that assignment. Major Brown, who had just been promoted to lieutenant colonel, was going over to the Gulf and taking along his A-Team, a select group of platoon leaders and pilots for this watershed mission. But even Fladry was being left behind, and he and DeMilia cynically called themselves the B-Team. Fladry, having already seen plenty of action in his life, shrugged it off, while DeMilia grumbled loudly.

By that time, Colonel John "Coach" Dailey had taken over as commander of the 160th. Dailey was determined to make sure that everything went right between the army and the navy on the other side of the globe, so he wanted at least one of his highest ranking officers always on scene. In the first month, nothing of significance took place out there, so Lieutenant Colonel Brown rotated home, to be replaced by Lieutenant Colonel Ralph Hyatt. Nothing much happened on Hyatt's watch, either. On a Friday night in late August, Bob Codney and his wife Cathy were at a unit cocktail party when Colonel Dailey sauntered over with a drink in his hand.

"Okay, Codney," he said with a smile. "You're next."

"Don't send me, Coach," Codney warned. "You know I have a magnet ass. As soon as I get over there, something's gonna happen."

Dailey just laughed, but Codney's wife chimed in with all seriousness.

"He's right, John," she said. "You send Bob over and sure enough, something will happen."

"Yeah, sure," Dailey laughed again. "You're both wacky."

"Whatever you say, boss." Codney grinned broadly, then he and his wife looked at each other and shrugged, as if they were biblical prophets in the presence of an agnostic.

Early in September, the A-Team came home. They had done a lot of nighttime, low-level flying over open water, but hadn't spotted any Iranian boats worth engaging, and certainly no minelayers. It was B-Team's turn. The aircraft had remained in theater, so Codney and thirteen pilots (two for each of the six Little Birds and one spare) embarked on various commercial flights for Bahrain, the port at which the navy was basing its operations. The Night Stalkers didn't travel as a group, but it would have been difficult to spot them as army pilots any-way; grooming standards for special operations personnel were consid-erably more "relaxed" than for the average soldier, and Fladry, DeMilia and their comrades looked more like oil rig wranglers in their cowboy boots, blue jeans and colorful short sleeves.

From Bahrain, Codney was flown out to the USS *La Salle*, a vessel type known as an Amphibious Transport Dock, which had been built to carry nearly a thousand combat-ready troops along with all their vehicles, fuel, ammunition and support cargo. The *La Salle* was more than five hundred feet long and nearly half of its aft deck consisted of a helicopter landing platform. Curiously, it was painted in a brilliant white glaze reminiscent of a Red Cross hospital ship and had already earned the nickname "the Great White Ghost of the Arabian Coast." The *La Salle* was the flagship of COMIDEASTFOR, the Navy's Commander of Middle East Forces, Rear Admiral Harold Bernsen. Codney was going to join Bernsen's staff, and as the only army special operations officer in a clique of "squids," he was already anticipating some head-butting. What he didn't know was that it had been Bernsen's idea to place the army helicopters aboard ship and back them up with patrol boats, SEALs and marines. That being said, early on in the mission Bernsen had had some doubts about whether or not the Little Birds would actually be stealthy enough to get close to Iran-ian vessels without being spotted. To prove him wrong, the Night Stalkers had chosen a moonless night and launched a pair of Little Birds on an alleged "patrol." Half an hour later, the pair of black birds, bristling with miniguns and rocket pods, suddenly appeared directly in front of Bernsen's bridge and announced over the comms: "Bang. You're dead." From that moment on the admiral was a believer and the Night Stalkers inherited their Prime Chance call sign: "Seabats."

Accompanying the *La Salle* on her tanker escort and mine-interdiction mission were a pair of FFGs, navy fast frigates called the USS *Jarrett* and USS *Klakring*. Since the frigates were deployed to cover, respectively, the southern and northern sea-lanes of the Gulf, DET 160 AVGP was also divided into two teams of three Little Birds each and dispatched to their assigned vessels. Bob Fladry and Paul DeMilia were assigned to the *Jarrett*, along with Tom Leedom, Steve Chilton, Brian Collins and Terry Pena. The four-thousand-ton frigate was a fast-moving, sleek ship just over 450 feet in length from bow to stern, with a pair of SH-60 Sea Hawk LAMPS helos, a MK-75 three-inch gun, torpedo tubes and a Phalanx 20mm antiaircraft system. There were more than two hundred navy officers and enlisted men aboard, so adding the Night Stalker pilots, backups, crew chiefs, maintenance personnel and their Little Birds made things very tight indeed. The Night Stalkers would soon find themselves "hot bunking," waiting for sailors to crawl out of their curtained racks and start their work shifts, so the army guys could quickly slip into the coffin-size beds and get some sleep. Fladry and his fellow pilots would be flying all night, then killing time by exercising their cramped muscles until it was time to stuff in some earplugs and fade away for eight hours. When they emerged from their racks, the 120-degree heat of the day had often melted and bowed the plastic console covers in their cockpits.

During those first few sweltering days at sea and some long, dark nights of recon missions, the Night Stalkers didn't see much more out there than a few lazy dhows, the ubiquitous primitive fishing vessels that wandered throughout the Gulf. Yet those nights were like nothing they had encountered before, and they needed the time to acclimate themselves to conditions that were unusually deceptive. The sun might set through crystal blue skies, yet two hours later the surface of the sea would be swathed in a blanket of chilled fog. You could take off for a night mission and have perfect, three-mile visibility through your NVGs. Then half an hour later you wouldn't be able to find your ship, even with its patrol lights blazing. It was common for novice helo pilots to experience vertigo when first flying over water at night, for the sea and sky would meld into an inky curtain with no discernible horizon, yet the Night Stalkers were grateful for the many hours they'd spent training and flying with their SEAL customers. Their over-water night-flying capabilities were already exceptional, but this was most definitely hairy.

On the evening of September 21, the Iranians launched a naval vessel called the *Iran Ajar* from the port of Bandar Abbas. The ship was two hundred feet long, a "roll-on, roll-off" cargo vessel with a drop-down ramp at the bow. The *Iran Ajar* had been modified to lay mines along the Allied cargo route in the Gulf, and fitted with heavy machine guns to fend off aircraft and small-boat assaults. By nine o'clock in the evening, its shape was just appearing as a dim radar blip in the CICs (Combat Information Centers) aboard the *La Salle* and the *Jarrett*. Fladry, DeMilia and their fellow pilots had just landed from their first "picket duty" mission of the night and were out on the *Jarrett*'s deck trying to let the cooler night air evaporate the sweat from their flight suits, when the word came down from the bridge to launch again. They climbed back into their cockpits, and the three Little Birds cranked up and took off.

Aboard the *La Salle*, Bob Codney was spending another long night in the command ship's CIC along with Admiral Bernsen. It was 2200 and the birds from the *Jarrett* had been vectored over to the slowly crawling radar blip, but Flapper hadn't reported anything but the usual marker buoys and dhows. "Aww, this is bullshit," Codney grumbled. "I'm going back to bed." The admiral concurred, and both of them went off to their quarters.

Fladry and the Seabats had been sweeping an area about twelve miles west of the *La Salle* for forty minutes, and they still hadn't seen anything. It was a perfect night for flying, with a five-thousand-foot ceiling, more than a nautical mile of visibility and "zero illumination"—no moon to interfere with their NVGs or cause reflections off the water. In the right seat of the lead MH-6, Flapper had the controls while Tom Leedom worked the FLIR, staring at the screen that would display any unusual heat signatures like sunspots against a ghostly white background. The two AH-6 gunships trailed behind Chalk One in a loose formation. DeMilia was pilot-in-command of the first AH-6, flying with Brian Collins, while Steve Chilton was paired up with Terry Pena in the second bird. They were all watching their fuel gauges drop and were just about to give it up when Flapper spotted the long flat silhouette of the *Iran Ajar*.

"I'm going in for a look," he reported to his flight.

"Roger that," DeMilia answered. He and Steve Chilton moved their two helos into a holding pattern a mile from the target while Flapper eased his MH-6 lower and closer.

The *Iran Ajar* was running into the wind, its work lights blazing up in the FLIR screen and Flapper's NVGs. He started reporting back to the *Jarrett*, and the officers in the *La Salle*'s CIC could hear it all as well. Aboard the *La Salle*, an ensign was already pounding on Codney's door.

"Better get up top, sir. Your boys've got something."

"Yeah, yeah," Codney mumbled, "dolphins and jellyfish." He had just drifted off and had to drag his uniform back on. The ensign briefed him as they climbed back up to the CIC, and Codney got on the intra-team radio to Fladry.

"Chalk One, what've you got down there?"

"She looks like an LST," Flapper said as he cruised three hundred meters off the port side of the vessel. "Crew's walking around on deck. There's a bunch of fifty-five-gallon drums stacked on the port side, and some sort of tarp covering the cargo area."

"Anybody got guns up?" Codney asked.

"Negative hostile action," Flapper answered.

"Roger that," Codney said. He figured he'd been woken up for nothing, but it wasn't his call to have the Seabats stand down. The commander of the *Jarrett*, Lieutenant Commander Blankenship, broke into the transmissions.

"Seabats, return to station."

Flapper acknowledged the order, shrugged and made one more pass over the *Iran Ajar*. The Little Bird's rotor system was relatively quiet, and with the forward motion of the ship, her rumbling engine noise and the wind, he didn't think the Iranians had even sensed his presence on such a pitch-dark night. As he passed the stern, heading back for the *Jarrett*, he glanced at where the ship should have been through his NVGs and saw . . . *nothing*. It was as if the ship had suddenly disappeared.

"Holy *shit*," he hissed into his boom mike. "They just turned all their lights off!"

No vessel would be running without lights in these waters, unless the crew had evil intentions. Suddenly all the night watch officers aboard the *La Salle* and *Jarrett* were very much awake, focusing intently over the shoulders of sailors working the communications gear and radar displays. Codney had been halfway out the door of the CIC again when he heard Flapper's transmission and spun back for the UHF transmitter.

"Chalk One, say again?"

"That ship just turned all their lights off," Flapper said. He was in a holding pattern two hundred meters astern. "It's slowed down and changed course, and there's some activity on the starboard side of the deck."

"Roger, wait one." Codney turned to the ensign. "Get the admiral up here *now*."

By the time Bernsen appeared in the CIC, Flapper's voice had risen in pitch.

"It looks like they're pushing shopping carts on deck."

"Shopping carts?" Codney furrowed his brow.

"That's what it looks like. They've got handles on 'em and wheels on the bottom, and in the middle's like a fifty-five-gallon drum with a round top."

"Ask him if they have horns on them," Admiral Bernsen said to Codney.

"Horns?" Flapper nearly laughed in response to the query. "What are you talking about?"

"Probes," the admiral said. "Ask him if there are probes on top of the round things."

Codney relayed the question and Flapper answered, "Affirmative . . . and now they're pushing them into the water."

"Those are *mines*," Bernsen said to Codney as he made a tight fist. "You tell your pilot to stay on top of this and get the guns ready."

Anti-shipping mines have not changed much since they were first used extensively during World War I. The bottom half of each system consists of an anchor, such as a fifty-five-gallon drum filled with cement. The top half consists of the mine itself, a metal sphere containing high explosive and dotted with protruding contact—or proximity—detonators, the "horns." When the drum sinks to the seabed, the mine itself is released and floats to a predetermined depth, held to the anchor by a steel cable. There it waits, until a passing hull activates one of the detonators. Flapper had never seen a naval mine being deployed before, but his description left no doubt. However, taking lethal action was a decision that would have to be made in Washington, so now they would all have to wait.

Flapper's helo was like an invisible black bumblebee, holding just aft of the *Iran Ajar*'s stern as he and Tom Leedom glanced at their FLIR screen and stared at the ship through their NVGs. Less than a mile behind them, Paul DeMilia and Steve Chilton flew their two attack helos in racetrack circles just above the waves. Each of the AH-6s had a minigun mounted on one side and a seven-shot rocket pod on the other. The rockets had solid-fuel navy motors with seventeen-pound army warheads, a hybrid that had been devised back at Dalgren. The warheads were of two types: high-explosive for destructive effect, and flechettes, deadly clusters of three-quarter-inch-long anti-personnel steel darts. A Little Bird gun pilot had to know exactly when to let those rockets loose; too far from the target, and they would drop harmlessly into the sea; too close, and the warheads wouldn't have time to arm, resulting in zero effect. As for aiming the weapons, the system was somewhat less than high-tech—a circle and crosshairs marked on the bubble canopy with a grease pencil.

"There goes another one," Flapper reported in frustration as he watched the Iranians drop another mine. He knew that each splash meant potential death for American sailors aboard those re-flagged merchant vessels. "Request permission to fire."

"Negative," Codney answered from the *La Salle*. Next to him in the CIC, Admiral Bernsen was talking on the Satcom to someone in Washington, and from the tone of all his "Yessirs" and "Nosirs" it was obviously someone very high up in the chain of command—maybe the secretary of defense or even the president.

"There goes the *third* one," Flapper said, his voice a barely controlled growl. "Request permission to *fire*."

"Negative, Seabat One." Now it was Lieutenant Commander Blankenship from the *Jarrett*. "You do *not* have to permission to fire."

There was a long pause and then everyone could hear Flapper's disgusted sigh.

"If we don't get permission to fire, we're *out* of here," Flapper warned. Hovering so close to an enemy vessel while it conducted hostile action was one sure way to get a missile up your ass.

Bernsen hung up the Satcom and Codney turned to him.

"Well, Admiral? Do we have permission to stop these guys?"

"You have permission to stop them from laying mines." Bersen nodded and smiled thinly. "You may use whatever force is necessary."

Codney snatched up the UHF mike. "Bob, bust those fuckers."

"Permission to fire?" Flapper's tone was suddenly like that of a kid in a candy store.

"Permission to kill those sons of bitches and stop them from laying mines!"

"Roger! Breaking left!" Flapper pulled power and banked the MH-6 away from the *Iran Ajar*'s stern. Paul DeMilia's voice immediately echoed inside both CICs.

"Roger, we are inbound hot."

The pair of Little Bird guns broke from their racetrack pattern and pitched noses down, racing for the Iranian vessel in a long, right-hand arc that would set them up perpendicular to its hull. Steve Chilton was flying the lead bird, and his gloved thumb poised above his weapon selector as the black shape of the minelayer loomed larger and larger in his NVGs. At a range of three hundred meters, he opened up with his minigun, sending streams of red tracers punching into the forward pilothouse and chunking back into the cargo section; then he fired two HE rockets and watched them burst against the hull as he banked hard to get out of the way and keyed his mike.

"I am clear right."

DeMilia was right behind him, hunched forward in his seat, watching Chilton's infrared position lights carefully to make sure he was clear. DeMilia had never before fired a shot in anger, but he told himself that this was no different than a hundred other runs he'd made out at Range 29. He opened up long, expending nearly half of his two thousand rounds of minigun ammo until the ship was huge in his vision, and he punched two more HE rockets into the hull, banking hard to the right as they exploded in blinding flashes.

"Chalk Three, clear right."

Suddenly Lieutenant Commander Blankenship's voice echoed from the bridge of the *Jarrett*. "Seabats, have you started engaging yet? *Don't* shoot. We want to call them on the radio and give them a chance to surrender."

"Uhh, you're a little too late for that, sir." DeMilia's voice crackled above the sounds of explosions and gunfire. "Sorry." His apology was less than sincere.

As the pair of gunships started lining up for another run, Codney asked Flapper for a situation report.

"Well, the crew's run up forward and hunkered down near the bow. . . . Some of 'em are down. I don't think they know where it's all coming from, like it's the hand of God or something. I think there's a fifty-caliber mounted up there—"

"Tell your men to cease fire," Admiral Bernsen ordered Codney. "Let's see what the Iranians do."

For more than ten minutes, Flapper and the Seabats hung back from the *Iran Ajar*, just circling, watching, like vultures above a fresh kill. There were some small fires on board, but no major activity, and it seemed as though the Iranians had had enough for one night. Then Flapper suddenly broke the silence.

"I don't believe this! They're getting up and going back to the mines. She's turning. . . . She's steaming again. . . . Yup, they're putting more mines in the water!"

"Stop them from doing that!" Bernsen jabbed a finger at Codney's radio. "I want that ship dead in the water."

"Bust 'em again, Bob!" Codney ordered. "Take out the engines."

"Roger," Flapper answered and broadcast to the guns, "You heard the boss. Cleared to fire."

This time DeMilia was in the lead. Half his ordnance was already expended, and Chilton's, too. They were getting fuel critical and would have to finish her off on this pass. DeMilia remembered asking the navy guys where the optimal targets were on a ship, and they'd said, "Find the smokestack, 'cause right below that's the engine room." He spotted the stack just aft of the cargo section, but first he raked the wheelhouse with the rest of his minigun ammo, fired two flechette rockets to keep the Iranians away from their machine guns, and then pierced the hull with a pair of HEs just below the root of the smokestack. He flipped the helo nearly on its side and skidded to the right as a plume of fire bloomed from the aft deck. Chilton followed up, spewing the remainder of his machine-gun rounds and rockets into the shuddering, smoking hull.

The Iranians gave up on their mine laying and began to abandon ship. Soon Flapper could see a huge round life raft floating away from the smoking stern, and he reported twelve or fifteen survivors swimming in the water and pulling themselves into the raft. DeMilia and Chilton circled above, with just a few rounds of minigun ammo left in their links.

"Hey," Flapper suddenly transmitted, "there's a Zodiac leaving the ship, and it's going like hell!"

"Are any of your guys wounded?" Admiral Bernsen asked Codney.

"Nope, our guys are all okay."

"Then tell them to find out where that Zodiac's going."

"You bet, Admiral."

Steve Chilton gave chase, and after ten minutes he reported the Zodiac dead in the water, with a tarp covering its floor. He hovered in closer, but just to be sure, he picked up his MP-5 submachine gun from under his leg case and flipped off the safety as he leaned out his open door.

"I don't see anybody down there," he called in, and just then the tarp flipped away and a man holding an AK-47 jumped up and opened fire at him, the muzzle flashes searing his vision in his NVGs. "I'm being fired at!"

"Well, *shoot* the sonuvabitch," Codney snapped.

The rattle of Chilton's MP-5 spat out from the radios, then silence.

"Okay," Chilton said. "He's down."

"Is there anybody else down there?" Codney asked.

"Negative."

"Then get your asses back to your ship before you run out of gas and splash."

"Roger that."

The Night Stalkers flew for ten hours straight that night, keeping watch on the abandoned *Iran Ajar* and returning to their ships only to refuel and get back out there. Codney himself flew one of the missions to give his guys a break, because even though Admiral Bernsen had ordered USMC Cobras from the USS *Guadalcanal* to relieve the Night Stalkers, the marine pilots were not NVG qualified and would only arrive at first light. Washington wanted the *Iran Ajar* captured and taken in tow as a prize. The Iranians wanted her back, and a flurry of livid accusations flew between diplomats and statesmen across the seas. It soon became a Mexican standoff.

The waters surrounding the *Iran Ajar* were laced with mines, so for the time being, none of the U.S. Navy heavy vessels or frigates could approach her. At dawn, she was boarded by a contingent of SEALs off of the *Guadalcanal*. Admiral Bersen wanted a BDA (Bomb Damage Assessment) of the Iranian vessel and as much intelligence materials as could be found, so he sent Codney, along with a contingent of Secret Squirrels who'd been flown out to the *La Salle* from Bahrain, cruising out to the smoking hulk aboard a wooden-hulled motorboat. They were halfway there when Bernsen called Codney *back* to the *La Salle* to pick up a group of reporters and photographers. Cursing all means and manner of media, while also understanding why Washington wanted the incident publicized, Codney, the intelligence officers and the sailors aboard the small craft immediately started tearing off name tags and unit patches and swapping headgear. They picked up the newspeople and resisted the urge to toss them all into the drink as they then made their way again to the Iranian minelayer.

Up close and aboard, the *Iran Ajar* was a filthy vessel, her decks strewn with refuse and the smeared blood of her dead. The corpses of a few sailors lay bloating in the early sun beside their machine-gun positions. Belowdecks, she looked like the unclean kitchen of a Third World falafel joint, and her latrines were nothing more than cut-out holes to let the feces foul the ocean. Above, still racked in the cargo area, stood thirteen mines, some of them clearly punctured by the Little Bird minigun rounds. Codney and his fellow pilots stared at them, realizing that only luck had kept the mines from detonating under the intense machine-gun and rocket fire. The resulting daisy-chain explosion would have evaporated the Iranian ship, as well as the Little Birds assaulting her.

The missile frigate *Jarrett* finally drew close enough to have a cable attached to the *Iran Ajar* and began towing her back toward the *La Salle*. Codney and his contingent were also heading back aboard their small wooden boat, when a fast-moving craft appeared on the horizon. It was a large Iranian battle hovercraft, racing to the area with all intentions of taking back the battered minelayer.

"You American pirates!" the hovercraft's commander called out furiously over his international radio. "We want our ship back, or we will engage you in combat!"

To Codney, the black-skirted hovercraft with its bristling guns looked about ten stories tall as it came on fast, its massive props and fans whipping up a halo of sea spray. His little wooden boat seemed like no more than a helpless dinghy, caught in the midst of a triangle of giants: the *La Salle*, the *Jarrett* and this furious flying monster. Suddenly the *Jarrett* opened fire with her five-inch gun, the rounds screaming overhead through the air and splashing up the sea before the onrushing Iranians.

"Do not approach any closer," Commander Blankenship warned the Iranians via ship-to-ship, "or we *will* sink you."

As a high-explosive round struck very close to the hovercraft's bow, she suddenly pulled to a stop and her skirts slowly deflated. Codney and his men reached the *La Salle*; he had never climbed a ladder so fast in his life. By this time, another contingent of SEALs had located the *Iran Ajar*'s life raft and brought thirteen survivors, many of them badly wounded, aboard the *La Salle*. The wounded men were arrayed on stretchers on deck, awaiting treatment, while the remainder were flex-cuffed and sitting up against the bulkheads. One Iranian crew member was a Special Forces officer, clearly in charge and the most hard-core of the group. He had a steel flechette round stuck in his jaw but was neither complaining nor asking for treatment. Codney summoned his pilots and an interpreter. He knew the Iranians would soon be repatriated, so he bent close to the prisoner's face and instructed the interpreter to translate his message precisely.

"We're the son of bitches that killed your friends, and we'll do it again if you keep this bullshit up. Understand that?"

The Iranian said nothing.

The next morning, Codney was abruptly reminded of an OpSec lecture he had given to his B-Team just before deployment: "This is a very high-level, low-key operation. Under no uncertain terms will you talk to any news media, and you will *not* get your pictures in the newspaper. If you do, I'm gonna burn your nuts." Now he cringed as he remembered that, for his wife had just called him from the States to tell him that his picture was not only on the covers of *Newsweek*, *Time* and *U.S. News & World Report* but there were multiple shots of him wearing a navy uniform and inspecting the mines aboard the *Iran Ajar*. Codney would be taking a gleeful "ration of crap" about that from his Night Stalker comrades for the rest of his career, and long after his retirement. . . .

WITH U.S. FORCES having scored a major victory against Iranian aggression in the Gulf, Operation Prime Chance was deemed a success and kicked into an even higher gear. However, it had become obvious that it wasn't sufficient to have warships and helicopters deploying from the port of Bahrain in response to radar contacts at sea. What was needed was not only patrol but *control:* some sort of permanently established presence, particularly in the northern waterways where the Iranians frequently operated off Farsi Island. The navy looked back into some of its successful operations of this type from the Vietnam era and revived the concept of Mobile Sea Bases.

Lieutenant Commander Paul Evancoe was selected for the job. At thirty-nine years old and at the pinnacle of his career as a SEAL commander, Evancoe was something of Bob Codney's doppelgänger—the navy's version of a battle-hardened warrior who could be depended on to handle any mission. As a young SEAL in the late 1960s, he had operated in Vietnam from the Mekong Delta all the way up to the Parrot's Beak in Cambodia, and had been involved in a navy experiment called the "Sea Float," a contraption of lashed-together pontoons that featured trailer-like structures for berthing, mess, supplies and a landing pad for Seawolf helicopter gunships. The Sea Float roamed the bay between Camron and Kanto, deploying SEALs, patrol boats and helos against the Vietcong.

As with Codney, Evancoe's commission wasn't something he sought out; it came to him as a result of his superior performance as an enlisted man. By the midseventies he was a SEAL platoon commander, working alongside such men as Bob Gormly, whose warriors would deploy from Bob Johnson's Blackhawks during the later invasion of Grenada. Soon, Evancoe was put in charge of multiservice operations called Task Units and made a lieutenant commander. The navy had a particular personnel designation called "Area Expert," and Evancoe was noted as such for Southeast Asia, Europe and the Middle East. He had also been through the navy's three-month Mine Warfare School, and all of these qualifications made him the perfect choice for what the navy had in mind for Prime Chance. A man didn't rise to the top of the SEAL food chain without being aggressive, smart, well respected and charismatic. At the top of his game, Evancoe was also tall, broad and sported a thick, bristling mustache. Everyone who met him said, "He looks just like Tom Selleck."

The navy didn't give him much time to prepare for Prime Chance. He had just taken over a new SEAL command down at Norfolk and was literally still drinking farewell beers with the outgoing commander when the quarterdeck watch ran up and told him he had a call on the red phone from the commodore. Evancoe thought it was a joke, until he heard the commodore's voice ordering him on a priority mission. He had only just returned from a three-year deployment, during which he had never set foot on American soil. Now he would have four days to load out all his SEALs, weapons, ammunition, equipment and everything else he would need to sustain operations in the Persian Gulf for three months. "Aye, aye, sir," he responded, and he went to work.

Evancoe left virtually nothing behind. He had been told only that he would be conducting countermining operations in the Gulf and that he would be working with the army's Task Force 160; they were every SEAL's favorite aviators, but when you heard their name you knew that action was afoot. An LPD vessel called the *Raleigh*, nearly identical to the "Great White Ghost" already in the Gulf, was stripped and prepared for his cargo. He had four MK III heavily armed sixty-ton patrol boats (PBs) loaded aboard. Then came his SEALs, plus enough weapons, gear, ammunition and explosives to fill twelve eighteen-wheelers, and as the ship got under way, it stopped in Charleston to pick up four MSBs—wooden-hulled minesweeping boats that were World War II relics and looked like the *Minnow* from *Gilligan's Island*. Evancoe, deciding that wasn't quite enough stuff, stayed behind and had two more Seafoxes—forty-six-foot stealth boats with radar-absorbent hulls—loaded aboard a C5-A, and when the *Raleigh* made port in Rhoda, Spain, he rendezvoused with the ship and added those to his arsenal as well.

When the *Raleigh* finally rounded the Horn of Africa and made port in Bahrain, Evancoe's mission was clarified for him. He was to make his way over to the construction yards of Brown and Root, where he would select one of two seagoing barges, the *Hercules* or the *Wimbrown*, and turn that platform into a floating fortress. Evancoe immediately chose the *Hercules*, an oil-platform servicing barge twice the size of a football field. It had an enormous crane attached and a small flight deck for medevac helos, but it would take twenty-three welders working around the clock to satisfy his requirements. A reinforced flight deck was added across the *Hercules'* girth. In a single day, a hangar was constructed to work maintenance on the Little Birds and hide them during daylight hours, with roll-up garage doors on both ends. Evancoe had forty-foot air-conditioned shelters brought aboard and made into berths, stacking them two high fore and aft. A ready room was constructed for the Night Stalker pilots and mounted atop their hangar, replete with a picture window so they could observe flight operations on the deck below; it would come to be called the "Bat Cave."

Evancoe was a seasoned sea warrior who believed there was no such thing as too much firepower. The *Hercules* had no engines of her own and would be towed to a position by a seagoing tug and left there, so if attacked, there would be no option but to fight it out. Paul DeMilia, who would soon relocate with his fellow Night Stalkers to the *Herc*, noted that every time a helicopter landed, it seemed like the commander was bringing aboard more guns. In a very short period of time, Evancoe would have a TOW battery, two Stinger batteries, sandbagged .50 caliber emplacements, 81mm mortars and the personal sidearms, machine guns and explosive ordnance of all of his SEALs aboard. His patrol boats and Seafoxes were additionally armed with heavy and light machine guns, mortars and 20mm cannons. A contingent of thirty-four marines would come aboard as a security detachment, and with the colorful mixture of army pilots, navy special operations warriors, hard-core marines, countermining, communications and intelligence experts, as well as the complement of twenty-six foreign nationals to service her generators, make repairs and run the mess, the *Hercules* appeared like something out of *Thunderball*. It was clear to Evancoe that this was the kind of mission he was born to run, and he loved it with the exception of one small detail: He would have to fly the Kuwaiti flag from her mast, for the operation was highly classified and the *Hercules* was not supposed to exist.

By the evening of October 8, 1987, the *Hercules* had been at sea for ten days. Evancoe's first mission was to anchor out past the Bahrain Bell, to which the *Iran Ajar* had been tied up while Washington decided what to do with it, and sweep the area for the mines that had already been laid. John Roark, one of Evancoe's PB officers, had discovered the Iranian's mine-laying chart aboard the *Iran Ajar*, which

precisely designated their mine placements. But the navy's mine warfare crew aboard the *Hercules* insisted on earning their pay and instead
methodically swept the sea in their wooden-hulled boats for six days.
Admiral Bernsen then ordered Evancoe to proceed northward and anchor the *Herc* a few miles off Farsi Island. He was to remain in international waters, but just astride the "Line of Death," and prevent any
further hostile activity or mine-laying. The *Jarrett* and another fast
frigate, the *Thatch*, would remain close by to shoot down any attacking
Iranian fighters that might launch from nearby Rashour, but aside
from those vessels, Evancoe and his task unit were on their own. The
rules of engagement were that he could not open fire first, and he
could respond only in kind; an AK-47 could be answered by an M-16,
a .50 caliber by a similar gun. *Bullshit*, Evancoe thought privately
when he heard the order. *Special operators don't work that way.* If a
single Iranian bullet came his way, he would bring every gun he had
to bear.

And so, the *Hercules* waited in ambush, but there wasn't a minute of
inactivity. During the daylight hours, patrol boat and weapons maintenance were in full swing, and the Night Stalker crew chiefs and "armament dogs" prepared the helos for another night of flying. Marines
filled more sandbags and upgraded their emplacements, making the
barge look like a floating Alamo, and the SEALs drilled and trained
and live-fired their weapons. The heat was so intense that it wasn't unusual for a crew member to faint dead away on the deck. But the only
thing that made the commander uneasy was that contingent of nearly
thirty foreign nationals working the vessel, none of whom spoke
English with the exception of their Irish foreman. Many of them were
clearly Middle Easterners, and Evancoe didn't trust any of them, but
they were part of the contract with Brown and Root. To suppress any
mutinous fantasies, he ordered that every single SEAL, marine and
Night Stalker carry a loaded weapon at all times. When an admiral in
command of the minesweeping unit arrived by helicopter to visit his

sailors, he witnessed the bargeful of "cowboys" and ordered Evancoe to belay that practice. Evancoe refused the order, and Admiral Bernsen backed him up.

Every evening as the sun set, the war in the Gulf woke up. Iraqi warplanes would streak across the Gulf to bomb Farsi Island, and the Iranians would answer with streams of antiaircraft fire. Taking note of the *Hercules* as a fixed object in the waters below, the Iraqi fighter pilots began using her as a navigational aide—roaring in low, banking left above the barge and making their bomb runs on Farsi. When Evancoe relocated the barge for his own tactical reasons, the Iraqis failed to note the positional change and inadvertently bombed a Saudi Coast Guard station nearby. The Iranians, for their part, were infuriated by the presence of the *Hercules*, made more so by the fact that the *Iran Ajar* had been towed up to Evancoe's position and anchored there. They were constantly probing his control area with fast-moving attack vessels, until his PBs and Seafoxes would chase them off. He was pleased to at last receive the order from Admiral Bernsen to scuttle the *Iran Ajar*, which his SEALs accomplished by towing her out to sea and using a very generous helping of C-4. She went to the bottom in less than half a minute.

The Iranians were watching from afar, and the sinking of their mine-layer really infuriated them. From the nearby oil fields at Faradune, they began deploying fast-attack craft called Swedish Boghammers, twenty-four-foot, aluminum-hulled, heavily armed boats that could make sixty knots and outrun anything the U.S. Navy had in theater. The Boghammers probed and raced around the perimeter of Evancoe's area, and he knew that it wouldn't be long now until they made their move. As the sun descended on the eighth, he ordered his communications men and a marine Farsi-speaker to board one of the Seafoxes and deploy to Middle Shoals Buoy, where they would tie up and listen to Iranian transmissions, giving him ample time to prepare for battle. Two of the larger patrol boats would accompany the Seafox, but all would huddle together to present a single, small radar blip, no larger than that of a dhow.

Fladry had already taken to the air that night, once again flying the MH-6 with its FLIR. Yet after the incident with the *Iran Ajar*, he was no longer satisfied with his and his copilot's MP-5s and pistols and had asked permission from Colonel Codney to mount a minigun on the helo.

"You can put a friggin' cannon on there, Flapper," Codney replied. "If you can mount it."

Flapper felt better with the mutlibarreled machine gun and two thousand rounds of 7.62mm in the belts, and he flew a low-level course over the water for nearly two hours, following a recon pattern that he and his pilots had planned along with Commander Evancoe. With Paul DeMilia and Brian Collins piloting one AH-6 behind him, and Terry Pena and Bob Witter piloting the other, Flapper swooped to the south and began tracking back over the predetermined waypoints, searching for the fast Iranian boats. They had seen nothing but flat, black water and were looking forward to getting back to the *Hercules* and taking a break. The last waypoint in their search pattern was the Middle Shoals Buoy, and they knew that Evancoe was deploying his Seafox and PBs to that position and expected to see them there. What they didn't know was that the navy boats hadn't arrived yet.

As Flapper closed the range, he could see through his NVGs what appeared to be three small boats clustered near the buoy. As it was standard procedure to report what he saw, he keyed his mike and spoke to his attack helos. The transmission was automatically broadcast on the secure Alpha net to all ships in the area.

"Uh, I've got a couple of boats in sight up here."

"Roger, I've got that, too," DeMilia replied as he hung back behind Flapper with Terry Pena.

"Continuing inbound," Flapper said. "I've got some personnel in sight . . . some weapons systems. They're not running any visible lighting, sitting low in the water."

In the lead AH-6, DeMilia and Collins looked at each other. They had established a procedure with Evancoe whereby his navy boats would have infrared strobes attached to their antennas for friendly identification, but Fladry wasn't reporting that.

"Damn navy," DeMilia muttered. "They forgot to put their strobes on."

"Well, should we go ahead and arm the guns?" Collins posed.

"Yeah, let's load up, just in case."

At a thousand meters range, DeMilia armed the weapons systems. He selected flechette rockets, but as he closed the distance the timing fuses of the flechettes would no longer be effective, so he switched to just minigun and high-explosive rockets. Still, he considered the boats below to be friendly and was just following his training and instincts.

Flapper was nearly on top of the buoy now. He could see the three boats nearby—two that looked like Boston Whalers and one long, sleek shape of a low-hulled, fast-attack craft. It looked like .50 caliber machine-gun barrels were tracking him, but American fifties had straight round barrels at the end, while these guns had that hex-head shape of . . . *Russian-made weapons.*

"Boghammers! Boghammers!" Flapper spat into his mike as he broke left hard, just above the enemy vessels. The Iranians immediately opened up on him, sending streams of red tracers right between his skids as he rolled away. "Taking fire! Taking fire!" he yelled over his radio.

"Roger," DeMilia answered. He didn't need Flapper to tell him he was being fired on; he could see the bullets lancing up at the MH-6 from the water, and he nosed his helo down and aimed directly at the source of the gunfire. "Inbound hot."

At five hundred meters, DeMilia opened up with his minigun, hammering a tight cluster of fire across the Iranians amidships. The boats were all gasoline-driven and a billowing, sun-bright plume immediately burst up into the night. Suddenly a star-shaped flower of white light popped from one of the hulls below and a missile arched up at him, but the range was so close that its warhead had no time to acquire the Little Bird and it bounced across the waters right beneath him. It was going to be a duel to the death.

Aboard the *Hercules*, Commander Evancoe was inside his own small CIC, a fifteen-by-twenty-foot steel trailer packed with communications gear and radar screens. Considering his own comforts to be the last priority, Evancoe hadn't even installed a window or air-conditioning, and he and his men just dripped sweat inside the box.

"Holy shit!" Flapper's adrenaline-surged voice boomed through Evancoe's command center. "It went right through my legs!"

"Engage, engage," came another pilot's voice above the buzz-saw roar of a minigun.

"Roger, engaging."

"Break off! Missile! Missile!"

Evancoe listened carefully, but he did not respond. It was not like in the movies, where the commander would immediately break in and take charge, managing the combat by remote control. This was precisely the time to say *nothing* and let the Night Stalkers do their job. Almost immediately, Evancoe's patrol officer, John Roark, reported in that he was taking his PBs and the Seafox and heading for the engagement. Evancoe swept off his headset, slammed the box's door open and peered out across his decks. He didn't need his NVGs to see what was going on just a couple of miles away. The sea was on fire, with forty-foot plumes of orange gasoline flames licking up at the sky. The thuds of detonating rocket warheads and the ugly buzz of miniguns echoed across the sea. Enemy gunfire was streaking up at his helos, and the Night Stalkers were giving it back in spades. He reported to COMIDEASTFOR that the *Hercules* was under attack and her forces were returning fire.

DeMilia had just blown up one of the Boston Whalers with his minigun and rockets. He broke hard right as the machine gun from the other Whaler tried to bring him down, but Terry Pena was already racing in at full power just above the wavetops. He held his trigger down and hosed the Whaler with bullets and rockets until its fuel tanks detonated, and he turned the Little Bird on its side and burst through the smoke. By this time, the Boghammer had taken evasive action, speeding away from the scene. It suddenly circled back, spewing up spray from its powerful engines as it came on, firing at the American helos darting through the night sky. It was a very nasty fight in very close quarters, between furious sailors and determined aviators.

"Boghammer's coming back." Flapper had broken left and was circling close, warning, advising and directing his gunship pilots. "Engage, engage."

"Roger, engaging." DeMilia completed his tight circle and raced back into it. He expended the rest of his minigun ammo at the zigzagging shape of the Boghammer and then fired his last two rockets. They missed their mark, but the range was so close that when the warheads detonated both he and Collins were soaked with spray through their open cockpit doors.

"I'm out of ammo," DeMilia reported. "Going back to rearm."

"Roger," Pena acknowledged as he set himself up for another run and checked his weapons. "I've got one more rocket."

"Terry," DeMilia said, "just get *real* close and sink that damned thing!"

"Take your time," Flapper broke in. "I'm going in."

"Roger that," Pena said.

If Pena was going to get a good clean shot, the Iranians would have to be focused elsewhere. Flapper broke from his pattern, rolled in and dove at the vessel, firing two long bursts of four hundred rounds each from his newly mounted minigun at the Boghammer. The Iranians tried to bring Flapper's bird down, but it was just enough of a distraction. Pena pierced their aluminum hull, dead center, with a high-explosive rocket. The Boghammer pitched up and slowly sank below the waves.

Flapper called a cease-fire. He could see some Iranians flailing around in the flaming waters below. "We're gonna need some prisoners," he reported to Evancoe. The commander advised him that his PBs were en route. With some ammunition left, Flapper stayed on station while DeMilia and Pena returned to the *Hercules* to rearm and refuel, but when they got there, it looked like the battle wasn't over quite yet.

John Roark had just reported in to Commander Evancoe from the wheelhouse of his racing PB.

"Sir, I'm holding about forty high-speed contacts coming out of Faradune in our direction." Roark was a Texas boy and his easy, cool drawl belied the significance of so many enemy boats. "Do you hold those on your radar?"

"Wait one," Evancoe answered. He was back inside his little CIC, and sure enough, his radar man was holding the same contacts, moving very fast in their direction. He confirmed that to Roark and told him to hold his position. Forty fast-moving craft could only mean Boghammers, or vessels very much like them, heavily armed and potentially very, very nasty. If it was a fight they wanted, they would get it, but Evancoe was going to bring in every asset he could. He called over to the *Thatch*, the fast frigate patrolling twelve miles south of his position, and identified himself as the barge commander by saying, "*Hercules* Actual."

"*Thatch* Actual." The frigate's commander was also doing his own radiowork that night and had already monitored Roark's alarming transmission. "Do you require my assistance?"

"I'll take anything I can get," Evancoe said.

"We'll be there as fast as we can. I'm going to launch our LAMPS, so bear in mind you've got a friendly inbound."

"Roger." Like all the American tactical seacraft and helos, the LAMPS would display an infrared light that could be seen only through NVGs.

John White, the captain of the *Raleigh*, was steaming ninety miles south of the *Hercules*, but he had also heard all the combat transmissions and the deadly news of an inbound assault on the barge. He raised Evancoe on the Alpha net.

"*Herc*, can you use some more helicopters?"

"Wouldn't mind at all." All three of Evancoe's Night Stalker birds were now rearming and refueling aboard the barge, but there were more aboard the *Raleigh*.

"I've got four Seabats on deck and they're looking for a fight," White said.

"Send 'em my way."

Support was now en route from multiple volunteers, but it would take some time. At a range of ninety miles, it would be forty-five minutes before the additional Little Birds were on station. The *Thatch* had not yet appeared over the horizon. The LAMPS helicopter now reported that it, too, was holding multiple radar contacts and they were closing on the *Hercules* fast. John Roark called Evancoe from his PB.

"Skipper, what are your orders?"

The only thing between the *Hercules* and those Iranian gunboats now was Roark and his two patrol boats. They were very heavily armed, and would each have eleven SEALs manning their .50 calibers, horizontally firing 81mm mortars, a 40mm Bofors rapid-fire cannon in each bow and a 20mm machine gun on each stern. When they took the Boghammers on, only the coxswains would be steering the boats; everyone else would be firing, including Roark, who would be exposed like a tank commander standing up in the turret. The PBs were very fast and maneuverable, but their hulls were aluminum. They would send a lot of Iranian sailors and boats to the sea bottom, but it was likely that they would go down with them. It was one of the hardest orders Evancoe had ever issued.

"John . . . turn and engage."

"Aye, aye, Skipper." From his tone, the Texan could have been responding to a request to pick up the morning mail.

Evancoe dropped the radio mike and went out on the *Hercules'* main deck. *They're going to hand me my ass*—he thought of the swarm of attacking Iranians—*and I'm gonna hand them theirs*. He looked across his structures and gun emplacements. There was no need to sound general quarters—every remaining SEAL and marine on board was already in full battle dress and pumped up behind his gun. Evancoe raised his eyes to the *Herc*'s highest radio mast and saw the Kuwaiti national flag whipping in the midnight air. He yelled out to one of his command master chiefs.

"Chief, haul down that fucking rag and run up the Stars and Stripes!"

"Aye, aye, sir!"

The *Hercules* was ready. Flapper, DeMilia and Pena lifted off in their fully armed Little Birds and headed back out to sea. Four more helos were inbound. John Roark and his PBs wouldn't be able to stop the entire flotilla of Iranians, but if the surviving Boghammers tried to attack and board the *Herc*, God help them. Evancoe went back out on deck as he checked the ammo in his own battle vest and jacked a round into his M-16. Then he turned to see the *Thatch*, coming on like gangbusters, an eight-foot bow wave curling over its prow and a thirty-foot rooster tail arcing up from its stern.

The Iranians saw the frigate as well. John Roark was running at them at full battle speed and was just within firing range when the Boghammers suddenly turned tail and ran.

"Skipper!" one of Evancoe's men called out to him from the CIC. "They're turning ass back to Faradune."

Evancoe nodded slowly. He could feel the adrenaline begin to recede from his veins. He knew he could still have Roark pursue the Iranians and take a lot of them down, but that might mean a fight in the oil fields and collateral damage he wouldn't be able to justify. He had already seen enough combat in his life to know that sometimes the best kind of victory is in the battle you never have to fight. John Roark was calling him on the radio, begging for permission to attack. Evancoe went back into his CIC.

"John," Evancoe ordered. "Break off pursuit."

"But, Skipper," Roark whined in his drawl, "they're in gun range. I can take 'em!"

"Break off pursuit, John." Evancoe grinned. He knew that feeling, being hot on the blood trail and then suddenly ordered to stand down.

"But, *Skipper* . . . Awwww, aye, aye, sir."

En route back to the *Hercules*, Roark picked up six Iranian survivors from the water. They were the only men he found and they were all horribly wounded, punctured by multiple minigun rounds and flechettes. They were also badly burned, having swum through waves aflame with gasoline fires. When Roark's PBs reached the *Herc* with the wounded, Evancoe tasked the young minesweepers aboard the barge to carry the litters from the PBs to the deckhouse. The night wasn't over yet; the *Hercules* was still at general quarters, and the commander had no warriors to spare for that task. The young sailors had never seen action at sea, or anywhere else, and they were stunned by the cruelty of blood and fire.

The Iranians were fortunate that Doc Jones was aboard. He was a master chief and legendary SEAL corpsman, and he quickly triaged the wounded Revolutionary Guards and began treating them in the sick bay just across from the deck house. When Evancoe arrived at the sick bay, his running shoes splashed through pools of blood. The first of his prisoners had just died and a pair of young minesweepers were gingerly folding his arms over his chest and carefully putting him into a body bag. Evancoe's executive officer, Lieutenant Pete Wikul, strode in, saw the scene and lost his temper.

"He's dead," Wikul snapped at the sailors as he shouldered them aside and stuffed the corpse into the bag. "Now get him the hell outta here before we lose another one!" There was only one gurney in the bay, and no room for pity.

Doc Jones began working on another patient. The man wasn't long for this world; he had multiple bullet holes in his chest and a flechette embedded in his forehead. Most of his lips and eyelids had been burned away, but he was still conscious. Evancoe summoned two of his Marine Corps radio recon translators to the bay.

"He's asking for water, sir," one of the marines said to Evancoe.

"Get him a cup of water." It was a hard-and-fast rule never to give water to a man with a head wound, but the commander knew it wouldn't matter. "With ice."

Doc Jones lifted the mangled head and helped the man drink.

"Ask him how many operations he's been on," Evancoe instructed the marine.

"He says this was his first one."

"Ask him what he does."

"He says he's the baker."

Evancoe knelt next to the wounded man and smiled as warmly as he could.

"Please tell him that I think he had a very *bad* first operation."

The marine translated, the man's eyes rolled back in his head, and he died.

Doc Jones managed to save four out of the six. A Marine Corps CH-46 arrived with a doctor and another corpsman. It was too heavy to set down on the decks, so it hovered with its wheels in contact while the wounded and dead were loaded aboard and then it flew away. Roark returned to the battle area with his patrol boats, seeking anything still afloat that might be of intelligence value. One of Evancoe's petty officers, Jim Kelse, was a Stinger missile–qualified SEAL and saw something floating in the water; it was nothing more than a small Styrofoam box, but he recognized it as a battery holder for the American-made missile system and dove in to get it. It was such a missile that had been fired at Paul DeMilia, and when Evancoe's divers later descended to the wreck of the Boghammer, they would find a completely intact Stinger still encased in its box. A flurry of secure messages would fly between COMIDEASTFOR and Washington, until matching serial numbers revealed a horrific fact: The Iranians were using American antiaircraft missiles to shoot down American aircraft. They were the very Stingers that Lieutenant Colonel Oliver North had supplied to the Iranians in exchange for hostages, a failed and one-sided deal at best that had nearly resulted in further Night Stalker names being etched into granite at Fort Campbell.

Bob Fladry, Paul DeMilia and their fellow pilots didn't sleep at all that night. They flew, returned to the *Hercules* to refuel, and flew again. During one break in the intense activity, DeMilia wandered into the quarters where the Marine Corps intelligence officers and translators were sifting through the blood- and water-soaked belongings of the Iranian dead and wounded. He picked up a wallet and opened it.

There was a picture of the Iranian baker, with his smiling wife and children. DeMilia shook his head sadly. It was his first taste of combat, and that photograph dissolved all the images of war he had once imagined. It wasn't about the helos and the guns and the high-tech duels in the darkness. War was very simple. They had all come very far, leaving their homes and families, to kill one another in this empty place at sea.

CHAPTER 4

UNARMED
AND SCARED
SHITLESS

PANAMA
DECEMBER 1989

MAJOR RICK "THE HAMMER" BOWMAN was definitely going
to die.

He was standing on the flight line at Howard Air Force base in
Panama, just outside Hangar 3, squinting in the sunlight at an armada
of Little Birds, Blackhawks and Chinooks. It was three o'clock in the
afternoon and the Panamanian sun was merciless, the jungle humidity
soaking the unit crew chiefs and armament men as they turned
wrenches and loaded up rockets and ammunition. Over the past three
days, flight after flight of C5-As had been landing on the baked tarmac, bringing in more helos, more support troops, more ammo. By
now there were nearly a thousand men bedding down in the hangar,
forming a crossword puzzle of endless cots and gear. Bowman had told

his crew chiefs that once the shooting started, they were to get their men out of there because the Panamanians would no doubt shell the hangar. But that wasn't supposed to happen until H-hour, exactly at the stroke of midnight.

At the moment, Bowman just stared at the yawning mouth of the hangar, where the men of Delta's B-Squadron were emerging into the steamy heat with all of their kit and lining up in the small formations of their various chalks. There were going to be dozens of missions that night, from the massive parachute assaults of the Rangers to pinpoint raids by the SEALs to capture Panamanian dictator Manuel Noriega, but Bowman's mission, "Acid Gambit," might well be the most dicey of all. His company of MH-6s was going to deliver Delta to the roof of Modelo Prison, smack in the middle of the Panamanian Defense Forces headquarters, the *Comandancia.* The Delta men were going to fight their way into the prison and rescue an American named Kurt Muse, a CIA operative who'd been suffering in a filthy cell for nine months. Once they had him, Bowman and his pilots would be coming back in to take them all out. They had all been training for this for a long time. Over and over, they had rehearsed it at various locations in Panama and on a precise mock-up of Modelo down at Hurlburt Field in Florida. Major Bowman was the company commander of the 160th Special Operations Aviation Group's A Company and the air mission commander for Acid Gambit, and he had no doubt that they could all pull it off. But it was supposed to go down in utter darkness—not in the blazing light of day.

Bob Fladry, Bowman's copilot for the mission, pulled his head out of their Little Bird cockpit and also stared at the Delta boys forming up on the gluey tarmac. There were four assault birds in the flight: Jim Dietderich's and Don Fox's Chalk One; Bowman's and Flapper's Chalk Three; and J. J. Holmes and Kelly McDougal would be flying Chalk Two and Chalk Four, single-pilot birds so they could haul more customers. All of them turned now, their jaws going slack, as they watched the ominous process of the Delta commandos preparing to load up. Yes, they were shouldering into their combat webbing, slinging their submachine guns, pulling on their black Pro-Tec helmets. They had their satchel charges with them and their radios and light antitank weapons. A crew chief sprinted through the flight line, calling out to his armament boys.

"They've pushed it up," he was yelling. "We're going *now*."

Fladry turned to Bowman, his eyebrows pinched together and high. "They've *got* to be shitting us."

Bowman couldn't believe it either. This mission was going to be hairy enough at night, with every gun barrel in the *Comandancia* blazing away at them as soon as the Panamanians knew what was happening. But in broad daylight? He had been wearing his flight suit opened up with the sleeves tied around his waist, and now he unfurled it and started stuffing his sweaty arms inside. He couldn't help himself; he just started to laugh.

"We are all gonna *die*."

One of the Delta men was dragging something out of the hangar. It had a wide metal base and a small glass bubble on it, and he set it down before the formation. The first of the kitted-up commandos stepped onto it. The crew chief ran back through the flight line, waving his arms.

"No, no, no!" he yelled out wildly. "They're just weighing in! Stand down, stand down!"

The Little Bird assault helos were very fast and flexible, but they were also fussy when it came to weight and balance ratios. The Delta men knew exactly how much each chalk could carry, so they were tailoring their loads and carefully weighing themselves on a bathroom scale. That was all. They were just being superprofessional, as always.

"Holy shit," one of Bowman's pilots hissed relief from somewhere. "I think I just wet myself."

Bowman and Fladry looked at each other, grinned and shook their heads. *Okay,* Bowman thought, *maybe I* am *going to live . . . for at least another nine hours . . .*

OPERATION JUST CAUSE, the American invasion of Panama, was about to be Rick Bowman's first taste of combat. And yet the cynical side of him still believed that at the very last minute it would all be called off. This gathering storm in Central America just didn't seem confluent with President George H. W. Bush's vision of social responsibility and multinational cooperation, "A Thousand Points of Light," unless the commander in chief was referring to muzzle flashes. And not that Bowman's personal misfortunes had any bearing on the matter, but up until this point in his career it seemed like everyone else was always being tapped for a mission, while he was always left waving goodbye.

He had been in the army for thirteen years—seventeen if you counted his four years at West Point—and whenever the call to action came he was invariably in the wrong place at the wrong time. It was infuriating and frustrating as hell, and on more than one occasion he had nearly packed it in.

"One more year," he would say to himself as he watched his birds and his pilots load aboard a C5-A, bound for glory. "One more year of this crap, and then I'm outta here."

Yet nothing in Bowman's life had come easily, and he had learned early on to stick it out or come up empty. Quitting just wasn't part of his lexicon. As a kid in Pennsylvania he had grown up in a house full of memories of World War II and stories about the ranks of small-town kids who had gone off to serve without a whimper. His mother had been an army nurse and his father had served in the navy, and Rick had always dreamed of going to West Point.

"Okay, sure." His high school guidance counselor had smiled sympathetically. "What else do you want to do?"

That wasn't enough to discourage Rick Bowman. He was only fueled further by the dismissive sneers of doubters, and if someone said

Major Bob Johnson's Blackhawk on the deck of the USS *Guam* after being hit more than forty times by small-arms fire in Grenada. DEPARTMENT OF DEFENSE FILE PHOTOGRAPH

Captain Keith Lucas, who was killed in Grenada, the first Night Stalker to give his life in combat. COURTESY ALICE LUCAS

Lieutenant Colonel (then Captain) Mike Grimm was the visionary who helped bring the 160th into being. COURTESY KARIN GRIMM TERRY

Major Bob Johnson (left) at the monument to the Americans who lost their lives in Grenada. When he returned in 1988, he found a friendly and exceptionally grateful population. COURTESY ROBERT L. JOHNSON

The governor general's residence on Grenada. Sir Paul Scoon and his wife were trapped here when violence erupted in 1983. Courtesy Robert L. Johnson

Bob "Wild Man" Codney in the cockpit of his Huey in Vietnam. Courtesy Lieutenant Colonel (ret.) Bob Codney

The AH-6 gunship can carry a variety of weapons, but the 2.75-inch rocket is one of the pilots' favorites. COURTESY 160TH SOAR(A)

The barge *Hercules*, used as a helicopter base during Operation Prime Chance. COURTESY OF COLONEL (RET.) RANDY COCHRAN

Colonel John "Coach" Dailey, Major Randy Cochran, and Chief Warrant Officer 2 Steve Koester during Operation Prime Chance. COURTESY COLONEL (RET.) RANDY COCHRAN

Daytime gunnery practice against a target ship—the *Iran Ajr* would experience the deadly accuracy of 160th gun pilots. Courtesy 160th SOAR(A).

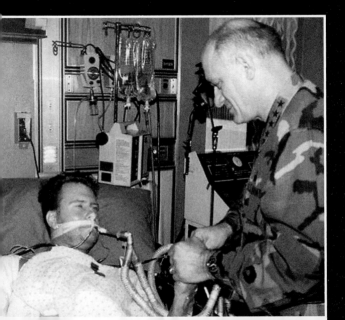

Major Rick Bowman is awarded the Purple Heart for wounds received in Panama, by Army Chief of Staff General Carl Vuono. Courtesy Colonel (ret.) Rick Bowman

Chief Warrant Officer 4 Bob Fladry receives the Silver Star for his actions in Panama. Major Rick Bowman, now mostly recovered, is at right. COURTESY CHIEF WARRANT OFFICER 5 (RET.) BOB FLADRY

Jim Crisafulli enjoying downtime in Saudi Arabia during Operation Desert Storm. COURTESY CHIEF WARRANT OFFICER 4 (RET.) JIM CRISAFULLI

Jim Crisafulli (second from left), Chief Warrant Officer 3 Randy Stephens, Private First Class Todd Diffenderfer, and Staff Sergeant Bruce Willard stand with members of the security team (all in camouflage) in front of "Lady Godiva" in a Saudi Arabian hangar.
COURTESY CHIEF WARRANT OFFICER 4 (RET.) JIM CRISAFULLI

Chief Warrant Officer 5 Karl Maier now serves as chief warrant officer of the regiment and close adviser to the commander. Courtesy Karl Maier

Chief Warrant Officer 5 Don Tabron is awarded the Silver Star for his actions in Afghanistan by Army Chief of Staff General Peter Schoomaker. DEPARTMENT OF DEFENSE FILE PHOTOGRAPH

An MH-47 in an Afghan valley. COURTESY 160TH SOAR(A)

Chief Warrant Officer 4 Greg Calvert in front of an MH-47E. COURTESY GREG CALVERT

Two MH-47s take on fuel

View from the pilot's seat of the MH-47 during refueling. The 160th is the only army unit that is equipped and trained to do aerial refueling. COURTESY 160TH SOAR(A)

Two MH-47Es on an overwater flight. DEPARTMENT OF DEFENSE FILE PHOTOGRAPH

The cockpit of a special operations helicopter is a busy place. State-of-the-art equipment allows flight under almost any conditions.
COURTESY 160TH SOAR(A)

The AH-6 "Little Bird" gunship, here mounted with two 2.75-inch seven-shot rocket pods. Gun pilots can put a rocket through a target

A flight of Little Birds. This photograph shows how troops are carried. COURTESY 160TH SOAR(A)

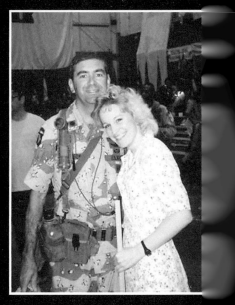

Lieutenant Colonel Bob Johnson, on his return from battalion command during Desert Storm, with his about-to-be wife, Julie. COURTESY ROBERT L. JOHNSON

Bob Johnson and the other love in his life—his "replacement," Robby. As Johnson found out, first-time fatherhood at age fifty-one is not for the faint of heart! COURTESY ROBERT L. JOHNSON

"Death Waits in the Dark"—the motto from the unit's unofficial logo. Many an enemy soldier has found the motto to be true. COURTESY 160TH SOAR(A)

The official unit crest of the 160th Special Operations Aviation Regiment. The crescent moon symbolizes nighttime operations, while the winged centaur represents the aviation mission. COURTESY 160TH SOAR(A)

operations in the

he couldn't do something, watch out. He made it onto the Point's admissions list as an alternate, went to Penn State for a year and then transferred to the academy. That guidance counselor was still scratching his head when Bowman graduated in 1976 as an infantry officer and volunteered for the 82nd Airborne Division.

Bowman loved being a paratrooper. The 82nd trained hard and it was go, go, go, all the time. The constant action fit his personality, and he was more than up to the physical challenges. He had already learned at the Point that when you'd expended your last joule of energy was exactly when you'd need it most, so he had developed a wrestler's upper-body strength and legs that could carry him way past the burn. He laughed easily, partied hard off-hours and was a habitual practical joker, but his temper was hair-trigger, and if a subordinate screwed up, his roars would rattle the windows. With his blond hair, blue eyes and flashing white grin, he looked like a killer Beach Boy. Rick Bowman could be your best friend, or your worst nightmare.

While still at West Point, he had enrolled in the cadet flight training program, where he filled his logbook with forty hours in an OH-58 and not only soloed but successfully executed cross-country flights. He knew then that he would someday want to fly again, so after one tour with the infantry he applied to flight school and breezed through the basics. Soon, he was flying a UH-1 for an assault company in Hawaii, and almost immediately regretted his decision. The infantry customers looked on their helo pilots as glorified cabdrivers, and the army was so risk-averse after Vietnam that they didn't even execute true air assaults; it was just flying at altitude, putting the guys on the ground and going away. After so much intense activity with the 82nd, three years in Hawaii had bored Bowman to tears and he decided to return to the infantry. He was back in the States at the Infantry Advanced Course when he ran into a friend, Joe Kautz, who was serving as the S-2 with a classified army aviation unit.

"You ought to come up to Fort Campbell and assess with Task Force 160," Kautz suggested.

"Task Force who?"

"Don't ask, 'cause I won't tell. Just get yourself up there."

It was over the Christmas holidays in 1982 that Bowman made his way to Kentucky. Colonel Barry Sottak, the Night Stalker commander, was away for the break, so Bowman endured a four-hour oral "interview" with a veteran Little Bird pilot named Randy Jones. In February of '83 he completed the process, but there were no slots available for assault pilots in A Company. He was a thirty-year-old captain with nowhere to go.

"I'll take him in my company." Bob Johnson had been serving as the unit's personnel officer since 1981 and knew a good candidate when he saw one. Johnson was about to take over command of the Blackhawk company Charlie 101, and the fact that Bowman couldn't yet fly that helicopter didn't seem to bother him. "I'll get him a Black-hawk transition, too," he told Sottak.

"Seems a little cocky to me," the colonel said, but Johnson hadn't yet picked out a poor pilot candidate, so the commander signed Bowman's paperwork.

Bowman had never seen an outfit like the 160th, or a more dedicated, aggressive, take-it-to-the-edge group of pilots. They would fly anywhere, anytime, over mist-covered peaks or under low-slung drawbridges. If the customers wanted to land on a submarine, at night, in the middle of January and a thousand miles from home, the Night Stalkers would do it. If the target was the size of a beach bungalow and hidden somewhere in a triple-canopy jungle, the Night Stalkers would find it. And the crews, rather than being the laid-back rear-echelon guys Bowman was used to, were just as wild as the pilots. The crew chiefs rode their door guns like cowboys gripping mechanical bulls, indifferent to the two-G banks and rolls of their helos. The armament guys were like deadly computer nerds, knowing every weapon's weight, rate of fire, ballistic capability and the proper marrying of tools to missions. The mechanics treated the helos like Formula One race cars, and kept them looking that way as well. They were all "A-types," or maybe even A-plus. It was a perfect fit for Bowman.

In the summer of 1983, Captain Bowman came aboard as Major Johnson's executive officer in Charlie 101. It was time for him to get a Blackhawk transition, but those slots were always reserved for warrant officers first. The warrants were dedicated solely to flying, while the commissioned officers like Bowman were expected to shoulder administrative duties and the multiple responsibilities of leadership. Finally, in October, he was in the middle of his Blackhawk training at Fort Rucker when he turned on the television to the news of the invasion of Grenada. No one had called him from Campbell or said anything about it, but he knew he had just missed a big one. It wasn't the last time he would be cursing as he waved goodbye.

Bob Johnson returned from Operation Urgent Fury, and while he recovered from his wounds, Bowman became the acting commander of the company. When Johnson was strong enough again to retrieve his command, Bowman remained as his XO for a year and was then assigned to take over the unit's Headquarters Company. After Grenada, there was no longer a question about the Night Stalkers' survival. By 1985, things were starting to happen "out there," and the "red phone" was ringing nonstop. International terrorists were making a habit of attacking American interests, hijacking airplanes and taking hostages. The Night Stalkers deployed more and more often, and even though that final green light rarely blazed, Bowman discovered the cruel truth about his new position: The HHC commander never went anywhere. He was the shop master, office manager and gatekeeper. If anything actually did go down, he was going to be left behind, right there at Fort Campbell. *Wave goodbye, Rick. . . .*

All right, so Bowman would try something else. He left his position at HHC and became the unit's LnO (liaison officer) to the SEALs. It was the kind of position everyone strove for, right at the tip of the spear, because once you linked up tight with the customers you weren't going to be left behind. Working with the SEALs was about as action-intensive as anything could be in peacetime. He planned with them, trained with them and flew them. On one nighttime mission at sea, he was piloting a Blackhawk and picking up a SEAL team from the deck of a rolling frigate, when the last naval commando to board the caving ladder inadvertently discharged a flare as he climbed into the helo. Bowman and his copilot, "Little Rick" Campbell, were temporarily blinded and the Blackhawk's rear wheel snagged on the ship's "overboard" net. The helicopter pitched violently from side to side and its turbines screamed, but Bowman managed to hold it until the gear strut finally snapped. He flew the bird back over to dry land and hovered, while his intrepid crew chief deployed the caving ladder again, climbed down and repaired the wheel. After that, Bowman couldn't buy his own beers if there were SEALs around. It most definitely wasn't a boring time, but he still had never deployed for anything "real world."

By this time, Bob Johnson had left for the Command and General Staff College at Fort Leavenworth. It was the path an army officer had to follow if he was ever to rise above the rank of major, even though it meant that you might never be able to return to the 160th; the army had its own quaint logic about personnel and assignments. Doug Brown had taken over command of Charlie 101 and asked Rick Bowman to be his operations officer. Bowman figured his karma might change with Brown's aggressive style, and indeed he enjoyed serving under another hard-charging Night Stalker company commander who could also fly with the best of them. But 1986 rolled into 1987 and he had *still* never heard a shot fired in anger. Hell, he hadn't even gotten to the point where you had to lock and load. He decided to leave the unit and go to Leavenworth as well.

"If you ever want to be a Night Stalker again," Johnson warned him one night over a beer, "don't do it."

"I've just got to break this spell, Bob."

"Well"—Johnson shrugged—"a man's gotta do what a man's gotta do." There was no reasoning with Bowman about anything once he'd made up his mind.

Bowman was in the middle of his C&GS studies when he found out that the Night Stalkers had not only deployed to the Persian Gulf but were already in some heavy action. He broke a few objects in his room.

Even before he had his C&GS College diploma in hand, the Hammer knew that he wanted to return to the 160th. He had just spent a year studying alongside officers from every branch of the U.S. Army, and nothing else appealed to him anymore. If he stuck it out, maybe somebody would rustle up a war somewhere. It was a very rare thing for the Night Stalkers to take on the army's bureaucracy and bring a man back to the fold, but they all knew Bowman too well; he would make such a pain in the ass of himself that it was easier to just get it done.

Lieutenant Colonel Bob Codney was serving as the unit's S-3, and he welcomed Bowman aboard as his assistant operations officer. The S-3 shop had the kind of action Bowman thrived on. Having so successfully executed their Prime Chance mission, the Night Stalkers were now the army's "secret celebrities"; everybody wanted a piece of them. The unit performed so much better than any other aviation outfit that once "chopped" to a theater CINC (commander in chief), those customers were very reluctant to let them go. Bowman became the "King of the LnOs," managing operations with a myriad of special tactics customers. And then, in the beginning of 1989, the Little Birds' A Company suddenly needed a new commander.

Bowman could fly the small and fast helos, but he wasn't nearly as proficient as the A Company pilots. That was all right; they would take him anyway. The only condition was that he would have to go through the Little Bird Green Platoon. He had already done Green Platoon with his Blackhawk company, but bringing that up only resulted in sneers and chuckles; Little Bird pilots were *different*.

A Blackhawk was a Cadillac; a Little Bird was a Porsche. A Blackhawk had all sorts of heavy hydraulics and compensation systems; you could trim it up and just take your feet off the rotor pedals and cruise.

A Little Bird made you work; after an hour, your left calf was sore from fighting the anti-torque pedals. A Blackhawk had all sorts of fancy navigational computers; plug in the waypoints and she'd tell you where and when to turn. A Little Bird still had "steam gauge" instruments; if you couldn't work a map, compass and clock, you were lost. Blackhawk pilots had the doors on most of the time, except when flying over water, and there were actually temperature control systems in their birds. Little Bird pilots were almost always freezing their asses off; the doors were never on because with that kind of low-level, pinpoint flying you needed to stick your head out and stare at the target. When it was really cold, the left-seat pilot actually wore a huge mitten to keep from getting frostbite as the wind slapped his collective. Bowman had always snickered when the Little Bird pilots screamed onto the post on their Harleys and Ninjas; they all thought they were "Top Gun." Now he knew why.

Near the end of Bowman's in-house transition into Little Birds, he was sent to SERE School (Survival Evasion Resistance Escape) for twenty-one days of torment in the North Carolina woods. The candidates were from various elite units of the armed services and the instructors were Special Forces veterans who very much enjoyed their work. First, the candidates were taught how to survive in the wild, while simultaneously deprived of food, water and cold weather gear. Then, they were broken up into teams and pursued by fleet-footed men with guns, who invariably captured them all. Finally, they were abused, tormented and interrogated. No one escaped. A number of the candidates fell out and failed. To Bowman, it wasn't much worse than his early days as a plebe at the Point.

He returned to Fort Campbell in March 1989 to take over A Company. There were eighteen Little Birds under his command and barely eighteen pilots, but Bowman immediately cranked up the training regimen. They were good, but you could never be *too* good. His peculiar style—sometimes understanding, sometimes the hammer—met with some resistance at first, which was typical when a new CO was being "tested" by his men. A group of his warrant officers thought they knew better than their brand-new major, and mutiny was afoot until Bowman confronted them.

"You think you're all irreplaceable?" Bowman roared at them in a closed-door meeting after he'd had enough. "I'll fire all your asses and just tell army leadership we're standing down for two months. Then I'll pull a bunch of green OH-58 guys in here and yank them up to speed. Just fucking *try* me!"

After that, it was all hearts and flowers.

Meanwhile, there was something brewing down in Central America.

Ever since the construction of the Panama Canal in 1914, successive American administrations had understood that the region's political winds would at times waft in their favor, and at times prove a challenge to maintaining this crucial access between the Pacific and Atlantic. The canal had clearly been constructed primarily to serve American interests, but nearly every seafaring nation on earth benefited from its convenience, and the income generated by the passage of trade bolstered Panama's economy. Throughout the twentieth century, U.S. Forces had maintained a healthy presence in the Canal Zone, cooperating and cross-training with the Panamanian military. Over the years, many of these Americans had married Panamanians and settled permanently in the slim isthmus of tropical forests and fine white beaches. In the century's last quarter, the Panamanians pressed their case to have the canal and its environs returned wholly to indigenous control, and a plan to do so was to take effect in 1990. Yet all in all, relations between the United States and Panama were stable, until Manuel Antonio Noriega came to power.

In 1983, Noriega had been serving as an intelligence officer under Panamanian dictator Brigadier General Omar Torrijos, until the overthrow and murder of his boss. After a series of power struggles, Noriega assumed the mantle of commander in chief of the entire Panama Defense Force (PDF), which included the armed forces, police, customs and all investigative services. A squat, physically unattractive character with an acne-ravaged face that had earned him the nickname "the Pineapple," Noriega soon began abusing his power. In 1987, accused of having fixed a national election and murdered his political opponent, the dictator turned his riot police on unarmed civilians protesting his reign. In turn, the U.S. Senate passed a resolution calling for the tyrant to step down, resulting in a violent attack on the U.S. embassy in Panama City. By that time, the dictator was barely bothering to conceal his intimate relations with the Colombian Medellín drug cartel, or the fact that his country had become a major conduit for drug smuggling into the United States. Early in 1988, he and his henchmen were indicted on drug trafficking charges by federal grand juries in Florida.

Noriega merely laughed at the notion of being indicted by a foreign power for crimes on his own soil. As tensions mounted, the Joint Chiefs of Staff began drafting a series of contingency plans to keep the canal open, protect U.S. lives and property in Panama, conduct noncombatant evacuations and assist any new government that might replace the recalcitrant bully. There were nearly thirty-five thousand American citizens residing in Panama, many of whom would shortly feel Noriega's wrath through intimidation, harassment, kidnapping and, eventually, murder.

Ever defiant, the Pineapple sought means to further aggravate his American detractors. Throughout 1988 and 1989, he engaged in mutual defense and cooperation treaties with Cuba, Libya and Nicaragua. Libya, in exchange for a relatively small sum of $20 million, was granted the use of Panama as a base from which to foment terrorist activities throughout Latin America. Cuba and Nicaragua contributed Soviet Bloc arms and expertise in building up Noriega's latest "project," alleged civilian defense committees known as the "Dignity Battalions," whose sole purpose was to inform on and intimidate the population. This quickly growing force of loyal arms substantially enhanced the fifteen thousand PDF troops under Noriega's command, four thousand of whom were well trained and combat-ready. American military planners predicted that in a fight, the PDF could be expected to aggressively defend its headquarters at *La Comandancia* in Panama City, as well as its positions at Fort Amador, Rio Hato and the Torrijos-Tocumen international airport. U.S. installations at Howard and Albrook air force bases, Quarry Heights, Fort Clayton and the Rodman Naval Station anticipated small unit assaults, shelling and sabotage.

After Grenada, no one in the U.S. Armed Services assumed that the Panamanians were going to see the Americans coming and just lay down their arms. Over the course of the nearly two years leading up to the invasion, numerous contingency and attack plans were drawn up, discarded and reworked. Eventually, the Joint Chiefs settled on a plan called "Blue Spoon," which involved a multifaceted invasion, spearheaded by airborne assaults and sustained by units already in place. Rather than risking the revelation of American intentions by a long-term buildup, the plan called for a three-day timetable from execution order to H-hour. President George H. W. Bush was far from enthusiastic about invading Panama, but realized that eventually it would become a necessity, unless Noriega was overthrown in some sort of coup. Such indigenous efforts to topple him were indeed attempted on more than one occasion; all of them failed. Dick Cheney, who was serving as the president's secretary of defense, would no doubt one day look back on the invasion and its immediate and conclusive results with some nostalgia.

There were to be multiple units from throughout the U.S. Armed Forces' order of battle participating in Operation Just Cause, but in many ways the invasion of Panama was going to be a special operations show. The decisive actions would be taking place within minutes of the opening shots, and most of those were to be performed by the army's Rangers, paratroopers, Special Forces and special missions units. The Navy's SEALs would also be among the first to fight, and all would be supported by the 160th and the air force's Special Operations Wing. General Carl Stiner, a paratrooper and special operations veteran warrior, had been pulled in to command the fight. General

Colin Powell had just recently been tapped as chief of staff. Powell was a firm believer in overwhelming firepower. If you were going to war, he believed, go with everything you've got.

Acid Gambit was only one of many high-risk enterprises tasked for the early hours of December 20. The army's 75th Rangers and the 82nd Airborne Division were going to parachute onto the airfields at Rio Hato and Torrijos-Tocumen, in the largest airborne assault of its kind since World War II. Special Forces would be hitting key blocking targets, such as the Pecora River Bridge to prevent PDF enforcements from reaching Torrijos-Tocumen. A marine rifle and light-armored vehicle company would capture the Bridge of the Americas to prevent the PDF from reinforcing the *Comandancia*. Army mechanized and airborne units would strike directly through the heart of Panama City to capture the PDF headquarters, while under strict orders by General Stiner to avoid using heavy artillery in order to minimize damage to civilian centers. The hunt for Noriega himself would entail numerous lightning assaults on his multiple mansions and safe houses, to be conducted by special tactics units, including an assault by Navy SEALs on the Punta Paitilla airport, where Noriega was known to park his private jet.

Rick Bowman's awareness of all of the various attack plans for Blue Spoon was relatively slim. His focus was narrowed to Acid Gambit, just as it needed to be, although he and his fellow pilots were fully pre-pared to have the mission canceled at the last minute and had to be ready to take on contingency operations. The 160th was going to be in-volved in many aspects of the invasion. Just prior to H-hour, two MH-6s, supported by another pair of Little Bird guns, were going to insert air force combat controllers with a navigational beacon into Torrijos-Tocumen. Four AH-6s were going to suppress enemy fire at Rio Hato just prior to the airborne assault, and an MH-60 Blackhawk would be landing there on a FARP mission to rearm and refuel the gunships. Two teams of 160th armament and refueling specialists were going to parachute onto Rio Hato and Torrijos-Tocumen along with their pallet-loaded FARPs, to support the Little Bird gunships working those strips. Nine Blackhawks and four MH-6s ferrying special tactics troops were scheduled to raid a PDF stronghold at Rio Hato, but as intelligence developed quickly in the hours prior to the attack, they would be tasked instead with a raid on PDF leadership at a beach house in Colon. Twelve more Blackhawks and Little Birds would be standing by on "strip alert" to respond to quickly developing missions, and the 160th's Chinooks would be tasked with moving special operators and supplies and executing emergency extractions.

Throughout that spring and summer, Bowman had pushed his men only as hard as he pushed himself. He was constantly flying with his instructor pilots, boning up on his Little Bird skills. Flying the diminutive helo was decidedly different from handling a Blackhawk; it was fast and flexible as a horse whip, but its power-to-weight ratios left no room for error. If you overhandled the bird on an assault, just tilting the rotor disk too much would have it biting less air and getting mushy on the approach. No matter which of the two pilots was actually flying the bird during an infil or exfil, both would have their hands on the controls, because just the momentary hiccup caused by one of them taking a stray round could result in a quick and deadly crash. The risk of flying a single-pilot helo with a full load of customers aboard didn't need to be verbalized.

Bowman was a strict adherent to the "train the way you fight" adage. He had his birds fly into clouds of black smoke from burning tires, because that was what he expected to encounter. He wanted his customers to use live fire as often as possible as they sat on the helo's slim benches, or "pods," because the gunfire was deafening and you had to get used to spent shells bouncing off your helmet. One of the cornerstones of the Night Stalkers' growing reputation was that its planners went "deep" into tactical contingencies, so Bowman posed every nightmare scenario he could think of: What if we lose a bird at this point? Suppose the customers can't make it back out onto the roof? What if the customers have to fight it out for an hour and our nearest FARP's been blown up? Where do we refuel and rearm? Bowman's MH-6s of A Company also trained constantly with the AH-6s of B Company, and he looked on the gunship pilots with great respect. They flew their heavily armed birds like fighter jockeys, and many of them could actually calculate the inertial effect on their weapons as they screamed through a tight bank, making their rockets swing out, curve and pierce right through a target house window. Bowman couldn't shoot like that and he knew it. But by the summer of 1989, he could fly with the best of his MH-6 warrant officers.

In October the Night Stalkers deployed to Panama in anticipation of a coup attempt against Noriega, which did not materialize successfully; the plotters surrendered, were tortured and then executed. It was clear that Blue Spoon would soon have to be implemented, and the 160th welcomed the opportunity to train and rehearse in the very AO in which it would fight. Bowman and his Little Birds were in demand for a number of anticipated operations, and the plans for Acid Gambit first centered on a Blackhawk assault, but developing intelligence indicated otherwise. Conveniently, the Gorgas U.S. Army hospital happened to be located in the heart of Panama City, and the flight path to its helicopter pad vectored close to the *Comandancia*. Medevac helos bringing "injured" troops to the hospital were often carrying pilots and commandos scribbling furiously on notepads. It turned out that the roof of the prison held a tall communications antenna, which meant that Blackhawks could not set down and would have to hover while their customers fast-roped. That kind of exposure was an invitation to disaster, so the rescue of Kurt Muse became a Little Bird job. By this time, the recovery of Muse had become nearly as high a priority as the capture of Noriega. Muse, supported by CIA funds and equipment, had been operating a clandestine radio network in the capital, rallying anti-Noriega dissidents until he had been captured early in the year. Red Cross representatives had been allowed to visit him, reporting back on the horrific conditions inside the overcrowded facility. Muse had already lost fifty pounds, was kept in a solitary cell, and his guards had been personally ordered by Noriega to execute him at the first sign of any rescue attempt. The odds of getting him out alive were slim to none, which meant that if Acid Gambit were to succeed, it would have to be fast and furious. A and B companies entered into an intense training regimen with the customers, working long nights assaulting an elementary school at Howard that closely resembled the prison structure. Naturally, live fire could not be used in those rehearsals — the rattle of gunfire and a pockmarked playground would certainly have telegraphed their intentions. Full dress rehearsals would be saved for the mock-up being constructed back at Hurlburt Field in Florida.

Early in December, Bowman and most of the unit flew home, grateful that at least they would be able to spend the holidays with their families. On December 15, the Panamanian National Assembly passed a resolution claiming that a state of war existed with the United States. Noriega anointed himself as Panama's "Maximum Leader." The next evening, four U.S. officers on a Saturday night outing inadvertently entered a PDF checkpoint outside the *Comandancia*. When the Americans refused to exit their vehicle and pulled away from the guard post, a PDF soldier opened fire, wounding two of them and killing Marine First Lieutenant Robert Paz. A U.S. naval officer and his young wife, who had witnessed the shooting, were dragged into a police station. The officer was repeatedly beaten, kicked in the groin and threatened with a loaded gun, while his wife was pinned against a wall and groped until she fainted.

At that point, President Bush regarded these blatant provocations as reasons enough to go to war. Still, discussions between his cabinet, the Joint Chiefs, national security advisers and seasoned diplomats continued all through that weekend, with the pros and cons of an invasion being carefully considered. At last, it was reckoned that Noriega would only be emboldened by a lack of response to his violent tantrums, that an American tragedy on a much larger scale could soon occur, and that U.S. Forces would not likely be better prepared or situated at a later time. Finally, late on Sunday afternoon, the president said, "Let's do it." It was not a facile decision; Bush had been shot down as a navy pilot during World War II, had lost his radioman and barely survived the incident. He knew what it meant to send good men into harm's way.

The Night Stalkers, along with all the other Blue Spoon elements, got the call almost immediately. The lumbering Air Force C5-As were soon setting down on the strip at Fort Campbell, which was suffering one of the worst ice storms in recorded Kentucky history. The huge jets had their nose cones and cargo ramps fully opened, and as the Little Birds, Blackhawks and Chinooks were folded up and loaded aboard, the resulting wind tunnel effect made the seventeen-degree freeze seem like a flat zero. Five hours after getting airborne, Bowman and his comrades stepped off the ramps into eighty degrees of soupy humidity.

H-hour was set for 2400 hours on the morning of Wednesday, December 20, so for two full days the trains of cargo aircraft stacked up into Panama like cattle cars at a railhead. Bowman, along with many of the other Night Stalkers, couldn't believe that the Panamanians didn't know what was coming, but then Noriega had flagrantly ignored every hint or threat that had crossed his gold-rimmed, cocaine-stained blotter before. Throughout those days, the Acid Gambit participants sucked up every bit of additional intelligence they could gather. Overhead photos showed a building near the prison with a colorful geometric pattern painted on its roof, which could be used as a reference point if Modelo was obscured by smoke. There was a cemetery located just outside the prison walls, and Bowman insisted on knowing if the flat expanse was free of telephone wires. When his birds came off the roof, loaded with the Delta operators and Kurt Muse, they would need to drop briefly into a clear area to gain some airspeed. The intelligence officers insisted that there were no wires; they would prove to be mistaken. At one point, the unit's S-2 came running over to the Acid Gambit pilots clutching a perfect, miniature model of the prison. It had been built for the Delta operators by their own in-house intel personnel. The excited officer popped the roof off the model and pointed inside.

"Look at this! They've got the stairs and the cells and everything. The doors even open the right way!"

"Hellooooo," Bowman sang as he knocked on the S-2's skull with his knuckles. "I don't really care! *We* don't go inside, remember?" He jabbed a finger at the model. "Tell me how high this roof is, and the retaining wall around it. Tell me where the wires are, that's what I want to know." Bowman thought that some of his intel guys had watched *The Dirty Dozen* once too often. One of them had given the pilots an exhaustive briefing on the PDF uniforms and patches and how to identify them. "Very nice briefing," one of the pilots commented afterward, "and if we're close enough to identify them, we're all screwed."

As the sun set on Tuesday evening, all the Night Stalker pilots and air crews ate their last meal. It was an endless chow line of men, and nearly all of the discussions were professional: reviews of procedures, execution checklists, radio calls. There would be virtually no comm chatter going in, to avoid giving anything away to PDF radio interceptors, but there would be plenty of it once the shooting started.

After dinner, Bowman and Fladry geared up and moved out to the four helos, as did Jim Dietderich and Don Fox, J. J. Holmes and Kelly McDougal. With weight and power ratios ever in their minds, they discarded every item that could affect the Little Birds' performance; their regular survival vests wouldn't be necessary, so they wore only their "bat belts" containing their radios, beacons, 9mm pistols and ammunition. They considered leaving their Heckler & Koch MP-5 submachine guns behind, then thought better of it. The Delta men were once again weighing themselves on their bathroom scale, but this time they meant it. At 9:30, the unit S-2 came bounding across the tarmac.

"Hey, by the way, there's a fifty-caliber machine gun right on your flight path."

"*What?*" the pilots yelled at him. "It's nice to let us know this *now*."

They followed the S-2 on the run, so he could show them the location on an overhead photograph. Flight paths suddenly had to be altered, and they were just hoping that no other surprises were in store.

At 11:30 P.M., the armada of Little Birds, Blackhawks and Chinooks was beginning to assemble into its various assault elements on the blacked-out runways at Howard. The night was steamy and thick and the lights of the capital winked in the near distance. The auxiliary power units of the bigger birds were already starting to whine, but the Little Birds had no such APUs; they started up by using a battery, just like a car, and that could wait until just minutes before launch. The S-2 appeared one more time.

"Now what?" Bowman rolled his eyes as he checked over his helmet and NVGs.

"H-hour's been moved up," the officer announced breathlessly.

"To *when?*" Fladry spat as he looked at his watch. They were scheduled to go in exactly half an hour.

"Fifteen minutes. You're going at 11:45."

General Stiner had personally given the order to launch earlier than planned. There had already been some sporadic shooting at U.S. Forces moving into positions, and the whole surprise was about to be irrevocably blown. Bowman hardly reacted to the news. It was better to go than to wait any more. He and Fladry pulled on their helmets and gloves and climbed into their bird. The Delta shooters jogged out to their respective helos, their boot leather pounding on the tarmac. Fladry cranked the engine and it caught, the sharp blades above starting to whip the air. Bowman was the air mission commander, but Fladry was the one with the combat experience, so he would be pilot in command and Bowman would defer to his experience, within reason. Fladry pointed to the forty-pound electrical battery on the floor.

"Hey, we don't need that weight anymore."

He was right. Once the helo's engine was fired up, if it failed in the middle of the mission they would probably all be killed. If they did manage to land it somewhere, they weren't likely to get a jump start from a passing taxi.

"Hell, yeah!" Bowman laughed, and he and Fladry yanked the battery and threw it out the door.

"What the hell are you guys doing?" their crew chief yelled as he leaped out of the way.

"Unnecessary weight!" Fladry shot him a ridiculous grin.

The Delta men were now hunkered down on the exterior benches, strapped in by belts with carabiners that clipped to the pods, and bristling with so many weapons, knives, grenades and gear that they looked like metallic porcupines. On each flank of all the helos, the lead operator shot the closest pilot a thumbs-up. The rotors of all four Little Birds spun into blurs as the cockpit clocks clicked over to 11:45. A single code word crackled in all the pilots' headsets. They lifted off the ground and headed downtown.

It was a very short flight, no more than ten minutes, but every second of it would linger forever in the minds of the men of Acid Gambit. Bowman was flying Chalk Three on the infil; Fladry would take it for the exfil. They hung back, along with Kelly McDougall's Chalk Four, for exactly ten seconds to let Dietderich's and Fox's Chalk One and J. J. Holmes's Chalk Two take the lead. Those first two birds would have to land on the prison roof, offload their commandos and immediately zip away so Bowman and McDougall could set their birds down. The timing had to be perfect; there could be no delays. There was a small cupola on the prison roof with a locked door, and as soon as Bowman's and McDougall's birds were clear, the Delta men would blow the door and charge down the stairwell into the prison. Simultaneously, operators remaining on the roof would ring-charge the high steel radio antenna and bring it down, just in case the backup Blackhawk, piloted by Steve Koester and Bob Welch and circling nearby in a holding pattern, might have to come in for an emergency extraction.

The four MH-6s, heavily laden with their commandos, began to gain airspeed as they pulled away from Howard. They were followed close behind by four AH-6s from B Company; two of them would attack the *Comandancia* to cover the raid, while two more would escort the assault birds. Fladry looked down to catch a glimpse of a small firefight at the airfield's perimeter. Bowman was in total focus, watching his airspeed, glancing at the clock. Whenever he and Fladry were on the ground, their relationship was formal: commanding officer and warrant. But as soon as they were airborne, they bitched like siblings without regard to rank.

"You're too tight," Fladry said. They had to be exactly ten seconds behind the lead birds going in.

"I am not."

"You're only seven seconds behind them."

"I'm exactly on ten!"

Bowman's heart was hammering in his chest and the incredible surge of adrenaline almost made him laugh. Flying the helo properly entailed very minute corrections to the controls, and here he was gripping the cyclic so hard he thought he might snap it right off. Yet even as they descended from the modest elevation of Howard, spotted the Bridge of the Americas and crossed the canal, he still believed that somehow it would all be called off at the very last second. After all, he was always the one waving goodbye. *Come on, George,* he silently implored the president, *don't bag it on me now!*

They were flying low and fast now, heading right for the *Comandancia*; they could see its low flat bulk looming in the distance. Up above in the black sky, a pair of Air Force AC-130 gunships was starting to hammer down into the PDF headquarters with multibarreled 20mm cannons and shells from their 105mm artillery. Their fire was being carefully directed by an insanely courageous air force combat controller hidden in a van in the streets below. Not one of their shells would hit Modelo. Bowman and Fladry saw one pair of the AH-6 gunships come from behind and zip by their flanks. The Little Bird gunners were looking for a high-rise apartment building directly in the flight path, where Panamanian snipers were known to have staked out the roof. Bowman saw the pilots make their "bump," suddenly swooping up to briefly show the enemy their bellies, then angling down and hard as they opened up with streams of minigun fire.

The entire world seemed to erupt. Tracers started flying up at them

from everywhere, lancing patterns across the sky like a holiday fireworks display. Explosions and fires were flashing up from the *Comandancia*; the light was so bright that it kept flaring out Bowman's NVGs.
He gritted his teeth, his head flicking like a lizard's as he searched for
the prison among the patterns of orange tracers leaping up from the
city. He no longer believed it was going to be called off. *We're in it
now*, flashed through his brain. *This is for real!*

There was Quarry Heights, off to the left. There was that geometric
pattern, painted on top of that reference building . . . And there was
the prison roof; he had it. The two lead birds were still sitting there,
but Bowman knew he wasn't too close; he knew his timing was dead
on. *Get the hell out of there, guys.* He pressed on at full power. He
could see a small connecting walkway leading from the prison rooftop
over to a guard tower on the *Comandancia*. Small dark figures were
rushing across the walkway, and then the Delta men on both sides of
their Little Bird started firing, their muzzles exploding right next to
Bowman's and Fladry's helmets. The Panamanians on the walkway
were spinning, falling, crawling away to die. The engine exhausts of the
two lead birds on the roof suddenly glowed brighter, and they lifted off
and turned away. Three seconds later, Bowman's skids scraped concrete and his commandos were instantly gone from the pods. Fladry
craned his head to the left, checking to make sure his bench was empty.

"We're clear left," he told Bowman.

Bowman craned his head to the right.

"We're clear right."

The bird felt so much better as Bowman pulled power and climbed
into the night. With the Delta boys and all their gear gone, it was like
having a fat man suddenly get up from squatting on your chest. Bowman could feel the sweat soaking the insides of his gloves and dripping
down his armpits. He was grinning from ear to ear—it was like nothing
he'd ever done in his life, or would ever do again. Then he remembered: They still had to execute the exfil.

They had purposely planned not to go into a holding pattern while the commandos rescued Muse; it would just be risking an engine failure or getting shot down. A mile away, at Quarry Heights, was a rectangular water reservoir with a concrete cover, where the four birds planned to wait it out until the Delta men called them back in for the exfil. Bowman nosed the Little Bird down so he could have maximum visuals through the helo's "greenhouse" as he chased after the two lead birds. They were already setting down on the concrete lid, facing his way. A swarm of huge black vultures that had been perching on the lid suddenly flapped and cawed and flew off into the night. Bowman and McDougall settled down on the far side of the reservoir, facing the other way. That was the security procedure, forming a perimeter facing all sides. The reservoir was surrounded by thick, dark jungle, and even though nothing moved there but the rustling trees, Bowman imagined the worst: a horde of Panamanians suddenly rushing them from the brush. When the heavily armed customers were on the pods, the pilots always felt protected enough to think just about flying. With them gone, the Night Stalkers were left with nothing but their puny pistols and MP-5s. They sat there in comparative silence, with only the sound of the rotors idling above and the wind whipping through the thick palms.

"Well, that was pretty good," Fladry said.

"Yeah." Bowman nodded. "Now we're just unarmed and scared shitless."

Flapper laughed. . . .

THE NIGHT STALKER pilots would not be the only unit members engaged in combat that night, not by a long shot. The helo jockeys were the tip of the 160th's spear, but without its shaft of crew chiefs, armament men, refuelers, aircraft mechanics, avionics experts, communications specialists, supply personnel and medics, that tip could not fly or fight. All of them were considered as integral parts of an elite organization—special operators who all wore the unit's distinctive red

beret. In particular, the senior NCOs, armorers, medics, comms operators and fuel and ammunition personnel all had to be jump qualified.
No matter how far the unit would have to travel to execute a mission, special operations aviation was regarded as a short-range, tight-turnaround
endeavor. Helos engaged in combat would have to be refueled, rearmed
and often repaired right in the middle of a fight. Their support personnel had to be exactly where the action was, often firing a weapon with
one hand and turning a wrench with the other.

Clifton "O.B." O'Brien and Donnie Calvery were two of the most
senior enlisted men in the unit, and had earned the respect and admiration of not only their younger subordinates but the pilots they
"mothered." In many ways, O.B. and Donnie were "twins"; their codes
of conduct were rock solid, army blood ran in their veins and they
often spoke as one. As a junior enlisted man, you couldn't incur First
Sergeant O'Brien's wrath and hope that Sergeant First Class Calvery
would save you. They had each other's backs, and even through their
raucous senses of humor, they demanded nothing short of perfection.

O.B. was born in 1955, Calvery in '54. When O.B. was getting into
trouble as a high school kid in Vergennes, Vermont, Donnie was doing
much the same in Mineola, Texas. O.B. was a wrestler: compact, powerful and not to be messed with. Donnie was tall and lanky with a
Texas twang. O.B.'s father had been an Army Ranger during World
War II, and although he never talked to his four sons about the war, he
knew that his errant seventeen-year-old needed some military disci-
pline and marched him down to the recruiting station. Donnie's father had served for thirty years in the air force, so the youngster
instinctively realized that the structure would straighten him out, but
the air force wasn't recruiting when he was ready to go. Both young
men joined the army in 1973, one month apart.

O.B. started off as a paratrooper, but he liked the aviation side of the
house and eventually switched to being a UH-1 aircraft mechanic,
working his way through all the schools and models that were coming
online. Donnie had always been a "gun guy" and became an aviation

armament specialist, one of those types who could make a weapon system hum when no one else could fix it. Separately, they rose through the ranks and gained reputations as two of the best in their fields. In the mid-1980s, each was "invited" to Fort Campbell to serve in an aviation unit that no one could tell them anything about. Both of them had only intended to serve in the army for a few years and then figure out what to do with the rest of their lives, but this Night Stalker outfit was something else. O.B. was going to be handling the hottest new airplanes around. Donnie was going to inherit a gunner's toy box, and they would put him through jump school as well, something he'd soon become addicted to.

"Well, this looks like home," O.B. said to Donnie soon after they met.

"Yep. Sure does."

By the time the invasion of Panama began spooling up, both men had already deployed on scores of training missions and real-world operations. A company might be able to rotate and switch out pilots, but the 160th's expert support personnel were coveted assets, so they were in the air and on the move all the time. Donnie, having come into the unit before O.B., had participated in the Night Stalkers' "debut" in Grenada. Both of them had been sent to the Persian Gulf for Prime Chance, as well as on a number of other classified missions, and by 1989 they had been serving together in B Company with the Little Bird guns for nearly three years. It was a small, tight-knit group of about forty men in all, including the officers, warrants and support personnel. The entire company could assemble in a space the size of a high school classroom. They knew one another very well, and would readily put their lives in one another's hands.

By late fall of that year, while neither O.B. nor Donnie knew exactly in which Panama missions they would participate, they did know that they'd be in the thick of it. Their pilots and AH-6s would be providing close support for special operations, so they would have to be in close proximity with rockets, minigun ammunition, fuel, spare parts and weapons. A FARP could be inserted near the target in many ways; you could load a fuel blivet in the back of a Blackhawk or Chinook, pile in rockets and ammunition, fly it all to an LZ, unload it all, hook up the hoses and start rearming and refueling the Little Birds as soon as they set down; you could do the same thing using a large vehicle such as a two-and-a-half-ton truck, if you had to, although driving such a juicy and volatile target through the middle of a combat zone was not the method of preference. The FARP delivery mode that required the most training and expertise was by parachute. All the cargo would be carefully stacked and strapped down onto a large metal pallet, which in turn sat upon a mattress of crushable cardboard resembling egg cartons. Three gigantic G11-B cargo parachutes would be rigged to the pallet and then the whole thing would be loaded aboard a C-130, along with a FARP team of generally nine or ten men, also rigged to jump. Flying over the target at approximately eight hundred feet, the cargo plane's ramp would open, and the team would push the FARP out the door and then leap right after it, invariably in the dead of night. Nearly all of B Company's support personnel were FARP team members. Their pilots thought they were nuts.

Donnie was in the middle of Jump Master school at Fort Benning when he got the call to return to Campbell. By then he had become a "jump hog," amassing more than four hundred entries in his logbook and already with Senior and Master wings. There had been a lull in Night Stalker mission activity for a while, but now the fun was over and it was time to work. Some of B Company's helos would be striking the PDF positions at Torrijos-Tocumen Airport just before the Army Rangers jumped in. The AH-6s would need a FARP set up near the runways, so Donnie, four "armament dogs," two refuelers and two ammo men would be jumping with the Rangers from a C-130. Jack Earls, the first sergeant of the 160th's headquarters company, would be joining them; almost no one in the unit was just a "desk jockey." The FARP itself, however, would be dropped separately from one of fifteen

C-141 cargo planes that would be spewing heavy gear from their bellies above the main runway. Donnie and his boys would have to find it, after midnight, in the midst of what was surely going to be a brawl.

It all sounded good to him. It was the kind of mission they'd all been training for over the years. He was thirty-three years old, married and had two kids, but he was totally focused on the mission. The only thing that worried him was if he would perform up to par, not screw up, set a good example for his men. And those men were some of the best he had ever met in the army. Ever since first going to jump school, he had discovered something about evaluating soldiers that would always stick with him. You could meet a man in uniform and know nothing about him, but if he was wearing jump wings, you already knew one very crucial thing: You could order him to do something he really didn't want to do, and he would do it anyway. He was surrounded by those kinds of men.

Donnie and his men joined the Rangers down at Hunter Army Airfield in Georgia. The FARP team was broken up and manifested onto two different aircraft; if one was shot down, there would still be someone to manage the FARP. Donnie and Bruce Lum, one of his armorers, would be jumping with the First Battalion of the 75th Ranger Regiment onto the Tocumen side of the strip; they would be the first two men out the door of the first aircraft. Right after that main force dropped, the train of heavy loads would stream over the Torrijos strip, dropping tons of vehicles, heavy weapons and, of course, the Night Stalkers' FARP pallet. Immediately following would be a company of the Third Battalion of the 75th, including the rest of Donnie's team. Early in December they performed a full rehearsal of the assault on Torrijos-Tocumen, jumping into Duke Army Airfield at Hurlburt Field, home of the Air Force's Special Operations Command in Florida. Then they waited, without any inkling of when or if it would actually happen. In the back of his mind, Donnie knew that if this thing actually went down, and he survived it, he would be able to wear the coveted combat jump wings with a gold star on the canopy. It was a very rare thing to earn, and more significant to a paratrooper than almost any other medal, but the thought was fleeting. *Just do your job and don't fuck up*, he told himself. And then the order to execute Blue Spoon flashed through secure channels; game time.

On the afternoon of December 19 down at Hunter, all the Rangers, air force combat controllers and Night Stalkers were miserable. It was 33 degrees and raining hard streaks of almost-ice, and they all just wished it would turn to snow as they packed their weapons and ordnance into drop bags and struggled into their parachutes. The C-130s were steady but relatively slow, and the seven-hour flight was like sitting in an overcrowded subway car, knees to knees, while the four huge engines drilled through your brain. Plastic jugs sloshing with urine were passed from man to man and the jokes were hollow. Less than an hour from the target, Lieutenant Colonel Wagner, the Ranger battalion commander, made one short announcement over the intercom.

"They know we're coming."

It got very quiet after that. And then, it all seemed to happen very quickly. The fuselage dimmed, the Ranger jump master on the aft ramp raised his palms. The men struggled to their feet, hooking their static lines to the long steel cables above. A bell rang and the jump doors on either side slid up and away as the thunder of the wind and the engines rushed into the plane. Donnie waddled with his gear bag toward that gaping maw, where the red lamp was glowing, the green bulb below it still dark. Someone was gripping his harness, holding him in position as he turned his hands, knuckles in and palms out, thumbs and fingers together, and hooked his wrists to the door frame as he stepped onto the steel tongue threshold. The moon outside was huge and bright, the wind as hot as a Texas summer. He turned to look across the fuselage, where the first thing out of the plane would be the trussed-up minibike of a combat controller. Through the black rectangle of that open door he could see the city below, the winking gunfire and the *Comandancia* already in flames. The bike suddenly disappeared, and then the bulb above his head flashed Christmas green and he was gone.

Donnie was in the air for less than half a minute. Descending at fifteen feet per second under his dark olive T-10 canopy, he barely had time to release his rucksack, which fell to the end of a "snake" line linked to his harness, and then he smacked into the tarmac like a sack of bricks. A sharp pain shot through his thigh, but he ignored it as he rolled to his feet, quickly shed his harness, shouldered his ruck and uncased his weapon. He jacked a round into his M-16 and spun around. More than seven hundred Rangers were in the air, streaming down onto the Tocumen strip, their boot soles smacking and gear bags thumping as their parachutes billowed and collapsed like giant jellyfish. From the north end of the runway and the Panamanian Air Force terminal, tracer fire was spitting up at the C-130s and -141s overhead. Swarms of Rangers were already forming up and charging toward that fight, but Donnie turned the other way. The north end of the Torrijos runway and the south end of the Tocumen runway paralleled each other in the middle of the vast airport. Between the two would be a small fire station, where the Night Stalkers were supposed to set up their FARP. But first he had to find the pallet.

He began to run. Bruce Lum found him on the jog, and a little Ranger sergeant suddenly joined them, breathlessly announcing that he'd lost his platoon.

"All right," Donnie shouted over the growing crackle of gunfire, "you're with us now."

They headed toward the tip of the Torrijos strip, where the Air Force Special Operations Low Level pilots were dropping their loads dead onto the tarmac, the tonnage of Humvees and Ranger Special Operations Vehicles sending shocks through the earth as they thundered onto the ground. Donnie spotted the colored strobe of their FARP flashing brightly near the northern end; they hadn't bothered to use an infrared strobe, knowing that at that point there would be nothing clandestine about their mission. The three men sprinted another half mile toward the FARP and were streaming sweat in the 90-percent humidity by the time they got there. The rest of the team had also vectored on the strobe and were just forming up when the Third Battalion's airplanes roared in over the strip and the sky filled once more with Rangers and parachutes. Indirect fire licked up at the falling jumpers from the PDF barracks, and a few rounds lanced in flat trajectories across the field, *whanging* off the vehicles. Donnie wanted to break down the FARP and get it into action right away; he didn't know how soon his birds would need the gas and bullets. In fact, the Little Birds would need both in short order, because they had opened the fight at H-hour by taking out the airport's PDF communications shed and guardhouse, killing all the occupants.

"Should we set it up right here, Sarge?" one of Donnie's armorers asked.

"Well, we sure as hell can't move it," Donnie said.

"You *will* move it, Sergeant." It was the voice of the Ranger battalion's S-4 supply officer, Captain Fuller, who was striding across the tarmac and jerking his thumb. "Don't care how you do it, just get it off the strip!"

Donnie looked around. There was a Humvee sitting close by, half-enshrouded by its collapsed chutes. He ran over to it with Bruce Lum, who pulled the driver's door open.

"Not *this* one," Lum exclaimed. "It's the Eighty-second's brigade commander's!"

"Well, he ain't here yet," Donnie answered as he turned the engine over. "So now it's *mine.*"

Within minutes, the team had linked some heavy web straps to the FARP pallet, hooked them up to the Humvee and were dragging the seven-thousand-pound hulk across the taxiway, spewing up sparks and gravel. They pulled to a stop at the fire station directly between the runways and began to unload as the Rangers assaulted the main airport terminal just one hundred yards to the south. The Night Stalkers had to duck behind the Humvee twice as Panamanian rounds reached out to them from the terminal buildings, but they just returned some rifle fire and went back to work. Ten minutes later they were ready to go as the first of the Little Bird guns swooped in and landed. The pilot leaned out his door and grinned at Donnie.

"Fill her up, Sarge."

"You need rockets and ammo, too?"

"Yeah. Put it on my bill."

O.B.'S FARP MISSION was considerably less glamorous than Donnie's, yet would turn out to be much more risky. On Sunday evening, as Donnie and his team were flying down to Georgia aboard a Chinook to muster with the Rangers, O.B. and the rest of B Company loaded their helos onto C5-As and took off for Panama. From the moment they landed at Howard, none of them slept for even an hour as they off-loaded the birds, built them back up and prepped all the machines and weapons for operations. By then O.B. knew that his mission would be running a FARP in support of the Little Bird guns attacking the *Comandancia* and supporting Acid Gambit, but the initial plan was to station it right there at Howard and let the birds come back in to rearm and refuel. Major Frank Whitehead, who had replaced Bob Codney as the Group S-3, called O.B. over to his map table.

"O'Brien, you're going to have to get that FARP closer to the target," Whitehead said. "We need to cut down on the air time."

"Okay, sir. Where do you want it?"

"Right here." Whitehead jabbed his finger at a spot on the map of Panama City. "At Albrook."

Albrook Air Base was a small military field located two miles north of the *Comandancia*. It was also less than three blocks from a major PDF station.

"Roger." O.B. nodded. "How're we deploying?" He assumed that

Whitehead would assign them to one of the 160th's Chinooks for transport.

"You're gonna drive. Pull a Sneaky Pete. We don't want to tip them off, bringing in a big bird full of rockets and ammo."

Drive? Despite the sweltering heat, a chill shot through O.B.'s spine.

"And get it done now," Whitehead added. "Don't wait for dark."

"Okay, sir, but you know we don't have any heavy wheels."

The major pointed across the airfield.

"Try the air force. They've got tons of big wheels. Ask 'em nicely."

"And if they say no?"

Whitehead just grinned.

"Roger that, sir," O.B. said. His wayward youth racing motorcycles and hot-wiring cars might come in handy after all.

As it turned out, O.B. didn't have to steal a truck. The air force loaned him one of their two-and-a-half-ton vehicles with an open bay in the back. He gathered up his FARP team. He had two crew chiefs, named Joe Burke and John McCutchen, three armament specialists, named "Smokin'" Joe Frazier, Bernie Nussen and Joachim "Big Dave" Davis, and a young commo kid named Perez. There was a supply specialist in the Group's S-4 shop named Jose Casanova, who spoke fluent Spanish, so O.B. recruited him for the job as well. Big Dave and Bernie Nussen were senior men already in their early thirties, but the rest of the men were barely twenty or twenty-one years old.

O.B. and his team piled all their combat gear into the truck and drove it across the airfield to where they'd initially intended to run their FARP. Two of B Company's AH-6s would be firing all the rockets from their nineteen-shot pods into the *Comandancia*, and probably using up a considerable amount of minigun ammo as well. The second pair of birds supporting the raid on Modelo Prison would also be expending a lot of ordnance. Setting up a FARP demanded muscle and lung power, especially in the turgid Central American heat. They loaded up two hundred rockets, six thousand rounds of minigun ammunition, two spare miniguns and fifty gallons of JP-4 fuel in five-gallon cans. They covered up the huge pile with a tarp and concealed their individual weapons and combat gear inside as well, then jammed their M-9 pistols into their waistbands, letting the tails of their camouflage shirts drape over the butts, and climbed aboard. They drove out the gates of Howard, riding aboard what was for all intents and purposes an enormous truck bomb.

O.B. rode shotgun near the tailgate, leaving Casanova up front in the cab, where he might be able to talk them through any rough PDF checkpoints. It didn't matter where you were sitting; if anyone opened up on them they were all going to be evaporated, so O.B. had decided to position himself where he could draw first if he had to. Perched all over the mountain of explosives, none of his men knew how scared to death their fearless leader actually was. Ever since the PDF shooting of the American officers, tensions had become palpable in the city. Noriega's radio and television stations were constantly broadcasting anti-American propaganda, and the only civilians on the streets were quick-marching with groceries. It was the longest two-mile drive of his life.

They made it almost all the way to Albrook and were nearly through the intersection directly in front of the PDF station when the light turned red. The truck sat there, idling in the thick afternoon swelter. A Panamanian soldier, gripping his AK-47 with both hands, his finger on the trigger, walked deliberately toward the two-and-a-half-ton vehicle and circled slowly toward the back. O.B. gripped the Beretta under his shirt. The Panamanian stopped and stared at him. The sweat was running in rivulets from both of their scalps. *Raise that barrel and you're a dead man*, O.B.'s eyes said. The light turned green.

They all began breathing again when they pulled through the guard gate at Albrook. Task Force Black, which consisted of elements of the Army Special Forces tasked with special missions in the city, had taken over operational control of the airfield. O.B. reported to the Green Beret commander, who told him he would have to set up the

FARP at the far end of the strip, which was unfortunately very close to the perimeter road. O.B.'s instincts warned him that there was going to be a fight that night.

"Gear up," he ordered his men into their combat equipment.

"All of it, Top?" one of his younger kids whined at his "top" sergeant.

"Yes, all of it."

"But, Top—"

"This is not a democracy," O.B. barked. "Happiness is not mandatory; participation is. . . . You will wear *everything*."

And of course, O.B. led by example. He donned his heavy body armor over his woodland camouflage BDUs, and over that went his ALICE load-bearing harness full of 5.56mm magazines, M-26 fragmentation grenades, two canteens, a red lens flashlight and a pair of standard air force survival knives, bundle-tied to his webbing with handles down; cutting through FARP bands would dull one blade quickly, leaving the other sharp for close-quarters combat. He hauled a ruck onto his shoulders, containing an extra uniform, two pairs of socks, a spare pair of black leather combat boots, MREs, a first-aid kit, matches and loops of 550 parachute cord. He carried no smoke grenades, because all their activities would be at night. He needed no strobes or flares, because the Little Bird pilots would be wearing NVGs and could easily spot a FARP pad by its shape. Finally, he smeared multicolored camouflage cream over his face and neck, strapped on his Kevlar helmet and slung his M16-A1.

With everyone kitted up to O.B.'s satisfaction, he mounted them up and drove the truck down to the far end of the strip. The concrete apron was indeed only seventy-five meters from the perimeter road. They unloaded the truck, parked it well off to one side, then broke into smaller teams and assembled two ordered piles of armaments: a large pyramid of rockets on one side, a landing area in the middle and a similar arrangement of ammunition cans and fuel cans on the other. As the Little Birds came in, the pilots would see the distinct piles and know exactly where to set down; one team would load rockets on one flank, a second team would load ammo or change out guns on the other, and a third would pour the gas in by hand, like filling a lawn mower.

By 11:00 o'clock, the FARP was set up and ready to go. O.B. didn't need to break radio silence and report that fact; Major Whitehead would know that it was so, unless informed otherwise. Task Force Black had contacted O.B. to warn him that the Special Forces had a mobile LP/OP—Listening Post/Observation Post—deployed onto the airfield to spot any intruders. O.B. gathered his men around him.

"Listen up. There's gonna be some Green Beanies out here crawling around. So if we take enemy fire, we don't return it without clear lanes of fire, and only on my orders. Clear?"

"Roger, Top." His men nodded and retreated to their respective stockpiles.

The night was silent and bright, the narrow grass fields surrounding the concrete strip rustling gently in the hot breeze. At 11:45, the men were standing there, letting the wind dry their sweat and looking south in the direction of the *Comandancia*, when a heavy vehicle pulled up on the road and stopped. Without warning, no less than eight AK-47s opened up, their muzzle flashes bursting the night apart as rounds whipped overhead and the FARP team slammed onto the ground. "Holy shit!" someone yelled as they all scrambled for cover; but the only things to hide behind were the high piles of ordnance and fuel. The rockets were least likely to explode from bullet impacts, so some of the men piled up there behind O.B. while the others just tried to belly deep into the grass. O.B. grabbed Perez's Satcom and called back to Howard. A Colonel Yuill answered.

"Go ahead, Black One."

"Has this thing started early?" O.B. inquired.

"Negative."

"Well, we're taking fire on this FARP."

"Impossible. You *can't* be taking fire."

"Okay, wait one," O.B. said. He thrust the transceiver up over his head and keyed the mike, holding it there as the Panamanians on the road opened up again with a horrendous volley. He jammed the handset back to his head.

"Believe me now, sir?" O.B. asked.

"Yes. Take cover."

"Roger. Thanks." O.B. rolled his eyes and clicked off. *Like I needed you to tell me that? We don't have any damn cover!*

The Panamanians stopped firing and sped away. O.B.'s heart was thumping like a jackhammer. He had seen plenty of tracers going outbound before, but this was the first time he'd ever seen them coming *inbound*, at *him*. He had never been in ground combat before, but he knew that the first thing to do after a firefight was account for your men.

"Frazier!" he called out.

"Here, Top!"

"Nussen!"

"Okay, Top!"

"McCutchen"

"Good to go, Top!"

"Davis!"

"Here, Top!"

"Casanova!"

"Okay, Top!"

Perez was right next to O.B. with the Satcom, so the sergeant knew he was okay.

"Burke!" he yelled out.

"Here, Top! And if I ever make it outta this alive, I'm gonna be the best fucking *clerk* the army's ever seen!"

The rest of the men howled with nervous laughter.

It wasn't long before a single Little Bird appeared overhead. O.B.'s team had assumed their positions, and the helo circled once and then settled onto the pad. But something wasn't right. There were supposed to be two birds. O.B. ducked low and ran to the open cockpit. The pilots were Paul DeMilia and Cliff Fisher, and O.B. called DeMilia "mister," as they did with all the warrant officers.

"Whatcha need, Mr. DeMilia?"

"Full load. And our gun's jammed up."

"Frazier!" O.B. yelled across the bird. "Change it out!"

Smokin' Joe was all of five-foot-six and 120 pounds, but he soon appeared hauling the spare minigun.

"Where's the other aircraft?" O.B. asked DeMilia.

"I don't know." The pilot shook his head. "They were with us."

None of them yet realized that Chalk One of the AH-6s hitting the *Comandancia*, piloted by George Kunkle and Fred Horsley, had already been shot down.

Joachim Davis started passing rockets to O.B., and the team leader began stuffing them into the pod. Their motors had to be hooked up to the igniters as well, and it had to be done right. Suddenly another blast of tracer fire sprayed across the pad from the direction of the road. A second passing PDF vehicle had pulled up short, and when the Panamanians saw the helo sitting there, they let loose with an incredible barrage. O.B. slammed down onto his back right beneath the pod, and Big Dave kept on passing him rockets, which he stuffed in the tubes as fast as he could.

"Okay, guys!" O.B. yelled as he and Big Dave rolled from right to left, passing and loading rockets. "Somebody shoot back at those fucking people!"

A few rounds popped back from some of the FARP team weapons, but all of them were very busy servicing the Little Bird. The Panamanian tracers were flying everywhere, but DeMilia and Fisher just sat in the cockpit, saying nothing, waiting as calmly as if they were getting their car washed. O.B. thought that to get DeMilia really excited, you'd have to pop him in the head with a hammer. On the far side of the bird, Smokin' Joe was standing straight up in the middle of the firefight. He changed out the minigun, put a new one in, dropped in a fresh ammo can, fed the belt and slapped Cliff Fisher on the shoulder. O.B. finished loading and rolled away from the bird as it took off.

The Panamanians disappeared into the night. O.B. and his men sat there, breathless, hoping the enemy would get themselves busy with something else. But after that, it just got worse. Now the PDF knew what the Night Stalkers were doing out there at the far end of Albrook, so word had gone out to increase their hits and runs on this "target of opportunity." Every hour, like clockwork, they would pull up on the road and let loose with tremendous, though inaccurate, volleys of gunfire, after which O.B. would call his roll once more and Joe Burke would consider a new career path in the army.

"Burke!"

"Here, Top! And if I ever make it out of this alive, I'm gonna be the best goddamn *cook* the army's ever seen!"

But it wasn't funny anymore as the attacks increased in frequency and volume. At one point the fire was so heavy that O.B. and Bernie Nussen had to take cover behind the truck, which was leaking diesel fuel all over from multiple impacts. Nussen and O.B. were hunkered down behind the wheels when the commo kid, Perez, rolled over O.B. and snuggled down between them.

"What the hell are you doin', Perez?" O.B. shouted above the fusillades.

"Top, you and Bernie are big boys." Perez grinned up at him. "You'll stop those bullets!"

"Thanks, kid."

At last, O.B. was forced to call back to Howard, cancel all inbound flights and have the helos redirected to an alternate FARP; it was just too dangerous at Albrook for the birds. He got up and sprinted down the strip to the main hangar, where the commander of Task Force Black told him that the airfield might soon be compromised. He then ran back to his team and led them to a spot in front of the main barracks, where they set up a blocking position to fight off the expected attack, which thankfully never materialized.

By dawn, they hadn't slept for three days and had endured multiple enemy assaults on their FARP. They were flat-out exhausted, yet amazingly unhurt. Not one of them had been wounded, though literally thousands of enemy rounds had been fired at them. O.B. received a radio call informing him that a Chinook would shortly be inbound to pick them all up. He moved his team back to the hangar, then realized that two spare miniguns and some ammo cans were still sitting in the shot-up truck at the end of the runway. By that time, he knew that B Company had already lost one bird; D-day was only five hours old and Group would need the weapons and ammo. He took Smokin' Joe and Big Dave and started running toward the truck when sniper bullets began plucking at their boots. They ran faster, the high-velocity rounds cracking the air around them, and dragged two guns and as much ammo as they could haul and started back.

The Chinook was already sitting there with the rest of the FARP team aboard, and all at once it lifted off and banked away. The pilots had started taking accurate fire in their fuselage and didn't realize that they had left three men on the ground.

O.B., Smokin' Joe and Big Dave jumped into a shallow ditch and lay there for an hour, while Panamanian snipers just outside the airfield's perimeter tried very hard to kill them. . . .

AT THE RESERVOIR cover on Quarry Heights, a single code word hissed inside Rick Bowman's headset.

"*Debby.*"

That was it, just that female name, issued from the mouth of a Delta radioman. There was no tremble in the commando's voice, even though the background clatter of gunfire was heavy as a jackhammer and sharp explosions *whumped* through the static. They had done it. They had freed Kurt Muse from his cell. They *had* him.

Bowman and Fladry had been idling atop the concrete slab for no more than five minutes. In that short span of time, the Delta men had executed their mission. They blew the rooftop door and charged down into the prison. Muse's cell was two floors down from the roof, and with all the gunfire and explosions coming from the *Comandancia* just outside his window, he heard no helo blades above. Then came the sounds of thumping footsteps and double taps of precision gunfire. His corridor suddenly filled with white smoke and slim flashlight beams lanced off the walls. Someone was at his cell door.

"Moose!" an operator called out to him, inadvertently giving him a new nickname. "You okay?"

"Yeah! I'm okay!"

"Take cover. I'm gonna blow the door."

Muse ducked into a corner and covered his head. The cell door flew off its hinges and the operator charged inside, dropped to his knees and gripped Muse's shoulders.

"Moose, we're here to take you home."

The team enveloped him and rushed him through the corridor. The Panamanian whose orders were to kill him lay dead, while another had been flex-cuffed alive and tossed into a corner. Someone slapped a Kevlar helmet onto Muse's head while another man stuffed him into body armor. They rushed him up the stairwell to the roof, surrounding him like an armored phalanx as the bullets flew everywhere, and called for extraction.

"*Elsie.*" It was the code word for the second group of two aircraft.

Fladry immediately pulled some power and the Little Bird went weightless, lifting off from the concrete cover and spinning around to face south. The two lead birds were already gone and he was itching to chase after them. He dipped forward and up, rising into the tracer-filled sky. Bowman started their traditional bitching.

"You're early."

"I am not."

"Give 'em the full ten seconds or we'll have to go around!"

"We're fine!"

If the formation was too tight, the two lead birds would still be on the roof loading Muse and his rescuers when Fladry, who was now flying lead, and McDougal, who was right behind him, swooped in to pick up the rest of the shooters. There wasn't enough room on that rooftop for four birds. If the timing was off, Bowman and Fladry would have to execute a "go-around," circling at a hundred feet above every exploding muzzle in the *Comandancia*.

But Flapper was on the controls now; it was his bird, and instinct told him they had to be there quick. Bowman swallowed his protest as a figure below darted from the black jungle and a rifle barrel flashed white stars at them. Fladry jinked hard to the left, then the eyes of both pilots saucered as one of the AH-6 gun birds, flying racetracks through the sky as it sought out targets, suddenly loomed dead ahead. Fladry and the anonymous gun pilot both careened to their starboards, missing each other by meters.

For an anxious moment, Bowman and Fladry lost sight of Chalks One and Two. The entire *Comandancia* was aflame, enveloped by a long blanket of smoke, tracers leaping through that woolly cloud like lightning through a thunderhead. The Air Force AC-130 gunships were chewing through the black sky above the maze of buildings, their cannons and howitzers spewing streams of answering fire. Flying from the left seat, Fladry zipped along at only seventy-five feet high, paralleling a ridge line off Bowman's side. Modelo was supposed to be right there, just off the left at eleven o'clock. Then, Bowman jabbed a gloved finger at a pair of glowing exhaust plumes. The two leads were roaring into the rooftop where the radio antenna had been freshly detonated and toppled. Their whipping rotors spun the smoke away, and there they were—those insane men of Delta, surrounding their liberated charge, Kurt Muse.

The bullet that entered Bowman was a 7.62mm round. It was long and hefty, nearly twice the size and weight of an M-16 round. It ricocheted off the Radar Warning Receiver before lancing into his upper arm, shattering bone, entering his chest under his armpit, bouncing off the anterior plate of his shoulder blade and lodging deeply inside his right lung.

It felt as if the largest man he knew had slammed him with an aluminum baseball bat. For a moment, his nervous system short-circuited and he slumped, unconscious.

Fladry knew instantly what had happened. Tracers were sparking off the helo from both flanks and a ragged bullet hole appeared right in front of his face in the Plexiglas. But Bowman's body was careening over onto his cyclic, so Fladry took Bowman's cyclic in his own left hand, stuck his right palm out and shoved his partner back against the seat. He reached for Bowman's inertia reel and locked it to keep him held in place by his harness, and then he kept on flying. They were almost there.

Through Fladry's chin bubble, the scene looked like a bank heist in the middle of Fort Knox. The flanking parapets of the PDF barracks were higher than the prison roof, and despite all the suppressing fire from the Little Bird guns and the AC-130s, Panamanian troops were lancing small-arms fire *down* into that unprotected rectangle. The access door in the cupola had been blown off its hinges, and just nearby the Delta boys were spinning and firing like Butch and Sundance in their last shootout. Muse, their precious slab of bullion, had been clapped with a flak vest and Kevlar helmet and was nearly obscured by the bodies of the men who would die before allowing him to be harmed or—worse—recaptured. They couldn't last long in that melee. Dietderich and Fox were just setting their helo down, with J. J. Holmes right behind them. Fladry banked left hard to execute a go-around. McDougal followed him.

Bowman woke up when he felt the still coal-hot bullet burning inside his chest. He shook it off, raised his head and tried to key his mike, but he couldn't move his right arm. It just flopped like a dead fish in the slipstream, and when he tried to hit the floor switch with his right foot it was all mucked up with dirt. He reached across to his cyclic with his left hand and pushed the button.

"I think there was a concussion."

"Yeah, okay." Fladry was very, very busy. No point in telling the major he was hit bad if he didn't know it yet.

"Did something just explode beside us?" Bowman asked. He wasn't feeling the pain quite yet. He was still numb with shock.

"Nope."

"Well, I guess I'm hit then."

"Yup."

Fladry charged down into one of the hottest LZs he had ever seen. The gunfire was unbelievable. Dietderich and Fox had just taken off with Muse and a full load of commandos. He watched their bird head off to the left, and then it turned back, started to fall and disappeared below the buildings. But they were still under powered flight. *Maybe they'll make it*, Fladry thought as his skids scraped the roof and a team of Delta boys charged toward him. They jumped onto the pods and hooked in. On Fladry's side, the nearest man stuck an upright thumb in his face. On Bowman's side, the nearest commando reached out and slapped the pilot on his freshly shattered arm.

"*Ohhhhh . . . wowwww!*" Bowman grunted as Fladry pulled power.

"Chalk Three, comin' out," Flapper announced over the comms. What he didn't yet know was that he only had five men on his skids instead of the planned-for six. It was the responsibility of the commandos to make sure the load was right and advise their pilots, because the aviators couldn't turn their heads far enough around to check. As Kelly McDougal came in to land, there were still *seven* Delta men left on the roof. He tried to load them all up. His bird was too heavy and wouldn't lift off. Three of them got back off the pods, set up a position at the roof's low retaining wall and kept on shooting.

Randy Cochran, who was a major by then and had battled the army bureaucracy to rejoin the 160th, was balling his fists in the TOC at

Howard. He had heard Fladry's call that Bowman was wounded and Dietderich's bird had gone down. There were still men on the roof and someone was calling frantically on the radio net, "Can anyone get them?"

"I'm inbound." It was Steve Koester's voice, cool and smooth. Koester and Welch, with Lee Pennington navigating, immediately banked their Blackhawk toward Modelo and landed. Their crew chiefs, Mike Gammons and Shawn Normandin, poured minigun fire into the PDF barracks while the remaining Delta men jumped on board, and then they were away.

But the rescue of Kurt Muse was not over. Dietderich and Fox had crashed in the streets below the prison. With Muse in their small cargo space and six commandos on the pods, they were just too heavy, and a skid caught a low-slung power line, just as Bowman had feared would happen. At first, they landed the Little Bird under power and bumped along the ground, then they tried to get a running start and take off again. This time, a volley of PDF gunfire slammed into their rotors and the bird crumpled hard onto its right skid. Dietderich and Fox tried to shut down the engine, throttle off, fuel lines cut, but the blades kept on turning no matter what they did. At this point, all the Delta men had been injured, some of them seriously wounded, yet none of them faltered. One of them, who happened to be wearing a standard-issue Kevlar helmet, was struck in the head by the spinning blades and fell to the road. He got up, blood streaming from his scalp, yet he was interested in only one thing.

"Muse? You okay?" he yelled as he pulled the shaken but unhurt CIA operative from the crushed helo.

"I'm all right!"

Along with Dietderich and Fox, the Delta men hustled Muse into the ground floor of a nearby building and set up a perimeter. One of them tossed an infrared strobe into the street, which was soon spotted by a Blackhawk flying overhead. The Blackhawk couldn't land in the narrow street, but after a very tense quarter hour, an M113 armored personnel carrier from a mechanized infantry brigade operating nearby picked them all up.

No one yet knew what had happened to George Kunkle and Fred Horsley, who had been shot down in their B Company gun bird in the opening minutes of the attack on the *Comandancia*. In fact the two Night Stalkers were using everything they'd ever learned in SERE school, plus their instincts and wits just to stay alive. Their helo had fallen into the middle of the PDF compound and smashed up against a security fence. Gripping their MP-5s, George and Fred slung their flight vests onto the razor wire and climbed over, making a mad dash for cover as the Spectre gunships above hammered every building around. They crawled under a portico. A PDF soldier spotted them, but just as the two pilots were about to shoot him, he threw up his arms and begged to surrender. Now, with a prisoner in tow, George and Fred escaped and evaded through the burning city blocks until they came upon a convoy of Light Armored Vehicles manned by Fifth Infantry Division troops.

George approached the armored vehicles, yelling the running password, "Bulldog! Bulldog!" But when they turned their weapons on him, he screamed, "We're goddamn Americans!"

Apparently, that was enough of a password. . . .

THE OUTCOME of Acid Gambit was still in question when Fladry set the helo down at Howard. He had already advised the 160th that Bowman was hit, and he settled the bird near the Joint Casualty Collection Site, where scores of wounded were being brought in and treated. The Delta men had no inkling that one of their pilots was badly hurt and immediately jumped off the pods and started high-fiving one another. They would soon learn that their comrades and Kurt Muse were down in the streets, still fighting it out, and would spend some time deeply concerned until the news about the armored rescue finally flashed over the comms.

"Hey!" Fladry called out to them. "I've got a wounded man here."

The stretcher bearers sprinted over from the JCCS as some of the operators grabbed Bowman by his right shoulder to extract him from the cockpit.

"*Awwww* . . . come *on*, guys!" he roared at them.

When the medical personnel triaged Bowman in the field hospital, they found an entry wound, no exit wound, and no evidence of a life-threatening condition. They assumed the bullet had lodged in some muscle, and there were critical cases requiring more attention. He was given some morphine and sent to the "back of the line," until he started coughing up bloody foam. As he lay there on a stretcher, he caught the sleeve of a passing medic.

"Hey, I think I need a second opinion over here."

The doctors discovered that his lung was collapsed and he was losing blood pressure. He kept asking about Dietderich and Fox, because he remembered hearing Fladry report, "Jim's down in the street," but no one could tell him anything. They prepped him to have a very thick needle inserted into his chest to reinflate the lung, and shook their heads when they saw that he was obviously a weight lifter; the muscle covering his rib cage was dense, but there was no other way to go in. They called six men over to hold him down.

It was not yet two o'clock in the morning when all the Night Stalkers and commandos outside the collection point turned their heads. Bowman was screaming at the doctors as they pounded the needle into his chest.

"*Awwwowww* . . . You're trying to fucking *kill* me!"

He would be flown out to a Texas hospital shortly after dawn and endure multiple surgeries for his compound-fractured arm, shattered scapula and pierced lung. Fragments of the bullet would remain inside him forever. His wife, Diane, who had spent a week with him in intensive care, said to him, "Since you have a collapsed lung, you won't be able to do this stuff anymore." He was breathing through a respirator, so he just cocked one eyebrow at her as if she'd suggested a sex change operation. He would be flying again by April 1990. In 1999, he would become the twelfth commanding officer of the Night Stalkers.

IT WAS WELL after dawn at Torrijos-Tocumen when Donnie Calvery watched the 82nd Airborne Division jump into the airfield. The paratroopers' mission had been considerably delayed by the necessity to deice their aircraft before they took off. By the time they began to tumble from their C-141s, the airport was completely in American hands and no more gunfire reached up at the airplanes, but they were all going to get those coveted combat wings anyway. That didn't matter to Donnie. He and his men would always wear theirs proudly, and he felt that they had earned them.

He called for a CH-47 to fly over from Howard to pick up his FARP team. When the Chinook landed, the Night Stalkers loaded up their empty fuel blivet, hoses and some minigun ammo and rockets that were left. When they landed back at the base, there was little time to rest, or to reflect on having just participated in a hefty slice of American military history. The hunt for Noriega was in full swing. There would be raids on his safe houses, mansions and the homes of his various female consorts across the country, all of them supported by Night Stalker helos. There were airplanes missing; some of them crashed, some, like Fladry's and Bowman's, too shot up to fly. Repairs had to be made quickly and new FARPs prepared. The search for Panama's "Pineapple," coined by special operators as "The Hunt for Elvis," would even take Donnie and his men to the Colombian border, where the Rangers would raid a jungle hideout and come up empty. Eventually, Noriega would come crawling to a Catholic monsignor and take refuge in the Vatican's embassy in Panama City, the Papal Nunciatore. After some days, he would be coaxed into surrendering, and a Night Stalker Blackhawk, piloted by Cliff Wolcott, would take him away to his fate: life imprisonment in the United States.

Clifton "O.B" O'Brien, Smokin' Joe Frazier and Big Dave lay in that ditch at Albrook Air Base for more than an hour, taking intermittent sniper fire until a Blackhawk from one of the other army aviation units flew in to pick them up. Curiously, it was piloted by a former Night Stalker named Jim Bandy, who had been a B Company Little Bird gun pilot and had then transitioned to Blackhawks and been rotated to Panama. O.B. didn't really care who was picking them up; it could have been a girl flying a hang glider, but he grinned very hard when he saw one of his old Night Stalker buddies at the controls.

Back at Howard, there was still no respite. The rest of O.B.'s team had already been tasked to another FARP somewhere and they were gone. None of them had slept for days. He found out that Kunkle and Horsley had indeed been shot down but had also been rescued. He breathed a sigh of relief. The company was too tight to have to lose anyone. The Group operations sergeant, Greg Lund, came up to him.

"O.B.," Lund said quietly, "you got a Little Bird down."

O.B. looked at him. "What's the tail number?"

Lund recited the number. It was the bird belonging to Wilson "Sonny" Owens and John R. Hunter. Sonny was a CW3 and J.R. a first lieutenant, and O.B. had been with them for so long, and on so many training missions, that their grins and laughs were embedded in his brain. He wanted to remember them exactly that way, before he finally asked the next question.

"What about survivors?"

"There are none," Lund said.

O.B. stood for a while, just breathing slowly. Lund told him that Sonny and J.R. had gone off on a mission to Colon to support a special tactics raid on one of Noriega's enclaves, and had been shot down right at the very beginning. They had a full load of fuel and ammunition and crashed in a marsh by the sea. The air force's CSAR team had already been scrambled and gone out there, but the Little Bird was burning and there wasn't much they could do. Dan Brown, B Company's commander, had also flown out to the site and returned, shaking his head and saying nothing more.

O.B. walked across the tarmac through the beehive of activity, watching crewmen work over the damaged helos and pilots gearing up for further missions. He found Donnie, who had also heard the news just after his Chinook from Torrijos-Tocumen set down. They shook hands and held those grips for a long moment, relieved to see each other alive. They were both filthy, their camo grease streaked with sweat streams, the "drive-on" rags around their necks soaked through. They both had stories to tell about the night just passed, but that could wait. They had an important task to perform.

O.B. and Donnie joined up with one of the other B Company pilots, Doug Snyder, and boarded a Blackhawk to fly out to the crash site. A Downed Aircraft Recovery Team climbed on as well, armed maintenance men from the company who would set up a perimeter and provide security. When they got there, the fire had burned itself out and the CSAR men had already pulled out the charred corpses of the pilots. The Group commander had told O.B. and Donnie that they should recover any personal effects they could find and bring them back. He also wanted what was left of the aircraft to be dropped in international waters. There wasn't much left.

O.B. and Donnie unfolded an A-22 bag, nothing more than a large tarp that could be snapped closed and slung from a Blackhawk. None of the remaining parts of the bird were too large to fit in the bag. As they were going through the wreckage, they found small bits of bone fragments and burned scraps of uniforms, and they knew exactly which were parts of Sonny, and which were parts of J.R., because they knew who had been sitting in the right seat and who in the left. They took their drive-on rags from around their gritty necks and laid them out. O.B. gently wrapped up Sonny in his rag. Donnie wrapped up J.R.

They called the Blackhawk back in and hooked up the A-22 bag to the sling. Then they boarded and flew out to sea. The Blackhawk cruised at a hundred feet above the gently rolling waves, and just as they reached the international boundary line, a sudden squall crowded the sky with charcoal clouds and it began to rain. A hard wind started to buffet the helo, and the A-22 bag began to swing from side to side below its belly. O.B. and Donnie sat in the cargo hold, while Doug Snyder pulled a small Bible from his pocket and read the Twenty-third Psalm over the internal comms.

The Lord is my Shepherd; I shall not want.
He maketh me to lie down in green pastures:
He leadeth me beside the still waters.
He restoreth my soul:
He leadeth me in the paths of righteousness for His
    name's sake.

Yea, though I walk through the valley of the shadow of death,
I will fear no evil: For thou art with me;
Thy rod and thy staff, they comfort me.
Thou preparest a table before me in the presence of mine enemies:
Thou annointest my head with oil; My cup runneth over.

Surely goodness and mercy shall follow me all the days
    of my life:
and I will dwell in the House of the Lord for ever.

When he was done, the pilot punched the release and the remains of the Little Bird splashed into the sea. O.B. and Donnie leaned out and dropped their drive-on rags, which fluttered into the foam below and disappeared. The Blackhawk banked and turned, heading back to Panama.

Almost immediately, the rain stopped and the wind died down to a mild flutter, leaving only the sound of the engines humming and rotors swirling above. Sunbeams flashed across the wave tops, and suddenly the arch of a giant rainbow appeared.

O.B. and Donnie looked at each other. They would keep that vision to themselves, for a very long time. . . .

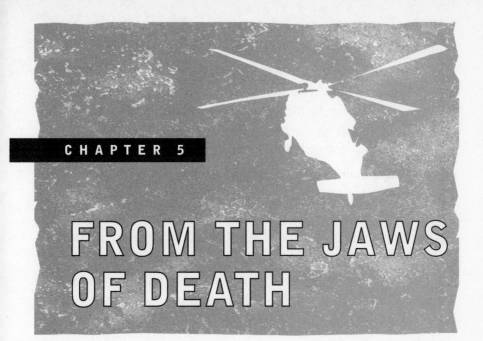

CHAPTER 5

FROM THE JAWS OF DEATH

**DESERT STORM
JANUARY 1991**

ON HIS VERY FIRST helicopter mission for the U.S. Army, Jim Crisafulli got lost.

He sat there all alone in the Huey cockpit, his hands slimy with sweat, his eyes darting furiously as he tried to locate the pickup point. It was only a mile and half from his post at Fort Knox to the radar dome at Snow Mountain, where he was supposed to simply pick up some major and deliver him to the Wilcox firing range. But he was already sure he was going to screw it up, lose his wings, get a dishonorable discharge and be sent home in disgrace. He wondered if his father had been right, that the army wasn't for him, that he would always be no more than his daddy's "little boy" and just couldn't make it on his own in a man's world.

A lot of that had to do with his size and appearance. In 1972 Jim was just nineteen years old and hadn't yet attained his full adult height of five feet nine and a half inches. At barely five-foot-seven, 120 pounds soaking wet, his soft cheeks still sprouting teenage pimples, he had always been doted on by his emotional and protective parents. So he knew full well that his determination to fly military aircraft was some sort of rebellion, a desire to prove that his heart and his courage were much larger than his physical stature. Jim's father had been a naval commander during World War II and after his retirement from the navy had gone on to a full career as an engineer for NASA. In 1970, when Jim was applying to colleges, his dad had tried to pull some strings with the senators in Montana to get his son accepted into the Naval Academy. That didn't happen, nor was Jim's application to West Point successful, so he decided to fly for the army.

"They'll treat you badly," his father had warned him. "I don't want you going into the army."

Like most teenagers, Jim heard those words of warning and pointedly ignored them. Just like Bob Fladry had done, along with so many other young men who dreamed of nothing but flying, he went from high school to flight school. At Fort Walters, Texas, he first learned to fly in small "mosquito" helicopters called TH-55s, then went on to advanced training in Korean War–vintage, bubble-canopy TH-13s at Fort Rucker. There he got his Huey transition, totaling up a modest twenty-four hours in that "big boy" bird, and finally graduated as a bona fide army aviator.

He went home on a short leave to Montana, wearing his wings proudly but expecting no more than gruff derision from his father. Yet his dad greeted Jimmy with a silk flying scarf and, fighting back tears, draped it around his son's neck.

"I went to flight school, too, once," Leonard Crisafulli confessed in a near whisper as Jim stood there dumbfounded. "It was near the end of the war, but I ground-looped a biplane trainer and washed out. Went to the navy as a navigator. Looks like you've done better than me, Jimmy."

Jim had never felt so tall in his life.

He showed up at his first assignment at Fort Knox, Kentucky, a spring in his step and ready for his first bona fide missions, but it seemed like he was the only one there who wanted to fly. Almost all the other pilots were Vietnam vets who never wanted to see another aircraft. All they wanted to do was drink beer, tell lies and go home. Jim knew full well that an aviator didn't really learn his trade until *after* flight school. Those eleven months of basic flight training and the wings awarded upon completion were merely a license to learn, and it was supposed to be during your first assignment and under the guidance of experienced mentors that you'd hone your skills. But no one at Knox was much interested in showing him the ropes.

"The whirly side goes up, the greasy side goes down," the burned-out vets would snidely remark to him when he asked questions. "If you can remember that, go fly the damn aircraft."

He was disappointed and disillusioned, until a man named Skip Ellerbrock came along. Skip had served three tours in Vietnam flying Hueys and been up to his elbows in death and danger, but he was still a helo pilot to the core. Almost immediately, Ellerbrock took Crisafulli under his wing, and they slipped into the master-and-disciple relationship that all young men and women need if they are ever going to be fine aviators and seasoned pilots. Ellerbrock never bragged about his combat experience. He had a quiet demeanor and a dark sense of humor that relaxed Crisafulli even under adverse conditions.

"Nope. I wouldn't do that again, Jim," Ellerbrock would calmly state as he corrected Crisafulli's mistakes while flying around the Fort Knox training areas. "That'll get you killed."

It didn't take long for Jim to absorb some of Skip's most basic wisdoms, or to unwrinkle his questionable habits. Within three days of dual Huey time, he was designated a Huey pilot-in-command, which was remarkable since he had never flown in the helicopter alone.

"On Monday morning, Crisafulli, you're going to fly up to Snow Mountain and pick up a major. Bring him out to Wilcox Range."

"Yessir," Jim gulped as he saluted his company commander. It was Friday evening, and now he'd be spending the entire weekend in a cold sweat.

"Uhhh, Skip." Jim caught up with his mentor as he and Ellerbrock left the commander's office. Skip was heading out for a beer.

"Yeah?"

Where the hell is Snow Mountain?" Jim whispered.

Ellerbrock laughed as he pointed to the glossy white cap of a radar dome in the distance. You could see it from twenty-five miles away, in any direction. He clapped Crisafulli on the shoulder.

"You'll be fine."

"Yeah. Sure. Roger that . . ."

The mission was scheduled for 0700 hours on Monday morning. Jim got to the flight line at 0530 and preflighted the Huey over and over again. He was so nervous that he somehow skipped an entire page of the checklist, but then he managed to strap himself into the cockpit. He cranked it up, hovered out from the apron, set it down again and called Ground Control for clearance. Then he picked it up again and moved the bird over to the active runway. Then he just sat there again, breathing.

"Uh, sir?" a voice from Ground Control crackled in his headset. "We do have a fixed wing coming in, in about twenty minutes. Are you gonna get off the runway?"

Blushing, Jim took off, got up to about three hundred feet and the engine failed—or so he thought. The rotors drooped and the turbine whined, and he started calling, "Mayday! Mayday! Mayday!" until he suddenly realized that his RPMs were only at 6,000 and should have been cranked up to 6,600. He spooled the engine up as the sweat ran in rivulets down his armpits, the Huey recovered, but then he realized that he'd already passed Snow Mountain and had to double back. When he finally set it down, he was amazed to have survived just the first leg of his first mission. It seemed like he waited another hour until his passenger finally appeared from inside the radar complex.

"Okay, kid. Where's the pilot?" the tall major asked him.

"Sir, that's me."

The major started to laugh. He was squinting at Crisafulli's over-sized flight suit, a helmet that looked like football gear on a toddler, and his pimply cheeks.

"No, really," the officer scoffed. "Where's the pilot?"

"Sir, really, sir. That's me."

The major's face fell. "Jesus, they're going to kill me."

Yet having no other mode of transportation and seeing no "adults" around who could fly, the officer reluctantly climbed in. Jim got them airborne, but his hands were preoccupied with the controls so he handed the major his map.

"Sir, would you mind holding on to this?"

"Just follow the damn road, kid." The major glared at him as he stabbed a finger at a thick strip of highway. "You want me to fly it, too?"

Jim flew the helicopter, and he got them there and back in one piece. Nearly everything that could have gone wrong on his first mission certainly had, but that hadn't dampened his spirits. He was nineteen years old, and he still believed that the sky was the limit, that he could do absolutely anything, that he could *be* anything he imagined. He was a goddamn *army aviator*. But he had no idea that it would take nearly twenty years to earn the respect he deserved. . . .

JIM CRISAFULLI'S aviation record was slowly assembled, block by block, with each piece enhancing the résumé of his skills. It was almost as if some higher power were choosing his waypoints, directing him toward something decisive, a crossroads in time where everything he knew and had learned would matter very much, as the sum total of many small parts. He wasn't very long at Fort Knox when his commanders switched him from Hueys to OH-58s, a much smaller helicopter that he "wouldn't hurt himself in." When the international oil embargo hit home in 1973, aviation gas was at a premium and for nearly two years there was very little flying to do. A group of pilots would pile into a single helicopter and take to the air, just so that everyone could log flight time and remain current. That was just fine with most of the other pilots, but Crisafulli wasn't happy when he wasn't at the controls. He soon got a transition into OH-58s and became an instructor in the fast little Scouts. He was excited when he finally received orders to deploy to Germany, where he'd be flying reconnaissance missions on the front lines of the Cold War.

Jim's wife, Linda, went along for the ride, but she was never really thrilled with his army career. She was an unpretentious farm girl from Wisconsin, and when they married early on during his service in 1972, army wives were still being informally sent to "Officer Wife Training School." Linda found herself at loathsome and boring tea socials, wearing white gloves and playing the dutiful army spouse. It was like some throwback to the cavalry and the Old West, yet at a time when most of the country's young women were burning their bras. Jim and Linda already had one child, Matthew, and they planned on having another. She had hoped to raise their children as normal American kids rather than army brats, but soon her dreams that Jim would eventually give it all up and fly commercial airplanes faded. She would be forever packing, unpacking, repacking, moving, putting the kids in the wrong schools, waiting for the next phone call bearing bad tidings. "We're going *where*?" Yet over the course of Jim's first decade as an army aviator, it became clear that despite Linda's complaints, she would be sticking with him. She was not old-school, but she was somewhat old-fashioned in that regard. He loved her with the devotion, gratitude and constant wonder that all military aviators have for the spouses who stick with them.

As the decade turned, they returned from Europe and Jim was ordered to Fort Rucker, Alabama, as a Huey instructor. After so many years in Europe and some very challenging flying over exotic terrain and in all kinds of weather, a mundane instructor's job in Alabama didn't sound very appealing, but it wasn't as if he had a choice. As it turned out, the Huey was the current platform for night vision goggle training, and Jim became an NVG instructor. The technology was relatively new and it stretched his aviator's muscles and challenged his skills. Because he was responsible for putting all the aviation crews through NVG training, Jim amassed more than eight hundred flight hours under goggles, an impressive record for a WO-3.

In 1983, he did not participate in Operation Urgent Fury. He had already received orders for a tour in Korea, which of course "thrilled" Linda to no end. All that combat flying in Grenada had apparently been done by some classified outfit that folks only whispered about over beers at the "O" Club.

"Hey, did you guys hear about some of that hairy, swoopy shit they did in Grenada?"

"Yeah, I heard something. But who was it? Who did it?"

"Nobody knows. Nobody'll talk about it."

Burn Before Reading.

Jim was just finishing up a senior instructor's course at Rucker when he was summoned to a phone call. An anonymous voice on the other end got to the point.

"Mr. Crisafulli, we've heard you've got some good goggle experience."

"Yeah, I suppose I do. . . . Who's *we*?"

"Would you be interested in a job in Special Operations?"

"Maybe. What's Special Operations?"

The anonymous "voice" seemed to like that. At least he wasn't dealing with some hotshot know-it-all.

"Look, we're going to call up your records and take a look at you. Tomorrow morning at ten, one of our selection officers will call you."

"Sounds like the heat," Jim said. In his personal parlance, "heat" meant "cool."

The telephone interview went smoothly, and by the time it was over, Jim was very intrigued by all this Secret Squirrel stuff. The Special Operations major who had spoken to him was ready to take him aboard. However, there was no way to get Jim out of his Korean assignment, and that was fine with him. Korea was front-line stuff, and this sort of scheduling was par for the course in the army. It wasn't like civilian life, where you applied for a job, got the green light and started the following week. In the army, your new position would generally begin after your next tour, which could be anywhere from one to three years long.

It was Jim's thirteenth year in the U.S. Army, and he was not only qualified, but an expert in flying just about every scout and utility helicopter in the inventory, including the new Blackhawks that were rapidly replacing all the aging Hueys. In Korea he flew missions for the Fourth Battalion of the Seventh Cavalry out of Camp Stanley, lifting infantry elements through tough mountain passes and often under horrific weather conditions, along a demilitarized zone that was constantly on the verge of going hot. In less than a year, he was summoned back to the States and sent to Fort Bragg, North Carolina.

No one informed Crisafulli officially that his career in Special Operations Aviation had just begun, but he knew that he was reaching a pinnacle, that he had come over to "the dark side." Fort Bragg was home to the army's Special Forces, the vaunted Green Berets. These soldiers operated in twelve-man teams called Operational Detachment Alphas, or A-Teams. They were schooled in the foreign languages of their Areas of Operation, experts in all small arms of domestic or foreign manufacture, medically qualified to the level of surgical assistants and so adept at dealing with allied bands of warriors that Jim regarded them as professionals who could turn from diplomats to assassins in the wink of an eye. Two Special Forces Groups were stationed at Bragg, the 5th and the 7th. Both Groups shared a flight element of eight Blackhawks, which were "tricked out" exactly like the Night Stalker birds at Fort Campbell. Jim was first hired on as the Fifth Special Forces flight platoon instructor and soon became their standardization instructor pilot. It wasn't long before he was the SIP for the entire detachment.

He was much different now than that pimply, nervous kid flying his first mission at Fort Knox. He was still diminutive in size, yet he had no Napoleon complex and no need to prove himself. He discovered that he needed only two obvious traits to be respected by the soldiers he flew and the commanders he served: being the best pilot he could possibly be and always saying what was on his mind. He had developed a reputation as a "sawed-off warrant officer with a big set of balls."

In the lexicon of the Joint Special Operations Command, there were two kinds of Special Operations Forces: White and Black. White SOF was comprised of the more conventional special operators, such as the army's SF and the Rangers. Black SOF generally referred to secret special tactics teams, such as Delta and the navy's SEALs. If there was a hijacking or hostage taking somewhere in the world, it was most likely that Black elements would be tasked to handle the crisis, as that was one of their main areas of expertise. If a sniper team was required to take out targets deep behind enemy lines, an insurgent force was to be quietly eliminated or allied foreigners needed expert training and guidance, this would most often fall to the White elements. Within the special operations aviation community, there was an ongoing, competitive argument about whether White or Black ops required more skill. But to Crisafulli, it made no difference and the argument was moot. He would be taking hard men into harm's way.

From 1985 to 1990, Crisafulli "dabbled near" the air space and borders of multiple countries, both allies and enemies, inserting Special Forces wherever they needed to work and bringing them back out again, without fail. He flew at night, over deserts and snowcapped mountains, or in hard blue skies and through near hurricanes. Years before, he had flown into East Germany when it was strictly *verboten*, and now he should not have landed anywhere near Syria or Mexico, but he did. In Honduras, he inserted his teams deep in the jungles along the Nicaraguan border, and all he knew was that when he roared back in over the Patuca River to pick them up again, they were carrying considerably less ammunition. There were always men in the back of his helo who meant business, and they depended on him and trusted him. In turn, he knew that if he was shot down or injured, they would bring him back out or die trying.

You couldn't fly these men for months on end without getting to know them intimately. He drank with them, partied with them and was regarded as an integral part of the Team. The Special Forces men were a particular breed of quiet professionals, yet the pressures of their missions did require a release valve. They were good-looking young men who rarely swaggered, yet they caught the ladies' eyes and were not always welcomed by the locals. Once in a small town in Texas, Jim was drinking with his comrades and sauntered over to the bar for a re-fill, when he suddenly felt the vise-like grip of a drunken cowboy on the back of his neck.

"Ya think you can drink our beer and fuck our women, huh, sol-dier boy?"

Jim tried to spin from the drunkard's grasp. He was wiry and solid and ready to fight, but he didn't have to. The cowboy's boots had al-ready left the sawdust floor and he was suspended by his throat at the end of a master sergeant's arm.

"You leave my fucking pilot *alone*, asshole."

There was no commendation that the army could give that would have swelled Jim's chest more than that growl.

In 1988, while still flying for 5th Group, Jim received a call from Lieutenant Colonel Dell Dailey, who was then a battalion com-mander in the 160th SOAR(A) and would someday lead all of JSOC's forces as a two-star general. Dailey was looking for another SIP to serve in the Night Stalkers' Third Battalion.

"I'd be honored, sir," was Jim's reply.

The Third of the 160th was stationed out of Savannah, Georgia. Back then and for some years thereafter, it was considered a bastard son of the Night Stalkers. The "Lost Battalion" was physically distant from Fort Campbell and handled mostly White missions, so pilots who flew for that outfit suffered an unspoken "you're not really part of us" attitude from some of the other Night Stalkers. None of that mattered much to Crisafulli—it was all junior high school stuff as far as he was concerned. He was quickly "validated" as a flight lead for the Third and then took up his position as an SIP, certifying other pilots and crews, including Dell Dailey himself in an overwater flight.

But soon enough, Dell Dailey decided that Crisafulli was going to have to go through the same assessment process as all the other Night Stalker candidates. Jim had a lot of respect for Dailey, but didn't quite understand the necessity and said so.

"I'll do whatever you say, sir. I don't get it, but I'll do it."

"It's like this," Dailey explained, which was something he rarely did as a combat leader. "Eventually you're going to be assessing other candidates for the unit. If you haven't gone through the very same process as them, it'll weaken your standing."

"Roger that, sir."

Assessment was not a pleasant experience for any Night Stalker candidate, and even less so for Crisafulli. Already a master aviator and at the age of thirty-five regarded as very young for a CW4, Jim knew that other special ops pilots would regard him suspiciously and might expect him to act like "the cock of the walk." But that had never been Crisafulli's style. The 160th assessment process was designed to weed out those very types of men, while seeking out pilots who were exceptionally skilled. For the most part, military pilots tend to have larger than average egos, so the combination of talent without braggadocio was hard to come by.

Mike Anderson, a CW3 with First Battalion, was chosen to be Crisafulli's assessment pilot. Mike was roughly the same age as Jim, yet still a full rung lower in rank, and he nearly snorted when he saw Crisafulli's master aviator wings. Anderson had been flying Black combat missions for the 160th while Jim's experience was strictly White, yet Jim had an enormous amount of flight hours and more goggle time than many "Black" First Battalion pilots. Anderson made Crisafulli's assessment flights as grueling as possible, giving him all sorts of convoluted waypoints, map coordinates, midnight NOE flights and nightmare emergency procedures that many other pilots would have failed. Crisafulli sailed through all of it without complaint or comment. He had never been in a college fraternity but to him this seemed like a frat hazing, and given his size and stature he had been through plenty of that kind of nonsense in his life.

The Assessment Board was another matter altogether. In a long, carpeted, harshly illuminated conference room on the Night Stalker compound, six officers, including the 160th unit psychologist, sat behind a horseshoe-shaped fixture of mahogany tables. Crisafulli, wearing Class A's and standing at parade rest at the far end of the room, was subjected to an endless hour of interrogation.

"You're a master aviator, Crisafulli," one senior pilot began. "You have more flight time than most of our pilots. Do you think you're better than us?"

"No, sir. I do not."

"You're probably standing there thinking this is bullshit," another Night Stalker chimed in. "You're thinking that just because we're all wearing a different patch than you are, we've got no right to put you through this crap, right?"

"Sir, that is not true," Jim said. He needed to immediately dispel the perception that his time, rank and experience made him think he was superior in some way. "I know I can learn a lot from the men in this unit, especially the ones here who have really been in the shit."

Another officer flipped through Jim's records.

"You've got over a thousand hours of goggle time."

"That is correct, sir. But a lot of that is pattern time, not mission time. A man with two hundred hours of real-world NVG time far surpasses my experience flying the traffic pattern."

It was what they wanted to hear. This man was aware of his skills, but wouldn't be lauding his rank or insignia over anybody.

There were other phases of assessment that Jim had to survive. You couldn't become a Night Stalker without proving your stamina and

passing the physical tests. Flying a Blackhawk, or any other special operations helicopter, could often demand eight or ten hours at the controls without rest. In addition, many of the missions would involve
flying over open water.

Jim had never been a very strong swimmer, but he was thrown into
the training pool along with all the other candidates. He was supposed
to tread water using only his arms for fifteen minutes, but basically he
just kept sinking to the bottom and staying there, until he had to kick
up, take a breath and submerge again.

"You there!" a very large noncom who was running the physical assessment screamed at Jim as he poked his head up for a breath. "Get
the fuck out of my pool!"

Jim lost his temper. "Shut up, you fat fuck! Why don't you come in
and get me?"

The other candidates whooped and hollered. Crisafulli had just introduced himself to his fellow Night Stalkers in a way they would not
forget. After a week of trials, he was officially accepted into the 160th.

In 1989, when many Night Stalker elements deployed to Panama
for Operation Just Cause, Jim had just assessed with the unit so he was
not "invited" to participate. In more than twenty years of flying army
helicopters, he had certainly flown into some places where enemies
were armed and dangerous, but he had not yet seen combat. But this
phenomenon was much more common in the special operations aviation community than one might think. Various elements of the 160th
were constantly training in one part of the world or another, often scattered throughout the globe, so if a mission quickly developed you
could easily be in the wrong place at the wrong time and miss the
"party." Getting tagged for a real-world operation was sort of like
roulette. Rick Bowman, who was regarded as a model, gung-ho, hard-
charging Night Stalker, had not seen action until he suddenly found
himself in the midst of Kurt Muse's midnight rescue in Panama. Bob
Fladry, on the other hand, had had the fortune to participate in nearly
every real-world mission that came up. In just a few years, many of the

Night Stalkers would find themselves battling for their lives in Mogadishu, a hellish introduction to combat for a number of pilots and their crews. It was like that. You never knew when your number would come up.

During this period, the entire 5th Special Forces Group was relocated from Fort Bragg to Fort Campbell, and Jim continued to ferry his ODAs as a flight lead of Fifth platoon, Delta Company of the Third Battalion. His four Blackhawks, now permanently transferred from Bragg, stood close by and ready to deploy for the Group. He lived in a trailer on a section of the post called "Destiny."

In early 1990, they deployed to the Kingdom of Jordan to instruct those allied pilots in night vision flying and Special Forces tactics. In June, they redeployed to Jamaica on training and drug-interdiction missions. Late that summer, Jim was sent out to Fort Chaffee, Arkansas, to straighten out a conventional aviation platoon that was having some bad luck and serious accidents. Saddam Hussein's armored brigades had just rolled into Kuwait, and Crisafulli wasn't surprised to get a phone call from Operations back at Campbell.

"Jim, come back on the afternoon flight. You've been assigned as the liaison officer to ARSOTF in Saudi."

The Army Special Operations Task Force was being stood up in the Middle East as the winds of war began to kick up. Being selected as the liaison officer to that body was somewhat of a compliment, yet as Jim returned via commercial air to Campbell, he already suspected that the position would mean "no flying." He wondered how that had happened and was already trying to figure out how to get out of it.

As it turned out, extracting himself from that honor was not going to be easy. Colonel Kraus, the commander of 5th Group, had personally asked for Jim to fulfill that role. The colonel had tremendous stature within the SF community. He was charismatic, well-spoken and steely, and when he issued an order, you executed it without question. He had just been assigned as the ARSOTF commander, a two-star position, and had called Dell Dailey seeking a pilot for the liaison position, which would entail cross-coordination with all Coalition aviation assets in theater.

"Dell, I need an army aviation liaison for ARSOTF."

"Well," Dailey replied, "I've got a couple of captains over here."

"No. Who's that sawed-off little warrant officer? He's got a big set of balls."

"Oh, you mean Crisafulli."

As soon as Jim set down at Campbell, he was summoned to Dailey's office.

"Crisafulli, you're going to be Kraus's liaison officer at ARSOTF. Better get on home and start packing."

"Yes, sir." Jim knew that it was a feather in his cap to have been personally requested by Kraus, but a position like that meant he was going to be grounded. If anything happened over there, he wanted to be in the air. He asked the superfluous question, "Am I flying?"

"No." Dailey already knew what was coming and a growl surged in his voice. These damn pilots were all the same.

"Well, sir," Crisafulli said. "I'll do what you tell me to do, but can't you find somebody else?"

"Negative. Kraus thinks you're good, and you've got more experience with the Groups than anyone else."

Jim tried to cut a devil's deal. "Well, if there's going to be any flying, will you bring me back up?"

"Yeah, sure, but there's not gonna be any flying. Everybody's going to be back in two or three weeks. Now go pack your shit."

"Yes, sir."

Jim wasn't happy about it, but he had gotten what he wanted from his commander. In Crisafulli's lexicon, a man's word was his promise and a promise was an ironclad contract. He would hold Dailey's feet to the fire later on, if he had to.

Linda wasn't very pleased with Jim's new set of orders. He often deployed to faraway places for stretches of time, and he could rarely tell her where he was going or why. But she knew the difference between cold times and hot ones, and this thing in Kuwait had evil potential. There was a lot of activity on post and the wives were talking, whispering, passing rumors along that made her skin crawl. Matt was now fourteen years old, an age when boys begin to really understand what their fathers do for a living. Rebecca was only six and a half, but her daddy's frequent absences still hurt.

"I'll probably only be gone for three weeks, maybe four." Jim passed on Dailey's flimsy assurance.

"Sure, Jim," Linda said. "And Santa Claus is coming over for dinner." Night Stalker wives were no fools. . . .

THREE LONG MONTHS PASSED, and Jim was still serving as a "staff puke" for ARSOTF at the King Fahd Airfield in Saudi Arabia. He basically lived underground in an enormous tunnel complex called "the bat cave," liaising between ARSOTF and SOCCENT—Special Operations Command Central. The cave was a hive of never-ending activity, where night and day were indistinguishable, where there were so many missions in the works that the pressure never diminished, but only cranked up as the gathering Coalition slid inexorably toward war. High-ranking officers of every nationality hurried between computer desks staffed by male and female communications personnel, operations officers, quartermasters and obsequious aides. Jim liked working for Colonel Kraus, who was one of the finest Special Forces commanders he'd ever met, but he still felt like a bird in a dark shoebox. Kraus sensed that and tried to give Crisafulli every opportunity to get outside and breathe some fresh desert air and aviation fuel. Jim's team coordinated practice C-130 drops and Cobra close air support training. He got to work occasionally with the guys from Group as they practiced pinpointing targets using laser aiming devices and called in close air support from Coalition partners, such as the British Tornado fighter-bombers.

But essentially, he didn't feel like he was doing anything worthwhile, and certainly not using the skills he had honed for twenty years. The real action was taking place up at KKMC, the King Khalid Military City, way up north and much closer to the Iraqi border. By now the entire Third Battalion had been deployed to that complex, while the Night Stalkers' First Battalion had also deployed to another section in theater. The Special Forces A-Teams that Jim usually worked with were all at KKMC, in particular ODA 523. The 523 was commanded by an SF captain named Chris Conner, but the team leader was Master Sergeant Jeff Simms. Crisafulli and Simms's team had been through a lot together in Group, and Jim felt like he had been amputated from his warrior brothers on the eve of something important, when they would need him the most.

As the aviation liaison, Jim had the flight schedules of all Coalition aircraft. He knew where they were going, when and how long they would be on the ground before they returned to King Fahd. One morning as he came off shift, he popped aboard a C-130 making a run up to KKMC and walked right into Dell Dailey's office.

"Crisafulli, what the hell are you doing here?" The colonel knew full well what his sawed-off warrant was doing there. "Why aren't you down at King Fahd?"

"Well, sir. That's why I came to see you."

Six feet tall and more than two hundred solid pounds, Dailey rose from his desk and reddened, looking like a furious Gargantua.

"Get the hell out of my office and get back down to Fahd!"

Jim obeyed half the order. He went outside and sat himself down in a chair. The C-130 he had hitched a ride on was going to stay on the ground for just one hour. At takeoff time, it would hold on the taxiway for its passengers, but only for an additional five minutes. If Jim wasn't on that flight, there would be hell to pay when he finally got back down to King Fahd. Dailey knew that, too, and he kept Jim outside for forty-five minutes until at last he called him back inside.

"All right. What do you want?"

"Sir," Crisafulli said, "you made me a promise. You said if we were here for more than a couple of weeks, you'd bring me back up to fly."

"Well, get your ass back down to King Fahd and I'll call you if I need you."

Jim didn't budge, but his eyes kept shifting to a clock on Dailey's wall.

"Sir, I really need to call you on this. You promised me I could fly."

Dailey drummed his fingers on his desk. There were pilots who would defy you, and pilots who would kiss your ass, but Crisafulli was neither of those. He rarely asked for anything, but if you'd promised him something he was going to dig in his heels like some stubborn little mule until he got it.

"Look, I'll get somebody down there. You cross train him, and if there's going to be any flying, I'll bring you up here in a couple of weeks or so."

"Yes, sir!" Jim saluted, spun on his heel and sprinted out the door for the flight line. His ride was already taxiing, but he made it aboard.

Sure enough, in late December a pilot named Eric Halverson showed up at King Fahd, having been ordered to do so by Colonel Dailey. Halverson was certainly no happier than Jim had been to pull the assignment, but the roulette wheel had just spun in Crisafulli's favor, with an honorable push from his commander.

The beginning of the war was looming, when the holding action of Desert Shield would turn to the assaults of Desert Storm—first from the air and then by ground forces. Military traffic on the byways from north to south was already increasing. Transport aircraft were taking off day and night, hauling personnel and matériel. Word came down from Third Battalion that a Blackhawk would come down to Fahd in about a week to pick up Jim, but he was itching to get moving and worried that Dailey might somehow change his mind. With the flurry of activity he didn't know if he'd get himself a passenger spot on a C-130. He decided to drive up to KKMC in a stolen car.

As the aviation liaison officer at ARSOTF, Jim had to constantly travel out to the distant ranges or the flight lines, and Fahd was a huge complex where a bike or a golf cart wouldn't do. Vehicles were at a premium and the quartermasters had just laughed at him when he requested one. He knew there was a junkyard outside the airfield, so he bribed the Saudi gate guard, let himself in and picked out a beat-up Blazer. He painted the Chevy up in desert camouflage, made up a bumper number that sounded legitimate, slapped it on and christened her "Sheila." In just a few short months Sheila had already racked up another 7,500 miles on her aging frame. As Jim packed up his footlocker, NBC mask, 9mm pistol and as many chocolate chip cookies as he could scrounge, he hoped she'd survive the seven-hour drive up to KKMC.

Schwarzkopf's armor brigades were on the move and the roads were packed. Coalition aircraft roared overhead and missile-toting Cobras kept an eye on the columns, kicking up even more dust and grit on the desert highways. Jim weaved Sheila in and out of the traffic, leaning on the horn and happy as a clam to be driving through a war zone, at last on his way to the front. After a full day of driving through a cloud of grit, he showed up at headquarters at King Khalid, looking like Pig Pen in a flight suit. Naturally, one of the first men to spot him was Dell Dailey, who glared at him like a bad penny that kept turning up.

"What the hell are you doing here?"

"Sir, you told me to come."

"How the hell did you get up here? I didn't send a bird for you yet."

"Well, sir, I drove."

"Jesus Christ." Dailey went off muttering and shaking his head.

Jim hardly bothered to unpack his gear and settle himself in. While down at King Fahd he had barely managed to steal enough flight time to keep himself current, so the first thing he did was to wrangle some Blackhawk time. He had flown the airplane in nearly all kinds of terrain and weather conditions, but he realized that he had never seen anything like the pure, rolling dune desert that stretched for hundreds of miles northward, its deceptively soft skin suddenly cracked by deep wadis or unexpectedly marred by craggy peaks thrusting up out of nowhere. One minute you could be cruising along in a clear blue sky, then the wind would kick up and you'd be enshrouded in a full brownout. At night, the challenge tripled. This stuff wasn't for the fainthearted.

The Third Battalion had established itself in force at KKMC, yet its Alpha Company was still under strength and had to be augmented. Dell Dailey, having flown with nearly every pilot in the battalion, cherry-picked instructor pilots and flight leads from all the SF Group flight platoons: 1st Group, 5th Group, the 7th and the 10th, crowning them the Delta Company contingent of A Company. These "leftovers" formed up into flight teams to augment Alpha's operations, and still being part of "the Lost Battalion," they knew that the hottest missions would still fall to the 160th First Battalion in another part of the theater. Yet they started to work hard and train with their customers, because they could tell that kickoff time was drawing near.

Jim paired up with a pilot from 10th Group, Randy Stephens, and as they started flying together they discovered that they made a good team. Almost immediately the other pilots and Green Berets started calling them Mutt and Jeff. Stephens was six feet four inches tall and had to bend his head like a freshly arrested criminal when he folded into the cockpit. Crisafulli's eye level was even with Stephens's chest. One morning after returning from a training mission, Randy looked down at Jim and made a doleful comment as they walked off the flight line.

"Well, if anything happens and you get hurt, Crisafulli, I'll be able to carry you out. But if anything happens to me, you might as well just shoot me."

Jim stopped dead in his tracks. He barely weighed in at 160 pounds, but it was all tight wire and he was much stronger than he looked.

"Randy," he said, "I will carry you out."

"Yeah," Randy scoffed. "That's a nice thought."

"Yes. I will." It was a crucial moment for a pair of combat pilots. Randy needed to know that Jim could do that for him, and Jim needed to prove it. "Bend over."

"What?"

"Bend *over*."

Stephens bent at the waist and Crisafulli hauled him up over his shoulder. Then he ran with him for two hundred yards, while the other pilots watched them like gawkers at an ostrich race.

"All right, all right!" Stephens finally gasped. "Put me down. You're hurtin' me."

"Hope it doesn't come to that," one of the other pilots remarked. "If Stephens isn't already dead, Crisafulli'll kill him."

Jim and Randy began flying recon missions along the border at night, using their FLIR to try to spot the heat signatures of any suspicious activity or substantial enemy movements. Norman Schwarzkopf was greatly concerned that before all of his divisions were precisely in place, Saddam's Republican Guard might strike out from Kuwait and stream into Saudi Arabia. He had good reason for concern, as the Iraqis had hundreds of Russian T-72 tanks and well-trained crews who only a few years before had battled it out with the Iranians, and they outnumbered his forces by a ratio of three-to-one. The Third Battalion "augmentees" never flew alone. In addition to their crew chiefs, manning four-thousand-rounds-per-minute 7.62mm miniguns on both flanks of each Blackhawk, there were always SF Search and Rescue men on board with plenty of medical supplies and guns.

When the air war started on January 21, Jim and Randy were flying a night recon mission and witnessed something they both thought was a nuclear explosion. The air force had dropped a "Blue 82" on a division of the Republican Guard twenty miles over the border. The Blue was the largest non-nuclear bomb ever devised, and its sun-bright concussion completely shut down their NVGs. Nothing within a five-mile radius could survive that detonation, and soon Iraqi soldiers who had been in the vicinity would start limping toward the Coalition lines, streams of blood running from their shattered eardrums and nasal passages. It was the 1991 equivalent of "Shock and Awe."

Soon thereafter, Third Battalion's "dirt missions" began. Schwarzkopf's armor commanders needed to know that the earth along their planned routes of attack would support their multi-ton vehicles, so the Blackhawk crews flew army engineers with sample gathering tubes and instruments into distant wadis far beyond the FLOT—the Forward Line of Troops. They encroached behind enemy lines, always at night, flying low and fast, and began taking some significant enemy ground fire when they did so. Dell Dailey, who always led from the front, flew one of those first missions himself.

Yet for the most part, the Third Battalion waited—for days, then weeks, while Coalition aircraft launched missiles deep into Saddam's underground Command and Control complexes, bombarded his divisions with thundering B52 strikes and strafed his armor with American A-10 Warthogs and British Tornados. Not having the "big picture," the Night Stalkers of the Third did not know exactly what they were waiting for, but they knew that the ground assaults had not yet begun. Schwarzkopf's master plan remained a mystery to them. The general was about to "make his bones" with a risky gambit; he figured that Saddam Hussein would expect the Coalition Forces to attack the Iraqis in Kuwait first, then attempt to drive straight up toward Baghdad. Instead, Schwarzkopf had planned a massive end run, swinging his armored and airborne forces to the west, then northwest, then ultimately circling back down to annihilate the Republican Guard. Schwarzkopf was one of those conventional ground pounders who mistrusted special operators of all types. He thought they were sneaky glory hounds and that if he didn't rein them in tightly, they might do something wild and start "his" war before he was ready. So the Night Stalkers held on the ground, with the maintenance platoons and armorer dogs checking and rechecking the helos, and the SF teams kicking the dust with impatience.

A few days before the thunder rolled, Jim and Randy and another

Blackhawk team relocated to Rahfa, a dusty pit of an airfield much closer to the FLOT. They had been assigned a mission that had to be executed just before the tanks began to move: infiltrating Strat Recon teams deep into enemy territory. Strategic Reconnaissance teams were comprised of very small groups of Special Forces who would be deposited in key locations to monitor enemy movements and report back to Coalition headquarters. Each Blackhawk would be carrying its own pilots and crew chiefs, a SAR specialist and two of these three-man, sub-ODA Teams. The teams, although small, would be heavily geared up, carrying their personal weapons, sniper rifles, grenades, LAW rockets, NVGs, binoculars, Satcom radios, camouflage gear and as much water and food as they could haul. The missions were supposed to be relatively short, perhaps only days long, but these SF veterans knew the first rule of warfare: No plan survives first contact with the enemy. They would be going in very deep, under cover of darkness, at ranges of 75 to 185 miles past the Coalition FLOT.

Jim had no idea what day of the week it was when the order finally came to launch. The helos were all gassed up and had been sitting on the cracked tarmac, their rotors drooping as if the birds were gloomy from the lack of action. Crisafulli's Blackhawk, Number 971, had been nicknamed Lady Godiva because the men regarded her as a "stripped bitch." She had come into theater as an afterthought, lacking many of the technical goodies that festooned other Night Stalker birds. Lady Godiva's FLIR had been taken off and mounted on another helo, and she had a beat-up, crappy navigation system, but she had a pair of motors like you wouldn't believe. What she lacked in toys she made up for with speed, and Jim was nuts about her.

As the sun swelled into an orange ball and sank behind distant desert peaks, Jim and Randy hopped into the cockpit, ran their checklist and started up the APU. Jim was in the right seat, Randy in the left. Manning the minigun behind Jim's seat would be Todd "Diff" Diffenderfer, a young PFC who had not yet seen any action, and certainly not tracer fire, so he would be needing some guidance on what to look for as they flew. Diff looked about twelve years old to Crisafulli, who suddenly harkened back to that day so long ago and his very first mission, when he had probably appeared very much the same way. He was tempted to say, "Hey, kid. Where's the crew chief?" But he just smiled to himself instead. Manning the gun on the other side was Bruce Willard, a steely-eyed veteran crew chief, battle captain and master gunner. Willard had seen plenty of combat, had been fired on often and had shot back to kill. He had eyes like a hawk and could tell the difference, at night, flying at breakneck speed, between a flashlight on the ground and an APC taillight. SF Master Sergeant Gordy Hopple climbed aboard as their SAR man, and then six more men from Group struggled into the bay with their loads. Jim knew every one of them.

The other Blackhawk in the mission was carrying an identical complement of men. It was piloted by a young lieutenant named Mike Miller and his stick buddy, CW2 Chris Durkin. Relative to the other pilots, Miller had a dearth of flight time, but as the only commissioned officer he automatically became the air mission commander. They all donned their NVGs, checked their comms and took off into the particular brand of night that seems to shroud deserts everywhere: a thick, inky blackness.

The pair of Blackhawks soon swept over the Forward Line of Troops, a "tripwire" of artillery pieces and machine-gun positions manned by very alert infantry, all facing north. Then came the berm, an endless sand hill winding its way from east to west, like the Great Wall of China. After that was a stretch of no-man's-land and pretty soon it would get dicey. Jim trailed close behind and to the left of Miller's bird, keeping track of its infrared position lights through his NVGs. Together, they would be infiltrating a total of four Strat Recon teams. At a predetermined point, the Blackhawks would bank away from each other, each heading for its two targets. Jim and Randy's drop-off points were at eighty-five and 125 nautical miles deep and the round-trip would take three and a half hours. That wasn't a particularly long mission, but when you were flying very low and fast, blacked out, with no moon and zero illumination, no serious hardware to hold your own except the miniguns and nothing but chaff to defend against missiles, it would be a challenge for any pilot and leave him totally wrung out at the end. But Jim thought mainly about his customers in the back and what they would soon have to endure. It was easy enough for him; he'd soon be back in the mess tent drinking fresh coffee and winding down. The SF guys would be out there hunkered down somewhere, hoping to remain undiscovered as they whispered into their Satcoms.

In particular, he worried about Jeff Simms and ODA 523. The night before, Simms and his men had been infilled super deep to Quam al Hamza. The target was 185 nautical miles past the FLOT, a full 50 miles past the Euphrates River. Simms's team was to set up just astride a major thoroughfare called Highway 8 and keep a close lookout for any significant Iraqi armored movements. Somewhere south of their position was an entire Iraqi tank division, but no one knew exactly where. When Schwarzkopf started his end run, he needed to know if that enemy division would start to move, because it would mean that his gambit had been discovered and the Iraqis would try to outflank him. It was the task of just these few SF men to spot that movement and prevent a fiasco, and they were hanging their asses out in a very bad place.

Jim forgot about Simms as the first burst of ground fire leaped up at the Blackhawks. The Iraqis couldn't really spot the birds as their silhouettes flashed overhead at an altitude of only fifty feet, but they would open fire as Miller's Hawk was already past, making Jim's helo the one they focused on.

"I've got some lights on the right," Diff's tremulous voice announced over the internal comms. Jim immediately jinked to the left.

"Those aren't lights, Diff," Willard coached. "Those are tracers."

"Oh. Then I've got tracers."

"Right," Jim said. "And remember that for every one you see, there are four more rounds you *can't* see." That was how nearly every army, allied or enemy, belted their machine-gun ammo—one tracer in every five rounds.

More "lights" appeared, more tracers, lofting lazily upward and looking deceptively slow, but they all knew that that was an illusion. Jim and Randy dropped the bird down to thirty feet to make it even harder for the Iraqis to lead them or draw a bead, but that also doubled the stress of flying. Their AN-PVS-5s were cutaways, but they still weren't state-of-the-art and the pilots wouldn't get much advance warning of high dunes or obstructions. A FLIR would have greatly helped, because its heat-seeking capabilities would spot enemy countermeasure screens being activated out forward, but Lady Godiva didn't have one. Instead, Jim was using an infrared searchlight mounted in the belly below. With the naked eye you couldn't see its projections, and using the NVGs helped to illuminate the immediate area to the fore. They were gambling, based upon intel, that the average Iraqi gunner didn't have NVG capability. Yet more than anything else, the pilots depended on their crew chiefs to spot any threats or obstructions and point them out.

"I've got vehicles hunkered down at ten o'clock," Willard said. "Four hundred meters."

"Roger." Jim shifted the bird to the right.

"And I've got a big fat dune coming up at twelve," Diff said as he stuck his helmeted head halfway out the open cargo door, his eyes bugged wide behind his NVGs.

"Shifting right," Jim said. Diff was learning fast and that pleased him.

"Tracers!" both crew chiefs spat at the same instant. There was nowhere to go but right up the middle, and after that Jim brought the bird down even lower, skidding along at an altitude of only twenty feet above an unforgiving landscape that could reach up and kill you just like that.

Two-thirds of the way to their targets, the two birds banked away from each other. Jim had the controls and was soon landing Lady Godiva in a furious cloud of dust on a barren hilltop. He couldn't speak to his SF guys as they scrambled off the bird, but he shot them a thumbs-up and a grin and took off.

Racing to the second target, Randy took the controls, but his landing was considerably more difficult. As they sank carefully through the second brownout, Jim spotted a deep crevice through the chin bubble.

"Randy, wadi, watch it!"

It was too late. The terrain suddenly pitched up just as Stephens was setting it down and something crunched hard into the belly of the bird. But the SF men poured out of the helo and this was no place to perform an inspection or repairs. All the instruments and controls were still functioning fine, but as they lifted off they realized that the infrared searchlight wasn't working. One of Colonel Doug Brown's axioms regarding combat flying was "Never rejoin in the air." Crisafulli had no other option. The only way to fly the return legs at low level would be to closely follow Miller's bird, so he broke comm security and called him in for a midair rendezvous.

The long return to Rahfa was a killer. Jim and Randy could barely see the terrain ahead without their searchlight, so they were forced to squint at the winking dots of Miller's infrared position lights and try to follow him as he careened along with the nap of the earth. Miller wasn't waiting for anyone and kept getting away, darting between outcroppings of terrain as his lights winked in and out. He would suddenly disappear, Jim would pitch his bird up, and sure enough a huge dune would appear just in front of his nose. Added to that, even though their exfil course was completely different from their insertion pattern, word of helos in the air had swept through Iraqi positions and it seemed like everyone and his mother was shooting at them. By the time they finally crossed the FLOT after three hours and twenty minutes of flying, they were nearly out of gas, trembling with muscle fatigue and flat-out spent.

None of that dampened the incredible rush of joy they felt as they landed again at Rahfa. Adrenaline was still coursing through their veins. They had successfully put their teams inside and they jumped out of Lady Godiva and high-fived one another. At four o'clock in the morning they were still in the mess tent, all wound up and debriefing the mission, until at last they went off to their racks to catch a few hours of sleep.

At ten o'clock in the morning, Randy arose to find Jim already awake and well past breakfast. It was a bright clear morning with just a warm breeze blowing from the north, and for the middle of January it felt like June back home as the sun warmed the tents and trailers. The two pilots wandered over to Comms, where for a while they listened to the sotto voce satellite communications from the Strat Recon teams somewhere out there. Everything seemed pretty quiet, but another order to infil or exfil a team could come at any time, and Lady Godiva still needed some fixing. Jim wandered around until he found Bruce Willard.

"Hey, let's go fix that dang light. We might need it tonight."

"Yeah, sure, sir." Willard smirked at Crisafulli. Pilots didn't generally get down and dirty under the helos. Bruce didn't know that Jim loved to tinker with mechanical things, which was precisely how his Blazer had gotten thrown together and made it all the way from King Fahd to KKMC.

"No, really," Jim said as they walked toward Lady Godiva. "I've fixed stuff before. I can help."

"Whatever you say, sir."

It was already getting pretty steamy outside as pilot and crew chief crawled under the bird. Jim had his flight suit unzipped, the sleeves tied around his waist. They managed to unscrew the infrared searchlight and extract it from the damaged housing, but apparently a gear for the slewing mechanism had been sheared off. Having no spare parts for that particular problem, they decided to just remount the light at a fixed angle. Tools, wires and bulbs were strewn all over a canvas tarp when Randy Stephens suddenly came bounding across the tarmac.

"We gotta go! We gotta fucking go! We've got a mission!"

"Oh, shit!" Jim cursed as he looked at the naked bulb in his hands and a fistful of wires. He quickly jammed the bulb into the housing, started setting two screws and then turned it over to the chief, who continued working furiously.

Jim jumped into Lady Godiva, flipped three switches and started up the APU. As the electrical unit whined and spooled up, he got the navigation systems on line and started up the Number One engine. He shimmied into his flight vest and was reaching for Number Two when he turned to look at Chalk One, Miller's bird. The pilots were cranking it, but one of its engines was on fire, pouring smoke and flame from the cowling.

"Holy shit! Lead's on fire!"

Jim grabbed for his helmet, stuffed it on his head and threw his mike switch.

"Lead! Lead! You're on fire! You're on fire! Put it out!"

Miller's crew chiefs and the ground boys were already sprinting for the bird with fire extinguishers and tools. They tore the cowling open and doused the sparks and flames, which roiled up in protest and engulfed them all in smoke. Jim could hear Chalk One's engines shutting down as his heart rate leveled out again. With one bird in the flight team obviously grounded, nobody was going anywhere now. You didn't launch any kind of mission at high noon, and certainly not without a wingman. They were Night Stalkers, not maniacs. It was not going to happen.

Still, they had to be ready. Another bird might be summoned from somewhere to join them. Randy had climbed aboard by now along with Willard, who had cobbled the light together. Diff rolled into the bay and got himself behind his gun, his eyes a little wide after seeing Chalk One burst into flame. Gordy Hopple was already in the back with his medical gear. The pilots looked over the instruments, checked the engine power and discovered they were still a bit low on gas, even after refilling upon their return the night before.

"Let's go get some gas," Jim said. "Just for the hell of it."

They ground taxied over to the fuel truck, which had been outcast to the far end of the strip in the event some lucky Iraqi gunner might blow it up. Their blades were spewing up dust and gravel and they brought it back to idle as the fuelers punched the hoses in. It was like gassing up a car with the engine running—they wanted to "fill to spill." As they sat there waiting, their headsets started to really chatter and they suddenly understood what they were facing. There was a Strat Recon team out there somewhere, very deep and in serious trouble. The SF boys were taking heavy fire and had asked to be extracted, something they rarely did until their mission had been executed. Jim and Randy listened carefully to all the confusing voices, the background roars of jet engines, the calls from fighters flying CAPs overhead. Jim hit his mike and called over to Operations and got Tim Childry, the ops officer at Rahfa.

"Who is it out there, Tim?"

"It's 523. And it doesn't look good."

Jim turned to Randy as his heart started to pound.

"It's Jeff's team," he said. "They're in the shit."

Jeff Simms and his two comrades were indeed in the shit at Quam al Hamza. He and his fellow SF sergeants, Roy Tabron and Ron Torbett, had settled into their hide site just a few hundred meters from Highway 8, at the crest of a craggy hill shaped like a reclining breast. For two days they had nestled inside a deep ditch and camouflaged their position as best they could, while using their field binoculars and night vision scopes to keep an eye on the highway. They had defecated into plastic bags and pissed into water bottles, trying to keep the scent sealed from wandering desert dogs. They could barely move or breathe, as at first daylight they had discovered that their position was virtually in the midst of a checkerboard of farmland, small villages and Bedouin encampments. Shepherds roamed the area all day long, coaxing goats and mules, their bells echoing back from the scruffy hills. On the third morning, a little girl who looked to be no more than seven years old wandered inexorably up toward the hide site while Jeff and his mates cursed under their breaths. She suddenly stopped, staring at something she knew did not belong there, something that hadn't been there before. Perhaps it was the unfamiliar texture of camouflage netting, or a glint of metal, but it was enough.

When prospective special operators of all branches of the services begin their first acceptance trials, they are interviewed by unit psychologists and asked a series of questions designed to root out the potentially unbalanced recruit. One of these questions is fairly universal to these tests: "You are behind the lines in enemy territory on a very important mission. Your hide site is discovered by a local child. Do you take that child prisoner, do you kill her, or do you let her go and hope to survive and accomplish your task?" There really is no "correct" answer to this conundrum, but the way in which operators answer it can be most revealing.

The girl who was staring at Jeff Simms's hide site was close enough to capture, and distant enough from her home that probably no one would hear her scream. Simms was also carrying a sniper rifle and a silencer, which he could have easily used and then buried the body, buying ample time for himself and his comrades to escape when night fell. He did neither. The girl spun on her heel and ran to sound the alarm. It wasn't long before the first truck full of Iraqi militia appeared on Highway 8 and stopped at the bottom of the wide hill. A soldier climbed to the roof of a nearby hut, raised a pair of binoculars and began to sweep the area, until he fixed his vision directly on the hide side and began to shout. At a range of 550 yards, Simms killed him with a shot from his sniper rifle, and then it all started in earnest. The Iraqis dismounted and began a frontal assault. It wasn't careful, it wasn't well executed, but there were many of them. Simms and his two partners began to kill them, firing their M-16s and M-24 sniper rifles, but more and more of them were arriving by the minute. The Americans called for some air cover and a pair of F-16s arrived, making close air support runs and strafing the Iraqis. The pilots told Simms that he'd better get the hell out of there, because they could see that mechanized troops were assembling a few miles down the highway, and that's when Simms had finally called for an exfil.

Lady Godiva was all topped off, but it just wasn't likely that higher headquarters was going to send a Blackhawk into an ambush in broad daylight. Men like Dell Dailey had achieved their positions by making cold, calculated judgments rather than knee-jerk decisions. Losing an entire Blackhawk and its crew in an effort to extract a three-man team from the jaws of death did not make sense. Jim and Randy suspected that any second Tim Childry was going to come up on the comms and say, "Scratch it, put it back on the chocks, you're done."

Jim and Randy looked over their codes and discovered that Simms's team was the deepest one inside Iraq, an hour and a half away. They didn't need to talk it over. Jim called Childry.

"Tell them we're gonna go," he said, meaning the C&C staff. "Tell them we volunteer. Let us go."

Nothing came back. They didn't know that Childry was already fiercely making that argument.

"Let's go, let's go." Randy was pounding his knee with a fist, then he covered up his mike and whispered to Jim, "Let's just *do* it."

This was strictly a no-no, taking off on a mission that hadn't been sanctioned, but Jim nodded as he reached up for the PCLs.

"Okay, let's just fucking do it."

Jim cranked up the RPMs and the big blades above began to really blur. Across the tarmac Rick Dietrich, who had been the SAR man serving on Chalk One, came sprinting through the prop wash hauling his SAR bag, an armful of weapons and bandoliers of ammunition draped around his shoulders like Pancho Villa. He threw himself into the bird as Jim kicked off the APU and then Childry's voice boomed in all their headsets.

"Okay! Go!"

Lady Godiva roared off into a clear blue sky. It was 1:15 in the afternoon. Jim and Randy pulled up their "spider route" on the navigation system. These were a series of waypoints they had preprogrammed into the system, which would lead them in a zigzagging pattern to avoid enemy elements that had the capability to shoot them down. They slipped the bird westward along the border, choosing not to cross at the same positions where Iraqis had shot at them the night before, and they crossed the FLOT at fifteen feet doing 130 knots. It didn't seem fast enough, but given that Lady Godiva was full to the brim with fuel, men and heavy ammunition, she was hauling.

Almost immediately they started taking fire. With their helmets on, 145 decibels of engine noise and the wind storming through the bird, they couldn't hear the weapons below and rarely spotted tracers in the bright sunlight, yet rounds were clipping the bird and they could hear that. For fifty miles they flew onward, checking off waypoints on the spider route: Alpha Two, Alpha Five, Alpha Nine, Bravo Three, until at last they started to pick up Satcom traffic from the target area. For some reason, they couldn't hear Simms, but they suddenly heard Pointer Six, the pilot of an F-16 flying Combat Air Patrol over the area.

"Chalk One, your men are surrounded and under heavy attack."

"Roger, Six."

"You need to fly faster."

Jim and Randy already had Lady Godiva cranked up to the max. She was still hauling a lot of fuel and until some more of that weight burned off, kicking her sides wasn't going to help.

On the ground at Quam al Hamza, Simms, Tabron and Torbett were preparing for their own private Alamo. They were all sniper qualified and fine shots, and they were picking off Iraqi militia and regulars as the enemy troops began to fill up the area, firing up at the hilltop incessantly with AK-47s, RPK machine guns and even shotguns. But the Iraqis were going for flanking maneuvers on both sides, encircling the hide site, and it wouldn't be long. SOCCENT had apologetically informed Simms that they didn't think they could get him an extraction until after dark. He wasn't going to last that long and he knew it. He also had no idea that Jim and Randy were on the way. He and his men were going to just fight it out to the end.

Pointer Six called Jim again.

"Chalk One, I'm out of ammo and running low on fuel. You need to be here *now*."

Jim and Randy were already sucking the guts out of the engines, doing over 140 knots. The twin turbines were screaming and the Turbine Gas Temperature gauges were running from yellow to red. They were flying as fast as they possibly could, and then Pointer Six came on again, the fighter pilot's voice almost a whisper in their headsets.

"Chalk One . . ." He paused. "If you can't be here in ten minutes, don't bother showing up."

Jim and Randy looked at each other. Jeff Simms was going to die. They knew what they had to do.

"Fuck the waypoints," they both said at the same time. They banked the helo, set the nose directly for the final grid position at Quam al Hamza, dropped her down to ten feet, then *five* feet above the ground, and charged. They knew that between that point and Quam al Hamza was an entire Iraqi armored brigade, and according to the map, maybe a full division. It suddenly appeared dead ahead in front of the helo's windshield, an endless sea of main battle tanks, armored personnel carriers, troop trucks and cannons. Hundreds of Iraqis were milling about their vehicles, their heads spinning toward the sound of rotors, ducking in disbelief as she careened just above them, nearly shearing off tank antennas. Jim just grit his teeth and watched the surreal vision splay across his windshield like some nightmare on an Imax screen. And then they were suddenly out of it. He saw the Euphrates River, wide and green, its waters covered with the white specs of darting birds. He pulled Lady Godiva up to fifteen feet to avoid kicking up too much spray, hoping that the squawking flocks wouldn't be sucked into his turbines. The river swept behind them and after that was an expanse of hilly terrain and suddenly a large sand dune. He pitched it up and over the dune, nosed it back down again to five feet, and missed the head of a donkey by mere inches. In the back of the bird the crew chiefs and the SAR men were holding on, white-knuckled. Jim settled on ten feet of altitude, figuring if he didn't calm down he was going to kill somebody.

They were getting very close to Highway 8. They could see it, a thin strip of black running from left to right in the distance. Power lines stretched along the south side of the highway, suspended from high metal stanchions. The target grid they'd been given was on the north side of the lines. The lines were about fifty feet high.

"We're going under them," Jim hissed in his mike, his jaw clenched.

"Roger," Randy said. "Do it."

Then Jim suddenly saw a second set of wires, suspended just below the higher, thicker lines.

"Negative! Negative!" he spat. "We're going over!"

Diff and Willard spread their feet wide apart and half-squatted, their fingers clasped around the trigger grips of their miniguns. Hopple and Dietrich crashed down onto the aft bench and curled their gloves around the knee spars in death grips. Jim pitched the helo's nose up and aimed straight for one of the stanchions, so he could clearly see the power lines, and at sixty feet he nosed it over the iron peak. Willard suddenly spotted a bright flash on the far side of the bird.

"Missile! Missile!" he yelled into his mike. "They're shootin' at us!"

Jim didn't say anything as he rolled the bird hard to the right and dove for the road, but Randy immediately started pounding the Chaff button, spraying the sky with shards of tinsel that would hopefully confuse the oncoming warhead. Jim threw her into a full evasive maneuver, hauling aft cyclic and rolling Lady Godiva *back up* and over the stanchion again, like a frigate zigzagging as a torpedo hisses toward it.

"No! No!" Willard came back on. "It's a flare!"

A *flare*.

It was Simms.

"Where the hell is it?" Jim yelled. Now he was on the *wrong* side of the road, so once again he pulled pitch and arced the bird up and over a second stanchion. He pitched it back down and pulled it back to 135 as he screamed down the highway, his wheels nearly furrowing the tarmac, craning his neck and searching for Simms. "I don't see the team. I don't see them!"

"Twelve o'clock!" Diff shouted in frustration.

Jim was going too fast He had to be in a position to land so he applied more aft cyclic and down-clicked, but he still couldn't spot anything.

"Where the *hell* are they?"

"One o'clock!"

"Two!" Randy yelled as he jabbed a finger past Jim's face.

Jim looked out his right window and there was Simms, standing atop a berm and waving an orange VS 17 panel. Jim zoomed right by him doing eighty knots. Now he could plainly see gunfire flashes and dirt kicking up everywhere. He hauled the helo around into a hard right bank, kicking left rudder pedal, making the tail rotor spin the airplane like a weather vane as he doubled back and slammed it into a landing right atop the berm. The tips of the rotor blades were spinning just above the ditch where Simms and his team had been hiding, and the three men came sprinting toward the Blackhawk from thirty feet away. They were hauling ass, dragging their rucks and their weapons. Simms hadn't been able to get the Satcom antenna off the transceiver so he was pulling it along and it just popped off and fell into the dirt.

I wonder if he signed for that, Crisafulli thought as Simms dove into the aircraft with Tabron and Torbett hot on his heels.

Bullets were raking through Lady Godiva. The men could feel them snapping into the rotor blades above and hear them piercing her skin. Glass shards flew through the cockpit as rounds shot up the console and blew the jammer off the aircraft. Jim and Randy could hear their crew chief's miniguns firing behind them at full rate, screaming like giant buzz saws. Jim looked over his left shoulder and saw Iraqi soldiers charging at them from the tail, so close they were nearly under the rotor system. Bruce Willard tore them apart with his gun, but more were coming up the hill, and Gordy Hopple jumped from the helo and started dropping them with his rifle at point-blank range.

On the right side an Iraqi suddenly appeared just meters from Jim's door. The window on Diff's side split into spider cracks and exploded in shards of Plexi. Diff swung his minigun and blew the man apart. Amazingly, a stream of bullets ripped through the grenade rack on the bulkhead but nothing detonated as they wanged through the fuselage, past Diff's forehead and out Randy's window. Rick Dietrich was firing his rifle one-handed as he dragged Tabron and Torbett into the bay. They were all aboard now, but Crisafulli wasn't lifting off.

"We gotta go!" everyone was yelling at once as they fired their weapons in every possible direction outside the helo. "We gotta go!"

Jim spun to Randy. "Where's the other three guys?"

"*What* other three?"

Jim didn't know that Simms had been inserted with only two other men. He hadn't infilled 523, so he somehow thought that a complement of *six* men had been together in that position, and he wasn't leaving without all of them.

"I counted them," he yelled back at Randy above the roar of gunfire. "There's only three on board."

"That's it! That's all!"

"Where's the others? I'm not leaving."

"There's only *three*, Jim! We gotta fucking *go*!"

Jim was finally convinced. He pulled pitch and the bird rose, her nose dipped and tail up as the crew chiefs hammered away at Iraqis still charging insanely up the hill. The SAR men and Simms and his teams were emptying their clips at a complete circle of muzzle flashes below, their spent shells spinning through the bird's interior, bouncing off the bulkheads like balls in a lottery globe. Jim turned for the Euphrates. He glanced back over his right shoulder and saw at least seventy-five shredded corpses laid out around the LZ like the petals of a bloody flower.

As they roared away, people were still shooting up at them madly from below. Jim felt something grip and shake his shoulder like a bear bite. It was Simms's fingers digging into his skin and jerking him back and forth as the sergeant shouted triumphantly, "All right! All right!" Simms's violent jerking was making Jim pitch the bird up and down, and at no altitude and top speed he couldn't fly, so he told Randy to take over. Someone was yelling into his ear on Satcom, asking if ODA 523 had survived. Jim turned and yelled back to Simms, "Are you guys okay?"

Simms looked around. Tabron and Torbett were grinning from ear to ear. Hopple and Dietrich were squatting, still popping off rounds at anything that glinted from below. Diff and Willard were still weapons tight, their eyes squinting over their miniguns as sweat streamed from their helmets and they kept on firing. No one had been hit. Not one of them. Simms looked back at Jim and spread his feet wide on the deck as the wind streamed through the open doors. He pounded his fists on his chest and howled like Tarzan.

Jim turned away and pressed his mike button.

"This is Chalk One." He could barely get the words out. "The team's okay. . . ."

ON THE WAY back to Rahfa, they decided to skip flying back over the Iraqi armor division. A Satcom call came through, asking them if they could reroute and pick up another Strat Recon team that was also in trouble. Jim and Randy wanted to go, but Lady Godiva's fuel tanks had taken some rounds and she was slowly bleeding out. Jim ran some quick numbers on the E6B computer and turned to Randy.

"I think we'd better count our blessings and get the hell out of here. We're not gonna make it there and back."

"Roger that," Randy said. They both prayed that another flight team would be able to reach those men.

They turned to the south, flying as low and as fast as they could. As they neared the border a small village appeared up ahead. A villager tilling the earth near his hut looked up and waved at them. Jim and Randy both waved back, then glanced at each other. Less than an hour before, they had killed everyone who raised his face to the sky.

Lady Godiva limped back into Rahfa and settled into the dust. When the men climbed out from the helo, they realized just how incredibly strong she was. The failing sunlight was streaming through shotgun blasts and large-ball ammo holes in the rotor blades. The flight controls were all shot up. The 144, a large glass countermeasures housing that looked like a disco ball, was completely shorn off the helo. Aviation gas dripped from the pierced tanks.

Jeff Simms and Jim stood on the tarmac for a long moment, looking at the Blackhawk, saying nothing. Simms turned and looked down at his pilot, slowly shaking his head as Tabron and Torbett joined them.

"We'd fly with you anytime, Crisafulli," Simms said hoarsely.

"Anyhow," Tabron said.

"Anywhere," Torbett said.

Jim didn't trust himself to speak. He turned to walk toward the mess tent and the SF men followed. The sun was just going down. . . .

SOME MONTHS after the war, Jim and Randy were asked to testify before Congress and the Senate Armed Forces subcommittee. It was not going to be an investigation or a reproach. The congressmen wanted to hear firsthand about one of the most successful and courageous missions of Desert Storm. John Glenn wanted to shake Jim's hand, and being that Glenn was one of Jim's boyhood heroes, he was honored by the former astronaut's kind words. It was clear that Jim and Randy, their crew and all the SF men who had nearly died together at Quam al Hamza, were going to be awarded many commendations and medals as well. Within the Special Forces community, their story would become legend.

But none of that mattered very much to Jim Crisafulli.

His father was very proud of him.

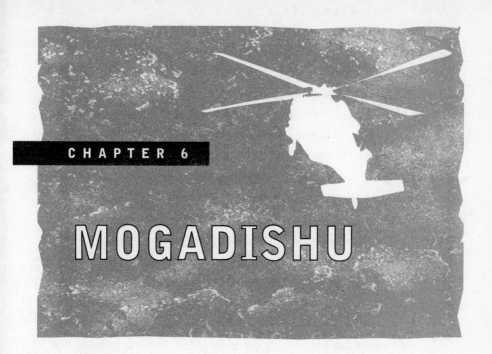

CHAPTER 6

MOGADISHU

SOMALIA
OCTOBER 1993

CHIEF WARRANT OFFICER 4 Karl Maier was taking fire, lots of fire.

It was coming at him from all directions: rooftops, street corners, broken windows covered with rusty grates and shanty shacks of broken cement and corrugated steel. He was sitting in his Little Bird, all alone in the middle of a street strewn with garbage. Dry dust and umber dirt were billowing through the air, torn newspapers being sucked up into his rotors and shredded into confetti. Behind him and somewhere around a corner, Cliff Wolcott and Donovan Briley's Blackhawk was down in the street. No one knew if the pilots or their crew or the Delta shooters who'd been aboard were still alive. But it didn't matter what their status was; someone had to get them out of there. Nobody in Task Force Ranger was leaving anyone behind, dead or alive. The rotors above Karl's head were still whipping at full speed and he had one foot out the left-hand door, both of his gloved hands gripping his MP-5 as he leaned out and shot back at every darting head and gun barrel that flashed in front of his windshield. He had the thing on full auto and he was going through an awful lot of ammunition. Someone from the air mission commander's bird was yelling in his ears to get the hell out of there, but he didn't know where his partner was. There was no point in answering. He wasn't leaving.

No way we're getting out of this one alive. . . .

Karl moved the submachine gun's selector to semiauto. Maybe he would actually *hit* something if he stopped spraying it like a garden hose. He'd always thought the German weapon was compact and cool, but now he was cursing it because it just didn't pack the punch he needed. A Somali militiaman suddenly darted out from the left corner of the intersection dead ahead, brandishing a gleaming AK-47. The man raised his weapon, its barrel suddenly looking as huge as a cannon maw, but this time Karl actually aimed before firing. The man collapsed in a heap, his gun clattering to the pockmarked street. Another man instantly darted out from a doorway, racing to pick up the precious AK. Karl fired two rounds and dropped him, too. Then, unbelievably, two more militiamen appeared in quick succession, and with just a few more rounds Karl piled them all up on top of one another.

That's a little better . . . but this 9mm peashooter still sucks. . . .

Sweat was running in rivulets from beneath his helmet and into his eyes. He reached up and swiped it away. How long had they been on the ground now? Five minutes? Ten? It seemed like a fucking hour already. For just a moment, he almost grinned as he mentally shook his head, remembering in an instant flashback his very first experience under fire. It had seemed back then that the whole world was exploding around him, but it was nothing like this. Nothing like this at all . . .

IT WAS PANAMA, in the first hour of December 20, 1989. Karl and his copilot, Captain Westphal, had taken off from Howard Air Force base in a flight of two Little Bird lifts, carrying an Air Force Combat Controller Team as their customers. They were headed for Torrijos-Tocumen airport and the timing had to be split second; put their CCTs on the ground so they could set up their radio beacon before the first C-141s roared overhead to drop their Rangers. Karl and West-phal banked the Little Bird to the south and headed out over the water toward the airfield. They were stunned to see Panama City suddenly erupting with tracer fire from the site of the *Comandancia*. It seemed as if all the Little Bird lifts and gunships had taken off virtually at the same time, yet the assault on Modelo Prison was already in full swing. There was so much fire spraying up that even at their range of a mile and half away and well over the water, rounds were zipping through their flight. Karl had been slated to participate in the Modelo mission, but was bumped when another, senior pilot took his seat. He had been pissed off and frustrated, swearing that if the opportunity ever came up, he'd never bump a younger pilot from a real world mission. Now, his regret at having missed the Kurt Muse thing waned as he saw what was going on over there and the collateral fire from it spit through the night air. He thought about Major Bowman and Bob Fladry, and his two close friends J. J. Holmes and Kelly McDougall.

Those guys are really earning their money. . . .

The flight to Torrijos-Tocumen was easy. The airfield looked quiet, nothing much moving, though that didn't keep Karl's palms dry. He thought of himself as a "wimp," though no one who knew him would have dared to characterize him that way. He was tall, muscular and had short brown hair with tips of grey and machine-gunner green eyes. He had an easygoing, self-deprecating nature about him, but you could be sure that if you did anything unprofessional under his tutelage, or dared to cross the lines of honesty or integrity, you'd hear about it from Karl. Even before his baptism by fire, everyone who worked and flew with him knew how he'd perform. As for Karl, he was actually never sure if he was going to do something right or well until after it was over. When he executed flying tasks in an exemplary manner, he sloughed off the compliments with shrugs and references to luck. So far on this mission, luck had been with him. He set down the bird in the correct position and let the CCTs hop off with their beacon. Then he spotted a passenger aircraft starting to taxi away from one of the civilian terminal gates.

"Uhh, that's not good," Karl said to Westphal as they hovered above the tarmac. "Somebody better call that guy and tell him he's about to take off into a sky full of paratroopers."

Even as he spoke, somebody from one of the other Little Birds was doing just that, raising the airliner pilot on the airport frequency. The big jet was a Panamanian carrier, but the pilot was an American and he had a full load of passengers.

"Is something going on?" the civilian pilot asked as he slowly rolled his plane to a stop.

"Hell, yes," Karl's flight lead answered. "You need to park that thing, turn it off and get the hell out of there!"

The Night Stalkers grinned. None of them had ever seen a passenger aircraft make such a hurried U-turn, pull up to a gate and unload like there was a fire on board.

With the CCTs on the ground, Karl and Westphal, followed by their wingmen, swung back out over the water to await a callback from the air force commandos. After the Rangers jumped, the Night Stalkers would have to go back into the airfield and move the combat controllers and their beacon to the other side of Torrijos-Tocumen, so the 82nd Airborne's jump planes could home in and put their paratroopers on the correct LZ. It didn't take long for the Rangers to hit the ground and move into action, and Karl had barely been in a holding pattern for a few minutes when he turned the Little Bird back for the second leg of his mission.

This time, it was as if he were flying toward an altogether different target. The calm and ordered civilian airport facility of just minutes before had instantly turned to chaos. The passive, steamy night had

suddenly become a sparking, thunderous day. All across the long tarmac, explosions were bursting up and flaring in his NVGs. Small-arms
fire crackled and the small figures of Rangers laden with heavy bur-
dens of combat gear rushed and waddled in leapfrogging squads, tracers spitting from their gun barrels as they charged toward PDF
positions. Karl pushed the Little Bird low and fast, but as he crossed
the outermost perimeter of the airport, his heart leaped into his throat.
Something huge and dark billowed up right in front of him from a
swath of elephant grass, and he pulled up just in time to avoid having
his helo sucked down into a crash. There were parachutes everywhere,
hundreds of them, surging and flapping like giant, punctured bal-
loons. There hadn't been a mass airborne drop of U.S. Forces in nearly
twenty years, and certainly no Night Stalkers had ever had to dart and
swoop like this between heavy loads descending from the sky and
deadly bouquets of cargo and personnel chutes. It was scary as hell,
and for a moment he pictured his buddies shaking their heads over his
grave.

Poor ol' Karl. Killed by nylon . . .

He spotted the CCTs waving a strobe at him. They weren't using
infrared, just a regular bubble-top strobe light; in the midst of a massive airborne assault and firefight, stealth was no longer a requisite. He
settled the helo down as the three air force men climbed aboard with
their radio beacon, and then he spun the bird toward the next target
coordinates across the massive field and started to hustle over there
just above the ground.

Off to his left, a .50 caliber machine gun suddenly opened up on
him. It was only two hundred meters away and mounted on the back
of a Chevy Blazer, which had pulled up in front of a PDF guard shack.
The Panamanian gunner couldn't clearly discern the black helo as it
cruised by, but he was ranging in on the engine sound, his heavy tracers starting to trail closer and closer to Karl's tail. Karl hit his transmit
button and called out to Leslie "Butch" Cassady, one of the Little Bird

gun pilots flying around there somewhere in support. Cassady had the reputation of being able to knock a beer can off a birdhouse with his minigun, while leaving the birdhouse intact.

"Hey, Butch. I've got a fifty chasing my ass over here," Karl said as calmly as he could. "You guys need to *do* something."

"Got it," Butch answered.

Karl couldn't alter his flight path. There was too much going on all over the target area and he'd be risking a midair or some other kind of catastrophe if he strayed. He had to get his guys into their next LZ and do it soon, before the 82nd's aircraft started roaring in overhead. The heavy tracers were lancing out closer to his tail and he just gripped his controls and felt his entire body go tight as he flew the damned thing and hoped Butch would show up *soon.*

He craned his neck around for a moment and spotted Cassady's bird banking in hard and fast out of the darkness. Butch lined up the grease-pencil mark on his windshield with the Panamanian machine gunner in the back of the Blazer, but when he squeezed the trigger on the minigun, it jammed. Instantly, he switched to rockets and let one loose. The flaming projectile lanced from the bird, flew across the tarmac, pierced right through the chest of the Panamanian gunner, kept on going and detonated inside the guard shack behind him.

Karl's eyes bugged. It was an impossible shot. He couldn't believe it, and he was oh so grateful. He got on the comms.

"Butch, I don't know how you did that, but you just saved my ass."

"Roger. Anytime."

The rest of that night continued without letup. All the Little Birds, both lifts and guns, flew scores of missions, going out to infil or exfil customers, coming back to a FARP for a hot rearm and refuel, receiving new orders and flying again. Karl flew for seventeen hours straight, until his body finally couldn't take it anymore and he just had to sleep. He finally set down at Howard on the evening of the twentieth, fairly crawled into the massive hangar, found an empty cot and crashed.

When he finally awoke, it was to the sound of an inadvertent gunshot inside the hangar. There were hundreds of men bedded down cot to cot—customers and pilots and crews all together; with all those loaded weapons, fatigue and adrenaline, someone was bound to have an AD—Accidental Discharge. Among the most elite units there were ironclad rules about such things. If a Delta boy or a SEAL accidentally fired his weapon in a rear area, he would be summarily dismissed from his unit. It didn't matter how long he had been there or how many acts of heroism he had performed under fire; as a professional shooter he was expected to be in complete control of his weapon at all times, and such errors just weren't tolerated. Karl witnessed two incidents of ADs by such men in the hangar; no one was hurt, but those unfortunate souls were soon packing their gear and on the next plane out. On the other hand, the Night Stalkers, while certainly regarding such incidents as grave, didn't hold their pilots and crews to such a cruel standard. One of the 160th's F Company officers also had an AD that night in the hangar, firing a round from his MP-5 into his own sleeping bag. Thereafter, every time the officer entered the hangar, Night Stalkers would toss their sleeping bags into the air and yell, "Pull!" A mountain of sleeping bags were piled up on the floor in the Night Stalker section and a sign was mounted: "Empty Your Weapons Here!" The officer took it all in stride, and he never had another AD.

There were some hard losses in Panama for the unit, but Karl wasn't the sort to dwell on them. He was a good-humored fatalist, knowing that in his business it was only a matter of fate and fortune. You could mourn a man who'd spent his life doing something he hated, and then died unceremoniously and essentially unhappy. But it was easier to grieve over someone who'd loved his work and knew the risks. They weren't social workers and they all expected to die on the job at some point, while flying low, fast and hard.

The rest of the operation never reached the fever pitch of that first night. There were lots of "Hunt for Elvis" missions, all of which came up empty. Karl, as was his wont, always remembered the "lighter" moments, although what was light to him might have been somber to the average civilian. After another mission to Colon with the SEALs, during which they again failed to snatch up any of Noriega's henchmen, customers and pilots took a break along the banks of the wide river mouth up north. From across the waters, Panamanian riflemen openly fired at them, but the range was too great and their bullets fell and skipped across the water. It was annoying, however, to the SEALs, who didn't appreciate being fired upon, no matter how ineffectively. A SEAL sniper with a .50-caliber rifle came down to the shore and lay down on a small rise, peering through his powerful scope for a full ten minutes. Suddenly, his "cannon" boomed once and across the way, a PDF gunman twitched and collapsed. The fallen man's mates started scurrying around in a panic, wondering where the shot had come from. The SEAL stood fully upright, holding his rifle over his head and pointing at it. The Panamanians disappeared and never came back.

Karl returned to the States in the early days of 1990, having just experienced his first real world operation after spending nearly fifteen years in the army. As a nineteen-year-old California kid in 1975, he had joined up primarily to get away from his small-town life and "see something." While his father had been a veteran of the Korean War, he hadn't heard a lot of thrilling war stories that might have led him down this path, yet perhaps he was unaware that such influences often skip a generation. Karl's grandfather had been a German aviator, fighting for the Kaiser during World War I. He had emigrated to the United States after that war, and when Karl was small he often heard stories about the early days of aerial combat, colorfully illustrated by his grandfather's thick Prussian accent. Flying as an aerial scout and radioman, the elder Maier had been shot down by British and American pilots on three separate occasions, yet it would only be much later in his life that Karl would consider the influence those tales had had on his choices.

In 1975, the army was hardly the place to be for a bright young man who had graduated from high school before any of his classmates. He really didn't know anything about the military, was unfamiliar with the

Military Occupational Specialties he might choose from and wound up being a military policeman. From there, he volunteered for jump school and was sent to the 82nd Airborne Division at Fort Bragg. The war in Vietnam was still a festering wound in the army's psyche. The draft had been terminated and it seemed to Karl that the only guys showing up in the paratroop battalions were those who were troublemakers back home and had been told by judges, "It's either the army, or jail." These guys, who broke into 7-Elevens and hot-wired cars, were risk-takers at heart, so they all seemed to volunteer for the 82nd, and Karl was stuck with them. So many of them were constantly strung out on something that his battalion earned the dubious moniker "the Jumpin' Junkies." The only good thing Karl got from the experience was his wife, another soldier in his airborne MP company. He soon gave it up and got out.

After a couple of years of civilian life and an economy that made it tough for a kid without a college degree to hold his own, Karl started thinking about getting back in. He remembered jumping out of Hueys at Bragg, and how he had always thought that those army pilots "had it made." Curiously, when he reapplied to the army and stressed his desire to fly, his prior record as a paratrooper had no bearing at all. There were sixteen other civilians applying for a single flight school slot from his civilian district, but as luck would have it, the three-man selection board was comprised of airborne officers. They weren't much impressed with Karl's jump wings, but when they heard that his *wife* was also an ex-paratrooper, they said, "Okay, you're in."

Karl showed up at Fort Rucker in March 1983. Halfway through that year of flight school, the invasion of Grenada went down and he and his fellow flight students watched it on TV. No one had any idea that the army pilots flying all those missions were part of a classified organization called the Night Stalkers. They didn't even know that such a unit existed. After graduation, Karl went to the First of the Seventeenth Air Cavalry at Fort Bragg, flying OH-58 Scouts for three and a half years. At the time, NVGs were being fielded in conventional units for the first time. Most of the older pilots weren't comfortable with the clumsy equipment, but Karl seemed to manage the strange night goggles without a fuss, so whenever a night mission came up, he was the one they sent out. He racked up hundreds of hours under goggles, and by 1987 his phone started to ring. Two of his instructor pilot mentors from the Cav, J. J. Holmes and Terry Pena, had already made the move over to the 160th, and they kept calling Karl at Fort Bragg and nagging him to come down to Campbell to try out. He already had twelve hundred hours in OH-58s and nearly four hundred hours under goggles, traits that were very attractive to the Night Stalker recruiters at the time.

Karl was totally stunned when he was accepted into the 160th. During the assessment, the only thing he did well was navigate to his targets and hit them plus or minus thirty seconds. By his estimation, he had screwed up everything else. He thought his performance on the written exams and briefs was sorry-assed, and when they took him out for his PT test and a run around Fryar Stadium in one-hundred-degree heat, he decided to pace himself, rather than run flat out. Other candidates were sprinting by him, taking a break to vomit, and sprinting again. Karl just jogged. The run was halted after two miles and Karl made the standard time requirement, but he certainly hadn't broken any records. When he finally stood before the Assessment Board, which at the time was located in a sun-baked trailer on post, the officers ripped him up.

"Your record shows that you usually max your PT test, Maier," one of the Night Stalker officers said. "Why the hell did you candy-ass this one?"

"Well, sir, I didn't know how long it was gonna be. Had to conserve energy."

"Right. Get outside and wait."

Karl stood outside in the summer heat in his Class A's, sweating for nearly half an hour, fully confident that he'd be on the next flight back to Fort Bragg. He could hear the officers inside laughing as they discussed his unusual demeanor. Then they called him back in.

Lieutenant Colonel Bob Codney took point, and he just reamed Karl up and down. He told Karl that he needed to get his act together, and his life as well. He challenged every decision Karl had ever made in the army, and then he called him a straight-out liar. Codney said there was no reason for a unit like the 160th to consider taking on such a lazy, good-for-nothing, sacrilegious, questionably talented pilot. It took a lot to get Karl's temper to the boiling point, but Codney's abrasive accusations were balling his fists. He had just about decided to coldcock the son of a bitch when Codney grinned, stuck out his hand and said, "Welcome aboard."

Karl stumbled back out into the sunlight, shaking his head and hardly believing that he'd just been accepted into the most elite aviation unit in the army.

This is a weird bunch of dudes. . . .

Indeed his first few months as a Night Stalker were stranger than he'd expected. Until you made it to the level of FMQ—Fully Mission Qualified—you were considered a nonentity and barely spoken to by any of the other pilots. He wasn't allowed to move his family or his belongings down to Fort Campbell, since new pilots had sometimes failed the rigorous initial training and there was no point in uprooting them for nothing. They wouldn't even give him a locker, so basically he worked out of the trunk of his car.

Socially, he remained on "probation," while professionally, he received the most intense and dedicated training he had ever seen. It was 1987 and the Night Stalkers were still operating over in the Persian Gulf on Prime Chance. Pilots were getting sick of the rotations, and A Company needed to get some new guys into the slots as quickly as possible. The 160th was still relatively small and barely seven years in existence. Many of the original pilots had already been older veterans when they came aboard at the beginning, so they were starting to move on to less demanding duties as their careers drew to a close. Yet the 160th's standards were incredibly high, so Karl's informal Green Platoon consisted only of himself, Kelly McDougall and Dan Brown.

Alpha Company's instructor pilots needed to get the trio up to speed as quickly as possible, so nothing was spared in their training regimen. In that respect, they weren't scorned like freshman plebes, but enjoyed the investment of a lot of time and effort in their skills. Within six months, all three men had racked up more than two hundred hours of over-water training time. By the seventh month, they were all Fully Mission Qualified. As it turned out, the 160th's participation in Prime Chance ended just as Karl was ready to deploy. Missing the action didn't faze him much, because he was certain that eventually the Night Stalkers would be out there "doing something" again. He was finally accepted into the fold and the entire atmosphere around him changed. He was a full-fledged Night Stalker, and he brought his wife and two small boys down from Fort Bragg to set up shop in a military community unlike most others. The Night Stalker families were as rare a breed as the pilots and crews. No matter where you were, or for how long, someone was always going to be looking after them, and Karl liked that. It matched his own values, which were rarely expressed but ironclad.

It was almost two years after his formal acceptance into the unit when Operation Just Cause finally went down. Karl had spent a lot of training time down in Panama in preparation for operations, yet when the balloon went up he was back at Fort Campbell and almost didn't make it. The ice storms that weekend were so heavy that many of the C-5s couldn't lift off. The air force commander of Karl's flight of C-5s, aboard which the Little Birds were already folded up and ready to deploy, was so frustrated that he joined the ground crews on the massive jet wings and got on his hands and knees, scraping off ice. At last they were airborne and made it down to Howard just in time to offload, build the birds back up, get one more briefing and take off for combat.

When Panama was over, Karl and A Company returned to the

States and a routine of intense training with their customers, preparing for the next emergency that would require their particular skills. There were lots of "almosts," but nothing as hairy as what he'd been through in Central America. A hostage-rescue mission to San Salvador was called off at the very last minute, because the bad guys were somehow tipped off that America's Best were en route to give them the fight of their lives; they surrendered. In 1991 when Desert Shield turned into Desert Storm, Karl and some of his mates were left behind with the "bullet": the emergency package of helos that had to be ready if a crisis suddenly popped up somewhere else in the world. He suddenly found himself with a Night Stalker role no one had ever mentioned to him: car mechanic, babysitter and child disciplinarian. Karl was one of the only men left behind on post, and all of the other pilots' wives came to him for help with household chores they couldn't manage. It seemed as if they almost resented him for being around all the time while their husbands were at war, yet they also loved the fact that he was there. He changed tires and diapers, shopped for women who had their hands full and warned their kids to do their homework and behave. He was more than a little awkward when it came to dealing with tearful wives and clinging kids, but he did the best he could. He figured if he'd ever deserve a medal for anything, it was for that war at home.

In the summer of 1993, the Night Stalkers and their customers began to prepare for a real world mission that no other force, American or foreign, had been able to accomplish. For more than a year, U.S. Special Forces, Navy SEALs and Marines had been working in conjunction with United Nations Forces in an attempt to bring relief and order to the war-torn and famine-ravaged African state of Somalia. Despite the fact that more than three hundred thousand Somalis had already succumbed to pestilence, hunger and thirst, battling warlords were still frustrating the efforts of the international community to bring relief to their starving nation. The worst of the culprits, Mohamed Farrah Aidid, had organized his Somali National Alliance into a band of

vicious thugs whose only true thirst was for power. The SNA was com-
mandeering U.N. supply convoys, controlling distribution to only
those who supported their vision of a Somali dictatorship and killing
all who opposed them. In June, Aidid's gunmen had ambushed and
slaughtered more than two dozen Pakistani soldiers of UNOSOM—
United Nations Operations Somalia. In response, American AC-130
gunships had pounded SNA positions and driven Aidid underground.
Yet even from his hidden nest of vipers, Aidid was still managing to ter-
rorize the capital of Mogadishu and assault U.S. forces with deadly effect. The result would be the deployment of a JSOTF—Joint Special
Operations Task Force—composed of U.S. Army Rangers, Special
Forces, Air Force Special Tactics personnel, Navy SEALs, Delta, and
the Night Stalkers. Task Force Ranger's mission would be the capture
of Mohamed Farrah Aidid and all his henchmen, thereby opening a
window for more moderate and socially conscious elements to step in
and heal the festering wounds that had driven Somalia to the brink of
chaos. When this Quick Reaction Force received its green light from
the U.S. secretary of defense, it adopted a mission moniker decidedly
more deadly than *Restore Hope*. "Gothic Serpent" would be the
checkmate mission to Somalia, one that would put an end to this
game of cruel despots and pawns. It was also the mission that would
hurl the Night Stalkers into a harsh glare of publicity and pain.

For the Night Stalkers, Gothic Serpent was exactly the sort of operation their early architects had envisioned. It would involve counterterror and counterinsurgency, precision and pinpoint targeting, and
the capture of deadly enemy insurgents in lightning raids performed
with the best on the menu of customers. The area of operations was
distant and the environment harsh, and planning would have to be
precise, the missions perfectly coordinated. With the exception of the
Chinooks, which due to their large "footprints" wouldn't be able to
effectively operate in the narrow alleyways and crumbling streets of
Mogadishu, every Blackhawk and Little Bird configuration would participate: Lifts, Guns, Assaults and DAPs. All the armament and naviga-

tion systems that had been perfected over the years would be brought to bear. It was as if a team of hard-training football players was finally being invited to the big leagues to compete. Everything they had ever trained for or learned or contingency-planned would be utilized in the "Mog."

The only thing the Night Stalkers and the task force couldn't plan for, and could not have envisioned, was the ability of Aidid's militiamen to so quickly learn the rules of the game, and to improvise and adapt to this new kind of special warfare that was about to arrive from the skies. The Americans were coming with multimillion-dollar flying machines, machine guns, rockets, cannons and armored warriors. But the Somalis already had an incomparable intimacy with death; and they had RPGs.

By the third of October, the Night Stalkers had executed six Gothic Serpent missions in Mogadishu without a loss. Task Force Ranger had settled into its fenced-in compound at the international airport, where Rangers, SEALs, Delta, Air Force CCTs, 160th pilots, medics and crews lived together, planned together, flew off on missions and returned victorious. They had developed a mission "template," which made it relatively easy to respond to fresh intelligence from paid informants inside the sprawling city. A task force TOC was set up in an old crumbling structure at the airport, replete with monitors and live feeds from P-3 Orions constantly in the air overhead. A hard-charging major general named Bill Garrison was running the show, and he seemed to be everywhere, all the time, night and day. If the general slept at all, there were no witnesses to his respites, and his determination to capture Aidid and his cohorts imbued the task force with an ambition that overcame the tough conditions, the long distance from families and home, and the oppressive heat. In most military organizations holding ready on the front lines of a small war, there would be long periods of mundane waiting between the calls for combat. But in Garrison's organization, if you weren't fighting, you were training. This was nothing unusual for the Night Stalkers, who never kicked back anyway between real world operations. If there was no "reason" to fly, they flew regardless, honing assault and gunnery skills.

The "template" consisted of a structured assault plan, whereby more than twenty aircraft would take off simultaneously for a mission downtown. In the lead were the Little Bird guns, followed by the Little Bird assault helos laden with Delta operators, the point men for any "snatch." Blackhawks were next in the formation, carrying Rangers to be inserted into blocking positions so that none of the wanted members of Aidid's militia could "leak" from the target area, and also to prevent enemy reinforcements from interfering with Delta's activities at the epicenter of the action. More Blackhawks flew cover with shooters and CSAR personnel aboard, and the air mission commander's UH-60 would circle high above and manage the missions. Every one of those six missions went off without a hitch, and all of them took place at night.

By this time, Karl's performance had elevated him to a position of heavy responsibility: flight lead of A Company's Little Bird lifts. There were other pilots of higher rank and more time-in-grade within the company, but apparently someone up above Karl had decided that the quiet Californian had the right stuff to lead men in a challenging combat environment. He didn't fully appreciate the breadth of that compliment. The four assault birds, with Karl in the lead, were the critical players on every mission. It was up to Karl to plot a course to the target, determining a route in accordance with prevailing winds, and set his operators down virtually at the enemy's front door. The rest of the formation depended on him to know what he was doing, and he tried very hard not to think about that.

At the time, the high-tech navigation equipment that would eventually replace maps and compasses had not yet been perfected. The Little Birds had just received brand-new GPS systems in their cockpits, three-thousand-dollar toys that didn't work. Eventually, a warrant officer named Tommy Dorris would figure out that the airfield's radar system was using the same frequency as the GPS's and causing computer chip confusion that told the pilots they were somewhere in New England, rather than Africa. Karl just shut the thing off and resorted to "stubby pencil mode," grateful that he'd paid attention in his high school math classes. When a mission was about to go down, the intel guys would show up with an aerial photograph of the target area, including latitude and longitude lines. Karl would pick his route to the target, select some checkpoints en route, whip out his Hewlett-Packard HP95 (not army issue), punch in the coordinates and write out instructions for everyone else on a TDH—Time/Distance/Heading card. Someone would copy the TDH for distribution, while Karl scratched his head and hoped his primitive calculations were correct. They always were, and he never once failed to get the task force on time and on target. At thirty-six, his hair was starting to go gray and he could no longer run as fast as the young armament dogs, but he was exactly at that point between the spring of youth and the stage where too much travel and work takes its toll. He would never be better than this, and other pilots aspired to his skills and his character.

Perhaps on that Sunday morning, the members of Task Force Ranger were trying to ignore the encroaching signs that things were changing for the worse in their AO. But back at Fort Campbell, Randy Cochran was greatly disturbed by the reports coming in of mounting casualties and losses of equipment by conventional forces in Somalia. Randy had left the 160th to become the commander of the Ninth Battalion, 101st Aviation Regiment. On September 25, just a week prior to Gothic Serpent's seventh mission, one of Randy's Blackhawks had been brought down in Mogadishu by an RPG. The Blackhawk, piloted by CW2 Granville "Dale" Shrader, had been assigned the "Eyes Over Mogadishu" mission, flying at only a hundred feet and a hundred knots, to spot and kill Somali mortarmen who were constantly raining shells on the airport. Shrader's bird had been hit square in the fuel cells by the rocket and the entire fuselage was engulfed in flames. Both engines failed, yet somehow the pilot had managed to auto-rotate the bird into a landing in the middle of the city. Both he and his copilot had sustained terrible burns while trying to extricate the crew, three of whom were killed in the crash, and then Shrader fought off repeated Somali attacks with only his pistol until at last a U.N. rescue convoy arrived. Randy would later put Shrader in for the Silver Star.

Early on the morning of October 3, another of Randy's Blackhawks spotted a Humvee overturned on the streets below near the Olympic Hotel, which was shortly to become the target of Task Force Rangers' next mission. The pilots set the aircraft down to discover a dead Somali interpreter in the wreckage, three marines huddled nearby and a fourth still trapped under the upended hulk. The Humvee had been ambushed by a command-detonated roadside bomb, and a mob of armed Somalis was quickly approaching to finish off the survivors, firing their AK-47s and warbling an eerie war cry as they marched. As the Blackhawk repositioned itself between the marines and the Somalis, its crew returned fire while the copilot, First Lieutenant Jeff Reidel, who would later assess for the Night Stalkers and be assigned to the Third Battalion, jumped from the helo with his M-16. Reidel scrounged around in the middle of the firefight for a long piece of lumber, and then helped the marines pry the Humvee wreck up high enough to extract the dead Somali and their injured comrade. The Blackhawk crew and their injured passengers barely made it out and alive, and Reidel would later receive the Bronze Star with "V" device for valor.

Such incidents of foreboding had certainly been occurring more frequently downtown, but Karl and his task force comrades could only try to glean tactical lessons from the incidents and press on. On that particular Sunday, most of them hadn't heard about the nearly fatal event of the overturned Humvee downtown. The Sabbath wasn't formally observed by more than the chaplain and a few die-hard believers, but it had started out as a rather languid morning. The skies were clear and an easy breeze was wafting in from the Indian Ocean. Many of the young Rangers and Night Stalker crews were outside in the compound playing volleyball or basketball, or jogging around the airfield perimeter to keep up their lung power. Others were lounging in the steamy hangar, writing letters home or waiting on line for a three-minute stint on the satellite phone. No one was firing on the ad hoc ranges and it was nice and quiet. By noon, the daylight was more than halfway done, and the Night Stalker pilots silently hoped that the rest of the day would burn away without any sort of alert that would force them to fly in broad daylight. In Somalia, the darkness was a potent weapon, as none of Aidid's militia had night vision capabilities. Yet fate was the hunter here, the time and choice of field was his, and very soon an unexpected mission was about to turn to mayhem.

Karl, as usual, wasn't having much fun that Sunday. There were four flight leads in the mission template: Randy Jones led the Little Bird guns, Karl led the Little Bird lifts, Cliff Wolcott was in charge of the Blackhawk assault force and Mike Durant led the Ranger blocking force. Someone had to know where each of these men was all the time, just in case something came up, so they couldn't just wander off and enjoy themselves somewhere. They had to stay fairly close to the TOC or inside the mess hall, which were hardly the epicenters of amusement. The alerts for an upcoming mission were accomplished the old-fashioned way, by a runner dashing through those areas where flight leads and Chalk leaders would be proximate. Karl was sitting outside the mess hall reading a Robert Ludlum novel when he heard the words, "Get to the TOC!"

In very short order, the compound shifted from a lazy lull to an adrenaline surge. Night Stalker copilots donned their gear and sprinted out to their fully fueled and armed birds, starting up the APUs and readying the nav systems while their leads hustled to the TOC for the briefing. The customers began gearing up: helmets, body armor, gloves, weapons, ammunition, radios, flash bangs and frags. None of them bothered to affix their Night Observation Devices to their Kevlar helmets because practice had proven that these missions seldom lasted longer than an hour and sunset was still very far away. Inside the TOC, aerial photographs were distributed and Karl and his fellow flight leads and customer ground commanders were told that a spontaneous meeting of some of the SNA's "heavy hitters" was about to take place near the Olympic Hotel. The mission profile was essentially the same as it had been on the previous six operations, with the exception that while the customers would be inserted by helo, they expected to be making quite a haul of enemy captives, so a portion of the exfil would have to take place by ground convoy. That was the only deviation from standard tactics that made Karl uncomfortable, knowing that some of his comrades might have to make their way out on foot, and through the nastiest section of Mogadishu, the Bakara Market. Other than that, and the fact that the sun was still high in a crisp blue sky, it would be business as usual.

He figured out his target coordinates and waypoints pretty quickly, and then he grabbed his vest and helmet and headed out for his bird, "Star 41." Keith Jones was his copilot and he already had the rotors turning and the systems up. Karl liked flying with Keith and tried to pair up with him as often as possible. Although already a CW5 and senior to Karl in rank, Keith easily accepted Karl as his "boss" whenever they flew together. He was a cool Floridian with a very calming nature. Their customers, four Delta men, were already settling onto the pods and clipping their safety belts in. Karl always marveled at the incredible poundage of equipment they hauled. Some of them carried so much gear and ammunition that they weighed in at more than 350 pounds, yet Karl was sure that even geared-up like that any of them could run him down at a sprint. Today, he noted that the Delta boys were relatively light, carrying only the necessities for quick and dirty combat. In the back of the bird, Karl made sure that a Squad Automatic Weapon was in its proper place, with plenty of extra ammunition just in case. Then he hopped into the left seat, strapped in, hooked up to the comms and waited for the code word, "Irene."

It was already after 1500 hours when the armada took to the air. An informant outside the Olympic Hotel had just confirmed that the SNA assembly was settling down for an afternoon conference and repast, most likely of purloined U.N. food supplies. The game was on, and every man aboard every helo hunched forward into the steaming slipstream, stomachs tense and trigger fingers twitching, like Thoroughbred jockeys poised on their steeds at the gate. At the apex of the flight, the Little Bird guns and lifts floated and bobbed, their engines sounding like heavy lawn mowers. Behind them, the Blackhawks hovered like larger siblings, black and sleek and ominous, their turbines and wide rotors thundering like the hearts of heavy beasts. Scores of combat boots dangled from the helos' doorless bays, and guns glinted in white sunlight. Inside the helmets of pilots and crews, code words crackled as updates and orders reached out to the force, and they flew on inexorably toward fate.

Karl took the flight in a long, easy arc out over the ocean, which was crystal blue, deceptively inviting and stocked with sharks. He slipped past the target area and continued for a bit; it wasn't much of a deception, but there was no time for finesse. Then the entire fleet of helos banked as one, circling north to swing around into the wind. They crossed the release point and headed straight downtown. Keith was flying the bird and Karl was navigating, because that was his primary task. He raised a finger and showed it to the Delta man nearest on the pod, who nodded at the "one minute" signal, passed it to his comrades, and unclipped his D ring. Carefully, almost gently, Keith dropped the bird lower. With operators unclipped and balanced so gingerly, there could be no sudden swoops or turns or banks. They descended past the lips of crumbling roofs as the dust began to swirl below and dark figures raised widened eyes, pointing, gesturing wildly and fleeing. And then they were nearly touching their skids to the untarred avenue, cruising straight along astride windows and cracked pastel doors.

"Straight down here," Karl said to Keith as he glanced back and forth from the photograph on his kneeboard into the cloud of dust and building silhouettes.

"Roger."

They arrived at a large intersection.

"Take a left here."

"Got it."

Keith carefully turned the Little Bird, spinning on its axis, and eased it forward again. He was glancing up and to the left, where Cliff Wolcott was inadvertently putting in his element a block short of his mark. The mistake temporarily threw Keith off.

"Which building is it?" he asked Karl.

"The big one on the left."

"Are you sure?"

"*That's* the building."

"Roger."

Keith set the bird down in a roiling cloud of shorn papers and grit. Instantly the Delta men were off the pods and racing into the doorway, as at nearly the same time Tom Wiese and Mike O'Connor landed Chalk Two. The dust was so heavy that Bob Fladry and Bob Witzler had to execute a go-around in Chalk Three before finally setting down, and then Ron Cugno and Joe Spencer put the last Chalk of Deltas on the ground. The operators had only just rushed through the doorways when all four birds were back off the ground and heading for their holding area, where they would hopefully have to wait only minutes before coming back in for their boys.

Karl thought everything was going exactly according to plan until he suddenly heard someone transmit that Super Six-One had been hit. He and Keith were holding about a kilometer off-target and they both turned their heads toward the city as they banked. It was Cliff Wolcott's bird, with Donovan Briley as copilot, a full crew and some shooters on board. They had taken a direct hit from an RPG as they circled above the target area, covering the men below. It was Cliff himself on the comms, his voice even and cool, informing everyone that Super Six-One was going down. *Oh, man.* Karl instantly knew that the entire mission would be screwed up now, but he could only think of his friends as he and Keith watched the smoking Blackhawk spinning and descending, until it impacted with the ledge of a building roof and disappeared below.

Immediately, Karl told Keith to bank the Little Bird out of holding and start heading for the crash site. Tom Wiese and Mike O'Connor rolled out behind him, while Chalks Three and Four stayed in holding. Karl should have asked permission to break from his position, but the idea of Cliff and Donovan being down there and probably injured had already taken control of his mind and his decisions. They were over the area where they'd seen Cliff go down in a matter of seconds, but at first they were unable to spot the fallen bird. Almost as an afterthought, Karl announced to the air mission commander that he was going in.

"Negative, Star Four-One," Lieutenant Colonel Tom Matthews answered. "Hold your position." Matthews wanted time to assess the situation before committing another helo to an obviously deadly area of the city.

"We're already here," Karl answered.

"I do not want you in there, Four-One," Matthews said.

Keith stabbed a finger at a street below, where Karl saw Super Six-One lying rotorless, battered and crushed like a minivan that had rammed into an eighteen-wheeler.

"I've spotted them," Karl snapped into the comms. "We're going in."

"All right," Matthews replied after an exasperated pause, "but only *one* of you."

"Roger."

Chalk Two rolled away and picked up a wide circle above as Karl and Keith made one more pass over the area, then nosed over and dove for the street. As they leveled off, Cliff's broken Blackhawk appeared directly below and out front of their windshield, lying in a wide strip of dirt avenue between low buildings. It was smeared up against a concrete wall, like a beached whale that had been shoved into a shoal after taking its last breath. There wasn't much smoke rising from the wreck, but the cockpit damage didn't look survivable. As the Little Bird zipped overhead, Keith had the controls and Karl was straining against his harness, trying to spot any signs of life down there. He saw sunlight glinting off a Pro-Tec helmet as someone moved outside the Blackhawk's bay and fired a weapon.

"We got survivors," he said to Keith.

"Good. Let's get 'em."

They zoomed over the wreck and Karl pointed up ahead, past the tail of the Blackhawk to where the dirt avenue broke into a wide intersection. Already they could see Somalis darting and sprinting along nearby alleyways, guns and rocket launchers bobbing in their bony, clenched fists. Even above the rotor buzz, Karl could hear the smatterings of small-arms fire. In his earphones he could also hear the ground convoy being redirected toward the crash site by the AMC bird above. A CSAR Blackhawk was also making its way over, but with enemy fighters converging so fast it was going to be a race for a prize. The Somalis were *not* going to get it.

In the middle of the intersection, Keith spun the bird to the left and popped the nose into the cross street, leaving the tailing rotor spinning in the open space where the avenues met. At least they would be able to defend one quadrant while they gathered up survivors. Karl looked over and saw one of the Delta shooters just meters away. He was still wearing his black helmet, but his face was a mask of blood and part of it looked crushed in. Karl leaned out, shouting to him and trying to wave him over to the Little Bird, but the wounded man just clutched his M-4 and shook his head. Then the shooter was out of sight again as Keith passed the corner building and set down.

"They're not gonna get on," Karl said.

"I know it," Keith said.

Karl reckoned there were four shooters on board Cliff's bird, plus the pilots and two crew chiefs. A single Little Bird couldn't possibly exfil all those men by itself, so the Delta men were going to defend the site to the death, or at least until they were sure that enough friendly forces had arrived to replace them.

At that point, Karl and Keith started taking small-arms fire. The

Somalis were converging from all points of the compass now, the heavy hammer sounds of their AKs echoing between the battered slum buildings. Karl grabbed his MP-5, cocked it, stuck it out the door and fired off a burst at an armed crowd that was advancing right at them from just a hundred meters away. Keith mimicked Karl from his right-hand door, and for a moment the Somalis scattered.

They both turned back to look behind them, hoping that the Delta men had heard by now over their radios that substantial help was on the way. Maybe they'd see the light and get the hell out of there. Karl wanted to tell them that he wasn't going to leave anyone behind, but just get them out piecemeal and keep coming back in. Yet above the rotor noise and the surging gunfire, there was no way to make himself heard.

To the right rear of the aircraft, Karl recognized the bloody shooter as an operator he knew named Dan. He was defending the near corner of the intersection, half standing and firing his weapon in precise double-taps. At the far intersection corner, another shooter named Jim was squatting and firing off in the opposite direction. Karl turned back to the front as the Somalis started to poke their heads out from broken doorways and pockmarked huts. They were shooting at him again and he shot back in long, urgent bursts, his spent shells clicking off the windshield and bouncing around the cockpit.

"What the hell's going on back there?" he shouted to Keith.

"Dan just got shot."

"Shit."

Dan had taken a round low in his body somewhere. He had col-lapsed to the dirt, unconscious. Karl was so busy fending off attackers from out front that Keith had to narrate for him.

"He's down. . . . Jim's running over to him. . . . He's picking him up."

Jim hauled his Delta comrade up in a fireman's carry and was now heading for the Little Bird as he spun and fired his M-4 with his free hand.

"Where *are* those guys?" Karl yelled as he changed magazines. The tension was starting to build, and he thought he'd soon be at the end of his emotional rope, which was usually a pretty long strand.

"They're comin'."

But the two Delta men stopped coming. Jim got shot down as he hauled Dan toward the bird. He had taken a heavy AK round in the shoulder and both wounded men had collapsed in a bloody, writhing pile.

Karl fired another long burst. Somali bullets were whipping past the cockpit, but the rotors kept on spinning. Nothing crucial had been hit, but he still didn't feel the familiar clunk of men piling into the lightweight aircraft.

"What's going on back there?" he demanded.

"Dammit, nothing good," Keith said. "They're both down."

For a moment, both pilots stopped focusing forward and shooting. They looked at each other, and they actually shook their heads and grinned foolishly. They both knew that it couldn't possibly get any worse than this, and that in all likelihood, they were not going to make it out of that place alive. Neither of them voiced it, but they knew it, and each of them was sure the other was thinking the very same thing.

"I'm gonna have to get out," Keith said.

"Okay, but . . ."

"I gotta get out, Karl." Keith shrugged. "Can I get out to get 'em?"

It was a ridiculous moment. Keith was actually *asking* his flight lead, in deference to rank, for permission to save two men's lives. Karl laughed.

"Well, yeah! But hurry up!"

Keith unhooked his ICS, left his MP-5 on the floor, unholstered his M-9 pistol and jumped out of the bird. Karl changed magazines again, unhooked his harness and got his left foot down on the skid as he leaned out and started firing in earnest. He had about three hundred rounds of MP-5 ammo and he was going through it fast. An RPG slammed into the building wall just outside the helo. It jerked his head hard to the right and he felt the incredible flash of heat, but he didn't feel any pain and he kept on shooting. His body armor was peppered with shrapnel and his copy of *The Road to Gandolpho* was shredded inside his flight suit pocket, but he wouldn't know that till much later. Rounds from the Somalis were kicking up dirt all over the place. He decided he was the perfect match for them; they couldn't shoot for shit, and neither could he. That was when he switched to single shot and started piling up the enemy in front of the bird.

Keith came back. He had gotten one of the wounded Delta men almost to the bird, but when he saw how much fire Karl was taking he thought he should join in and help or there'd be no bird to fly. He dropped down on one knee outside the right-hand door and started double-tapping with his M-9. Karl thought he was incredibly cool, looking just like 007 as he carefully aimed and dropped enemy combatants. Then he disappeared again.

Karl desperately wanted to drag the SAW from the back of the aircraft and indulge in some serious firepower, but he couldn't risk the time it would take to get it and set it up, so he kept on shooting. On top of it all, people "upstairs" were nagging the hell out of him in his earphones. He had no idea how many men were watching the event on live feeds back at the TOC, but the consensus was clear.

"Star Four-One! Star Four-One! Get your ass in the air and get the hell out of there!"

"Roger. Can't leave right now."

"They're all over you, Star Four-One!"

"Roger. My copilot's not in the aircraft. Not leaving without my copilot."

"Star Four-One. Your orders are to leave immediately!"

"Roger. Not leaving."

Keith showed up, dragging Jim with all of his gear still on and blood streaming down his arm from his shoulder wound. He eased the Delta man into the small cargo hold and sprang away again. Karl kept turning back to his left between his gun duels, trying to wave two more crash survivors toward the Little Bird, but they weren't coming. He twisted farther around and spotted Keith dashing toward the helo between geysers of dust that were popping up all around his slamming boots. He had Dan, the unconscious Delta man, completely draped over his shoulders and when he reached the helo he dumped his limp form in the back next to Jim. Keith knelt down beside the cockpit and fired some more from his M-9, then he and Karl "cross-ammoed": Keith gave Karl all of his MP-5 magazines, and Karl handed over his pistol mags. At this point, they were both disconnected from the ICS and shouting at each other. They were giddy with adrenaline and the near certainty that at any moment they were going to die together.

"What the fuck are we doing?" Karl yelled as he laughed.

"What we usually do," Keith yelled back, "something stupid!"

Keith spun around and ran back into the fight, looking for more men to rescue. Karl just shook his head. It was like some weird Olympic event concocted by a satanic joker upstairs, and he kept on fending off bad guys with his MP-5. The only place from which he hadn't been receiving fire was the right side of the cockpit at close range, where the corner of a near building obscured an alleyway. Suddenly, out of the corner of his eye, he spotted a head popping out and a gun barrel glinting. He swung his MP-5 from outside his left-hand door and into the cockpit, hesitating for only a split second because he didn't want to shatter the windshield. Through the black reticle of his weapon, he realized he was taking aim at the face of a Ranger. Lieutenant Tom DiTomasso dropped his M-16 and threw his hands up high, mouthing "Whhhoaaa!" There was so much gunfire in the streets that he hadn't even heard the Little Bird's engine from around the corner. Karl grinned from ear to ear and lowered his submachine gun as DiTomasso and a squad of Rangers spilled into the street and rushed past the bird for the crash site. Karl had no idea how the Rangers had made it so fast from the Olympic Hotel, but they had to have been sprinting like devils. He was ecstatic to see them, and of course relieved that he hadn't killed any of them. With a force of Rangers in the area now, he and Keith could get Dan and Jim to the Joint Medical Augmentation Unit at the airport compound. Keith appeared again and hopped into the cockpit.

"Guess we can leave now," he said as he strapped himself in and scanned the instruments for bullet holes.

"Yeah," Karl answered as he, too, climbed back into his seat. "Might be a good idea." He glanced back into the bay at Dan and Jim, who didn't look good at all. He started to apply some power.

"Think she'll fly?" Keith grinned. Both pilots were stunned to be still alive and actually about to get out of there.

"Guess we'll see." Karl hauled the bird up and away in a cloud of dust and tracer fire snapping through the skids. It looked like hundreds of Somalis below were turning their guns on him, and Jim sat up in the back and poured small-arms fire back at them with his good arm. Karl hit his external comm button.

"Star Four-One, coming out . . ."

ON THE WAY to the JMAU, Karl changed his mind. He kept looking back into the cargo hold at Dan, who seemed to have been hit somewhere in the groin, maybe his femoral artery. There was so much blood, his face was ashen and his eyes had rolled up. At the university there was a full-fledged army MASH unit set up, so he told Keith to head over there instead of to the airfield. On the way to the university, Karl raised the MASH on his radio and advised them of his situation.

"We're one minute out, and you need to get everybody you can in there because you're gonna be busy today."

They weren't on the ground at the university for long. The doctors and medics rushed out from the MASH with litters and quickly removed the wounded Delta men from the bloodstained helo. Karl and Keith then took the bird back to airfield to the nearest FARP to gas up.

Their crew chiefs had been watching the entire debacle on the monitors in the TOC and they came rushing out to the bird with more ammunition. They had the pilots shut the bird down so they could look it over, and although there were plenty of shrapnel gouges and bullet holes, it seemed to be flyable. Karl cranked it back up and they rejoined their flight over the city.

Another Blackhawk, Super Six-Four, was soon shot down in another part of Mogadishu. Once again, Karl and Keith witnessed the crash from a distance. It looked really bad and neither of them believed there would be survivors, but you couldn't judge that from a kilometer away. Having just barely survived one such incident, perhaps another pair of pilots might have decided, "That's enough for one day." Karl and Keith rolled in on the new site. A pair of Delta snipers had just been inserted to defend the downed crew until substantial help could arrive, and Karl was directed to land in the same LZ where Randy Shughart and Gary Gordon had hopped from another Blackhawk to struggle their way to the crash site over broken fences and through piles of burning tires. The two Delta men would soon fight to the death defending the crew, all of whom would die as well, with the exception of the captured pilot.

Karl and Keith sat on the ground for what seemed like a very long time, waiting for the Delta men to show up with the crew members from Super Six-Four. Karl kept calling back up to the AMC's bird, hoping to hear that his comrades were making progress toward his helo. No one ever showed up, and as the Somalis started gathering in force and taking shots at the bird, he and Keith were ordered out of there. There was no one left to rescue.

As night descended, the Little Birds were recalled to the airfield and the Battle of Mogadishu became a siege. There were Rangers still out there, hunkered down and surrounded, and no one could get to them. The task force didn't have any of the heavily armored vehicles that General Garrison had requested of his commanders, so the Americans were left to negotiate with United Nations Forces over quick re-

action convoys and additional troops. In the meantime, all the Night
Stalkers could do was to try to keep the Somalis from overrunning and
slaughtering their comrades, as they had so recently done to the Pa-
kistanis. Back in the States, the images of American corpses being
dragged through the streets were already appearing on CNN. Karl's
wife had been patient and supportive as a saint for all of his army career, but when she found their two young boys staring at the television
and trying to spot any of their father's familiar tattoos on the corpses of
those butchered Americans, it was just too much. The illusion of
America's overwhelming military prowess had just been shattered by a
band of enraged African militiamen, and Karl's marriage was irrevocably torn as well.

Karl and Keith were desperate to do something, so they nagged
General Garrison for a rescue mission until he finally threw them out
of the TOC. He wasn't going to insert any more shooters unless it
made tactical sense, and the only helos he'd allow up in the air were
Blackhawks to zoom in briefly and resupply the trapped Rangers, or
the Little Bird guns who could keep the Somalis from completely
overrunning them. Left with nothing but empty hands and frustration,
Karl and Keith ran over to the FARP to help the ground crews rearm
and refuel the gun birds. They brought coffee and sandwiches to the
pilots, who barely spoke between sorties, taking only enough time to
relieve themselves and grab something to eat. Randy Jones, the gun
bird flight lead, would later be cited with so many medals and commendations for his actions that night that they couldn't all fit on one
page. He didn't have much to say at the FARP; he was totally "in the
mode." But the windshield of his Little Bird was smeared with blood
and bits of bone, because that's how close his birds were making their
gun runs on the enemy. The Little Bird guns flew for eighteen hours
straight, until at last at daylight the Rangers were exfilled, some via armored convoy, and some by foot, all the way back to the Mogadishu
soccer stadium. The gun birds, a total of four, had fired 170,000
rounds of minigun ammunitions and seventy-seven rockets.

The next morning, Karl and Keith flew cover for the convoy that was extracting the Rangers from their hellish redoubt of the night before. Karl had never seen an area so shot up. It was as if that square block of the city had been squeezed through a meat grinder, and he realized that without the support of the Little Bird guns, every one of those Rangers would have died. He also suddenly remembered that during one of the task force's frequent "deception flights" before October 3—the helos would take off and make a run around the city, just to acclimate the opposition to their presence and reduce the sense of alarm when they lifted off on an actual mission—he had actually witnessed an RPG "class" being given somewhere down below. A man in an Arab *kaffiyeh* was holding up the launcher, instructing an eager group of militia in the proper technique for shooting down American machines. Perhaps of all the images from Somalia, that one would stand out in his mind.

When it was all over, the atmosphere in the compound had completely shifted. They had lost many men and suffered many wounded, and although there was still occasional laughter, it was darker and brief. There was a tradition in the task force called the "Amnesty Barrel." If an inspection was about to be performed of all personnel and equipment, any "contraband" you might have could be placed in the barrel and all would be forgiven. It was usually half full of extra ammunition, non-regulation gear, alcohol and the occasional "over the line" pornography. Prior to October 3, the Night Stalkers had flown with a myriad of non-lethal devices to try to keep the Somalis at bay from target areas without harming them. Cliff Wolcott in particular had done a lot of crowd control from Super Six-One, using harmless flash bangs to prevent curiosity-seekers from interfering with missions where they might get hurt. The Amnesty Barrel was now overflowing with those non-lethal weapons, as every one of the Night Stalkers had replaced such harmless toys with heavy weapons and hand grenades. But they would never get to use them, because Gothic Serpent was over.

After more than ten years in the dark, the Night Stalkers were suddenly thrust into daylight by the events in Somalia. Before that day in October, most Americans had never even heard of such a unit, and now they were all over the news. Reporters fought with one another for a chance at interviews down at the compound. Authors appeared, books were written and films made. Yet Karl, who had been raised in a Night Stalker culture where no one spoke about his work, rebuffed all such approaches. He simply went back to flying, as he'd always done after every other mission.

Karl and Keith were both put in for the Distinguished Service Cross. As often happens in the U.S. military establishment, the awards were downgraded to Silver Stars, but Karl didn't really think he deserved that either. He reckoned that the only thing he really had coming to him was an "Article 15"—disciplinary action for refusing an order, because he had gone into a crash site against the instructions of his commanders.

Karl thought that if anyone should get a medal for Somalia, it was Keith. After all, he reasoned, Keith was the one who had gotten out on the ground and dragged wounded men back to the aircraft.

From Karl's point of view, he himself had been nothing more than a "dumbass mushroom," just sitting there in his seat and watching things develop. . . .

CHAPTER 7

A COLD AND DISTANT PEAK

TAKUR GAR
MARCH 2002

ATOP THE HIGHEST SUMMIT in the eastern mountains of Afghanistan, the morning was bright and clear. Light winds had swept the crest of frozen fog and charcoal clouds, leaving a craggy panorama thrusting into silver blue skies. A high white sun lanced its sharp light into two feet of whipped-cream snow, and here and there green pines poked up from slits of earth between sharp stones. At over ten thousand feet in altitude above the Shahikot Valley, the air was very cold and thin, yet pure as unspoiled air could be. And still, there was no beauty in any of it. Sergeant First Class Cory Lamoreaux had already been shot eight times, and it was not yet noon.

Lamoreaux was the senior medic of the Night Stalker Regiment, and until just moments before, he had been successfully managing his casualties in the midst of a five-hour firefight. Some of his men had died instantly at dawn with the first onslaught of enemy gunfire, and there was nothing he could do for them. Yet those who had survived, he had kept alive, and he had just begun to think that this hell at the top of Takur Gar might turn out all right after all. But now the worst had happened. A burst of enemy machine-gun fire had slammed him in the belly and he was curled up, fetal, with the kind of pains only Satan could devise firing through all his nerves. His legs were soaked in steaming fluid. He was gut shot and impossibly far from any type of surgical care, and he knew exactly what that meant. He ground his teeth and swallowed his moans as one thought flashed through his mind.

This is really gonna suck for Laura and the kids. . . .

And still, at the very edge of his own death, and at the apex of his career as an army medic, Cory Lamoreaux had no doubt that this was where he was supposed to be. It wasn't until this very moment that he fully realized how everything in the thirty-five years of his life had been guiding him to this point in time. It was as if for all those years he had been pushing on through a maze of high hedges, and only now could he see that pattern from above. Here on this small and lonely battlefield, each professional decision he made was crucial to the lives in jeopardy around him, and every ounce of courage he summoned would be fuel for another minute. Gunfire still hammered like mallets on oil drums. Just behind where his own spine curled and jerked in the snow, Jason Cunningham, the air force pararescue jumper who had become his partner medic on the peak, lay writhing from the same burst of AK-47 bullets that had taken Cory down. Not far below his feet on the slope, two of his badly wounded patients lay strapped to litters, helpless. The hoglike laughter of the enemy fighters who'd just shot him and Jason echoed from behind a rock not two hundred meters away, as they praised Allah's wrath upon the infidels and loaded fresh magazines. It infuriated Cory, and that anger spurred a question: *What would Dad do now?* He knew the answer to that, and he pulled himself to his knees and felt for his wounds beneath his body armor, prepared to find the worst, yet finally ready to face it.

Cory's father had been an army combat medic with the Americal Division in Vietnam. When Cory was two years old his parents divorced. His mother was a government employee, so they moved from Utah to Illinois, Alabama, New Jersey, Korea and Hawaii, while he spent each summer with his dad. As with most of the Vietnam veterans Cory would come to know, his father never spoke about the war, except from the dark turmoil of his nightmares. Yet over the years, through boyish questions innocently posed, the lad would unearth his father's past. He had served one tour in Vietnam, a hellacious year in which he went from being a buck private to a staff sergeant and infantry squad leader. He had been awarded the Combat Infantry Badge, Combat Medic Badge, three Bronze Stars with the "V" device and two Purple Hearts. At the time, the army also awarded one Air Medal for every fifty combat air assaults; Cory's dad had two Air Medals. And yet the bond they formed was simply one of father and son and had very little to do with a boy's admiration for a hero, for the war was very rarely discussed.

Cory wasn't much of a student. He barely made it through one semester of college, then went off to live with his dad, working odd jobs throughout the summer of his nineteenth year. It was as if he were delaying the weight of responsibility he knew he would soon embrace, until at last he surrendered to it and joined the army in January 1987. He knew two things: He wanted to be a medic and he wanted to be a paratrooper, and as he earned those special skills and silver wings he found his new home at Fort Bragg, where he would serve for the next eleven years.

His first taste of combat was, ironically enough, also his first exposure to an elite army aviation unit he had heard of only in acronymic whispers while working as a medic at Fort Bragg. As the invasion of Panama spun up in December 1989, the colonel in command of

COSCOM—the Corps Support Command that would be handling all logistics for the deploying paratroopers—selected Cory to be his personal driver. Being some "full bird's" chauffeur might have been an insult to a less mature troop, but Cory reckoned he'd be ranging all across the country and seeing the battlefield from every angle—a fine introduction to warfare. Just after midnight on the twentieth, the C-141 with the colonel's Humvee aboard landed at Howard Air Force Base and taxied to the end of the strip. As the ramp dropped down and Cory walked off, he found himself facing a brace of GP-medium medical tents, the Casualty Collection Point for the battles that had just begun. In the near distance beyond the base, the flames from the burning *Comandancia* were rising into the black sky. Suddenly, a Little Bird assault helicopter appeared out of the night, its battle-damaged engine straining as it bounced onto the tarmac in a barely controlled crash. Commandos leaped off the pods, and within a few moments men were rushing from the tents to haul one of the injured pilots onto a stretcher. Cory had no idea that he had just witnessed Bob Fladry returning from the Modelo Prison raid, or that the wounded pilot was Rick Bowman, who would someday be his own regimental commander at the 160th. For the moment, the young sergeant's mouth fell open and all he could say was, "Wow . . . Now, that's pretty *cool*."

For the next few days and weeks, Cory did indeed see Just Cause at every angle from behind the wheel of his Humvee, at times straying too close to the action as his colonel strove to visit his troops on the heels of firefights. On the morning after D-day, he and his fellow drivers found themselves outside the headquarters of an American military compound, while their colonels and generals held meetings inside. The drivers smoked and joked. All of them were STRAC (Strategic Army Corps), an expression that meant sharply creased and spit-shined. They suddenly stopped talking and stared as an army Blackhawk appeared over the trees and deposited a squad of paratroopers on the manicured lawn. The men had just been extracted from combat and were dazed and filthy, with guns up and still jangling with adrenaline. Two of the paratroopers were being carried by their comrades—one dead, the other shot in the back. Cory, as always, had his aid bag in his vehicle and he quickly joined the squad's medic, treating his first combat casualty.

Those young soldiers would forever remain in a corner of Cory's mind, not only because they were the first Americans he had seen suffer from combat, but because of what they stood for. When he returned the next morning to deliver his colonel to a second strategy conference, the squad was *still* there on the lawn. Their killed and wounded were gone, but it was as if they had done their duty and been forgotten. The stark contrast between the pristine buildings of the post and the sweat and bloodstained men seemed like something out of *The Twilight Zone*. A young paratrooper who clearly hadn't shaved in days rose from the group and walked up to him, clutching his M-16.

"Hey Sar'nt," the kid said, "do you know if they're gonna put the flag up?"

Cory followed the soldier's finger to a tall white flagpole with nothing at the top but a brass ball. It was already well past eight in the morning.

"I don't know, man," Cory drawled.

"Well, I'm tellin' you right now," the bridling veteran warned, "if they don't get it up there in the next few minutes, I'm goin' in there with my rifle and put it up myself."

Cory nodded slowly, respectfully. He could see in the young trooper's gleaming, bloodshot eyes that he had witnessed much in the past few days, but this was what he cared about.

"Dude," Cory said, "you go right ahead."

Some minutes passed. The soldier got up again, picked up his rifle and strode into the conference building. He came out clutching an American flag, and he and his comrades raised it and saluted it. That image would remain with Cory forever. *That* was the American soldier.

For the next nine years, Cory remained at Fort Bragg as a medic, gaining experience, improving his skills and taking every advanced course his commanders would allow. Early in 1990 he was sent to San Antonio for the "91 Bravo" course: sixteen additional weeks of medical training designed to take regular army medics to the next level. He graduated on August 5, 1990, and by the twelfth he was in Saudi Arabia for the beginning of Desert Storm. His platoon led the way for the medical support of the 18th Airborne Corps, but the invasion moved so quickly and successfully that most of his casualties had only moderate bone fractures or minor wounds. But his most significant experience of the war was passing the time with the pilots and crews of the Night Stalkers Third Battalion at KKMC. The unit was clearly "swoopy" and at the sharp end of the spear all the time, and he knew that was where he would also be someday.

After that short war in the desert, Cory returned again to Fort Bragg, where his world began to widen. Doctors liked working with him. He was that lanky kid with the spiky blond hair, the soft western drawl and a toothy grin, who laughed under pressure but knew his stuff. To his commanders, he was the kind of soldier you could assign to any mission and know he'd do you proud. He was airborne and jumpmaster qualified, air assault qualified and a medical expert by regular army standards. He was always up-to-date on the latest field techniques, and he never complained about humping his hundreds of pounds of medical bags, but only added more gear to the mix. No one ever wondered if he'd get the job done or be there when he was needed. He was invited to move from the regular army to the "dark side" of the fence and the Joint Special Operations Command, and for four years he would execute tasks he would never discuss.

One day in the mid-1990s, during a lull between wars, Cory was participating in a major training exercise that involved the 160th SOAR(A). His men were operating as CASEVAC medics aboard conventional assault helos and he was short two men for the exercise. CASEVAC was a very particular expertise, which involved caring for a wounded raider from the moment he was loaded aboard a helo at the target area to the moment he was off-loaded at a Combat Surgical Hospital. Cory wandered over to the 160th staging area, found the Night Stalker operations officer and introduced himself.

"Sir, I wonder if I could borrow a couple of your medics for this mission."

"Doing what, Sergeant?"

"CASEVAC, sir."

"Sorry, son." The officer shook his head. "Our medics don't do that."

"They don't?"

"Nope."

"Well, sir," Cory said, "if you don't mind my askin', what *do* they do?"

"They take care of our pilots," the Night Stalker said as he turned back to his maps and ops orders. "What else?"

"Uh, roger," Cory said.

He walked away, scratching his head. Sure, the 160th was an aviation outfit, and the best in the business at that. Its pilots were its primary focus, so of course they had to be looked after properly. But Cory had seen them; they all looked like triathletes. When they weren't flying, they were either running or lifting weights, and the crews were the same. What the hell were their medics doing other than handing out Motrin?

So they don't do CASEVAC, huh? Cory mused as he hustled back to his exercise. *Well, watch out, boys, 'cause things are gonna be different when I get there. . . .*

It wasn't long before he got there. In late 1997, Cory had finished up his tour with JSOC, and his seniority and reputation now meant that he could have his choice of serving with any unit in the army's order of battle. He decided to attend the Special Operations Combat Medic course, an intensive six-month course taught at the Special Warfare Center at Fort Bragg. When he was done, he would be able to perform every emergency technique short of major surgery, and all of it in the toughest field conditions and under fire, if he had to. While there, he'd be looking for a new home. Although the United States

Armed Forces is a mega-monster, its Special Operations Forces comprise a relatively small community of operators who encounter one another throughout their careers. At the time, the Night Stalker regiment command sergeant major was Cliff "O.B." O'Brien, who had been crossing paths with Cory Lamoreaux for years. When Cory's JSOC commander called O.B. to inquire if a medic slot was available, O.B. said, "For Lamoreaux? You bet."

Cory arrived at Fort Campbell as the new senior medic of the 160th medical section and almost immediately started "secretly" developing his vision to revamp the organization. There were three doctors, one physician's assistant and twelve medics on staff, all of whom had to handle more than a thousand medical records for the pilots, crews and support personnel. While the doctors were the officers and technically in charge, their tours were short and they rotated in and out, so it was up to Cory and his medics to provide continuity, a difficult task considering the unit's operational tempo. Typical army medical sections trained together and deployed as a unit, but the Night Stalker medics were always scattered to the four winds—one a firing range, one a parachute jump, three managing sick call, two flying on a training exercise. What he found there was barely controlled chaos, with no one trained up to the exact same level.

But he was a patient young man with a plan. There was a "hole" that needed to be filled and his commanders were ignoring it because no one had shot at them for a while. You had CSAR (Combat Search and Rescue), which was basically a long-range helo with air force PJs aboard. A CSAR bird would fly to the site of a downed aircraft, extract the crews, treat the injured and get them out of there. You had Medevac, which was an unarmed flying ambulance that had to be summoned to the scene, a time lag that could often prove fatal. The "hole" was CASEVAC. Cory wanted every Night Stalker mission to have 160th medics aboard the assaulting Blackhawks or Chinooks (there was rarely room aboard a Little Bird for anyone but shooters), so the wounded pilots, crews or customers could be kept alive between the objective area and the CASH.

"Lamoreaux, get out of my ear and go treat an ankle sprain."

For nearly three years, that's what Cory heard whenever he made a pain in the ass of himself, trying to convince his Night Stalker commanders of the need for his CASEVAC capability. But he had been an army medic for a long time and he was used to the attitude. Medics were like cops: You didn't want to see one till you needed one. Eventually, he knew the crap would hit the proverbial fan, so he started sending his medics out to every combat medicine course he could find. He trained them hard, and exactly the way they would fight when they had to. If you had to stop an arterial bleed, you'd better be able to do it at night, on your belly, and assume that your NVGs had been shot right off your helmet mount. If you had to start an IV, you'd better be prepared to do it in the middle of a swamp somewhere while the enemy shot at you from the banks and mortar shells rained all around. If you were wounded yourself, you'd better be able to assess it, treat it and carry on, because the unit's pilots and crews would be depending on you. In his heart, he knew that's what his dad would have done, and most probably had done in Vietnam.

Despite the small frustration of not having his "harebrained" scheme taken seriously, Cory loved the unit. It was a special operator's dream. Night Stalker missions were daring, complex, totally "out there" and often "deep black." In training exercises, they would come up with a scenario no one could possibly execute, and then they'd do it. All the crews had highly tuned combat skills and most of them were paratroopers. The pilots were as smart and skilled as fighter-jocks, but a lot tougher and much less fussy than those guys who flew F-16s and lounged around their pools when off-duty. If a Night Stalker pilot asked him for an aspirin, it was likely he had a fracture somewhere and didn't want to reveal it and possibly miss some action. Cory was very proud to wear the Night Stalker red beret and unit crest.

On September 11, 2001, he was at home with his young family when the news started to break. His wife, Laura, had gotten used to having him around. He frequently deployed on training missions with his unit, but they were of relatively short duration and she rarely worried about something happening to him. Their daughter, Bailee, was three years old and their son, Hunter, was about to turn seven. Of all the family, Hunter was most upset by the recurring images he kept seeing on the television.

"Daddy?" he asked as Cory donned his uniform and felt his pager vibrate. "How come we can't put up a force field around all our tall buildings so this can't happen to us?"

"I don't know, son." Cory smiled sadly and shrugged. "But it's a heckuva good idea."

The Twin Towers and the Pentagon were still burning, but his mind was already elsewhere. Someone was going to pay for this, and he knew that the Night Stalkers would be delivering the bill. . . .

ON THE WEEK in October when the Night Stalkers began to deploy for Operation Enduring Freedom, the unit had been in existence for exactly twenty years. And throughout those two decades, the 160th's Chinook pilots had always been at the back of the line. Their twin-rotor, fifty-foot-long MH-47s were powerful, but they weren't "sexy" like the high-speed Blackhawks or "hot" like the flexible Little Birds. They could deliver plenty of operators and hardware, but they couldn't fit into tight spaces. They weren't exactly stealthy, either. An enemy combatant holed up in a safe house might not hear Little Birds or Hawks until they were right over the roof, but approaching Chinooks made the earth rumble. They couldn't be used to take down hijacked airplanes or ocean liners, nor could they slip between the buildings of a hostile city. They needed large open spaces in which to operate.

It wasn't that the special operations Chinooks hadn't done anything in all that time. In the spring of 1988, U.S. intelligence learned that a most coveted piece of Russian military equipment had been abandoned in North Africa, ripe for the picking. For the previous fifteen years, Libya and Chad had been warring fiercely over an oil-rich and uranium-embedded swath of border territory called the Azouzou Strip. The Libyans had just been driven off, leaving behind a fully intact, though unflyable, Russian MI-24 Hind attack helicopter. The Chadians agreed to let the Americans have the helo, if they could get it out of the desert.

A number of different schemes were tried, until inevitably the phone rang at Night Stalker HQ. It was clear that only the 160th's Chinooks could manage such a heavy load, but the CH-47 pilots and crews weren't about to just take off for Africa; first they had to plan, train and rehearse. CW4 Juergen Stark was chosen to command the mission. A pair of Chinooks were loaded aboard an Air Force C-5 and flown out to White Sands Air Force Base, where they were "built up" and then flew a desert course identical to that of the planned operation. To simulate the weight of the Hind, six five-hundred-gallon fuel blivets were filled with water, sling-loaded below Chalk One and both birds flew back to the simulated Forward Staging Base. Early in June, Stark and his team began making their way to Ndjamena, Chad, where they kept a low profile and awaited the arrival of the C-5.

At midnight on June 11, Operation Mount Hope was launched. Juergen Stark and his men flew their Chinooks five hundred miles to the target area over featureless deserts. While one helo landed and maintenance crews spilled out to configure the Hind, the other hovered just above, whipping up a hurricane of pebbles and sand as it awaited the hookup. En route back to Ndjamena, the Chinooks had to set down twice to refuel, then encountered a raging sandstorm with clouds of grit rising to three thousand feet. The operation lasted a grueling sixty-seven hours, and then the Americans disappeared with their

captured Russian helicopter. The mission was so secret that many of
the Little Bird and Blackhawk pilots who often snickered at their Chinook brothers would not even learn of it for years.

Night Stalker Chinooks had also participated in Operation Desert
Storm in 1991, inserting Special Forces teams behind Iraqi lines and
rescuing downed Coalition pilots. Perhaps to their good fortune, they
had not been "invited" to Somalia in 1993, though they were utilized
in Haiti in 1994 and in limited numbers in Bosnia in 1995, and had
helped evacuate nearly five hundred American citizens from war-torn
Liberia in 1996.

But the opportunities for glory were rare, and for the most part, the
MH-47 pilots felt like bench warmers on a Super Bowl football team.
In a highly competitive atmosphere of type A personality pilots, they
were often regarded that way as well. The Chinook jockeys were the
unit's "bus drivers." But in Afghanistan, all of that was about to change
forever.

The mountain range was called the Bear, and in order to penetrate
the northern border of Afghanistan you had to fly over it. There was no
way to skirt it, no inviting cleavage between its twelve-thousand-foot
peaks you could hope to slip through. If you looked at its outline on a
standard aviation Joint Operations Graphic map, it was shaped like
the head of a grizzly.

Greg Calvert and his fellow Chinook pilots thought that was appropriate, because if you weren't on your game every second while flying
over the Bear, it was going to eat you alive.

The pile of rubble at the World Trade Center in New York was still
smoldering when Greg deployed to Karshi-Kanabad in southern
Uzbekistan. He was tall and lean, freckled and friendly-looking, with a
quick wide smile and a hair-trigger laugh. At thirty-seven, he still had
the unmarred expression of a college grad student, and it was probably
his "Why not?" attitude that had gotten him into the 160th. In fact,
Greg had barely completed a year of college before deciding that it
bored him. In 1983 he joined the army and spent four years as a line

medic in the 82nd Airborne Division. From there, he served another two years as a flight medic aboard medevac helos, where he realized that he really wanted to be in the front seat. He came out of flight school piloting Hueys, then Cobras, and ultimately Blackhawks.

Greg loved flying, but not having that college degree bugged him, so in 1993 he moved over to the North Carolina National Guard as a full-time pilot and part-time student. In 1998, he was going through the Blackhawk Instructor Pilot course at Fort Rucker when a classmate named Casey Ragsdale, who happened to be a Night Stalker, "recruited" him for the regiment. Greg had heard about the unit but had never imagined joining it; rumor had it that the Night Stalkers did not take reserve or National Guard pilots. His wife, Dana, was a successful CPA who had always been supportive of Greg's flying. They'd just had their first child, a little girl, and while Dana had her concerns about Greg working for the Night Stalkers, she thought he should go for it; when Greg was happy at work, he was happy at home. *Why not?* he thought, and he went for the assessment.

The week of testing at Fort Campbell seemed like one endless night of relentless pressure, but Greg knew that was the idea and had fully expected it. While in college and at the Guard, he had also been flying a Hughes 500 executive helo for extra cash and had gotten used to having high-tech navigational aids, a GPS and Loran system. The Night Stalkers put him into a Little Bird, blacked out all his displays and gave him a map, a compass and a clock. He had to plot a course to two targets, cross every checkpoint en route within a two-minute window and hit each target in plus or minus thirty seconds of his plan. There were grueling oral exams on pilot knowledge, a PT test, psychological tests and a swim test. He was ordered to prepare a briefing on a particular aviation subject and then deliver that briefing to a classroom of evaluators. None of the pilots or examiners said more to him than was necessary; there was no small talk or a single hint about how he was doing. He had told his examiners that he was primarily a Blackhawk pilot. They told him that if he came to the 160th, he would be flying Chinooks, and they handed him an MH-47 manual and said, "Tomorrow, you'll be taking a check ride. Better study limitations and emergency procedures." The next morning they walked him out to one of the big birds. He had never even sat in a Chinook cockpit. The instructor pilot had him run up the bird, perform takeoffs and landings, and then he turned off the AFCS, the Automated Flight Control System that gives the pilot boost and feedback in the controls, like automatic steering in a car. Without it, the bird was a monster to fly, and when he was finally done Greg thought, *Okay, I'm gone. No way are they gonna take me.*

But he wasn't done yet. After days of hands-on testing and very little sleep, Greg dressed in his Class-A's and made his appearance before the Assessment Board. Every building at the 160th compound is named after a fallen Night Stalker, and Greg's final examination was held in Tidwell Hall, named after a Chinook crash in 1996 that took the life of Staff Sergeant Tracey A. Tidwell. The boardroom was long, cold and meant to be uncomfortable, with a large horseshoe table at one end and an empty spot at the other where Greg stood at parade rest. The president of the board, two instructor pilots who had tested him, the unit psychologist and representatives from the 160th battalions fired questions at him for two hours. They poked, prodded, challenged his abilities as a pilot and tried to piss him off, but it wasn't easy to get Greg's ire up. They asked him what made him think he was so hot, and he politely stated that he didn't think of himself that way at all, but only as a man who could be counted on to exceed his own limitations. They told him that they had never, ever, accepted a pilot from a reserve component, and they sent him out of the room. He waited for thirty minutes until they called him back in and fired another salvo of questions.

"Well, Mr. Calvert," the president of the board said as Greg fully expected to be dismissed without apologies, "we would like to invite you to join the regiment."

"Thank you for the invitation," Greg heard himself say as he came to attention. "Yes, I'd like very much to join the regiment."

"And you have no reservations about flying Forty-sevens?"

"None at all, sir." Greg was trying hard not to grin.

"Better get on home and start packing, then."

In October 1999 he arrived at the Compound, was in-processed and immediately sent to Fort Rucker for his Chinook transition. After that came Green Platoon, where he was trained in the particular skills required of all Night Stalker pilots and crews; weeks were spent on basic combat and navigation skills, including the infamous SERE School, and then he proceeded to a course for the MH-47 Echo model, an upgraded special ops version of the big bird. Finally, he reported to Bravo Company of the Second Battalion and company commander Captain Joe Garst, whom Greg quickly recognized as a natural-born combat leader. Garst believed in doing everything "real world," just as one would have to do in wartime. The "op tempo" at what was known as the "Bravo Project," due to its small size, was intense, and as soon as Greg dropped his duffel and reported in, he was off on an over-water training mission to Key West.

He never looked back at those other, sleeker, smaller birds he had flown before. The Chinook wasn't sexy, but it had "legs"; you didn't have to land or link up with another aerial platform to refuel every two or three hours. The Chinooks were incredibly reliable and had a great reputation with the customers. But the best part was the interaction with the crews, as each bird was a flying "community," a team. Up front were the pilots, but they couldn't handle the helo alone. In back were four able men: the flight engineer, who monitored the systems panel and doubled as a crew chief and right-door minigunner; on the left-door minigun was another crew chief; two ramp men in the rear controlled the on-off loading of customers and equipment, as well as manning additional machine guns from their smaller side windows or the ramp. The helo was so large that the pilots couldn't land it without callouts from their crew members, counting off the altitude and warning of obstructions, telling them either "Okay, set her down," or "You ain't gonna make it." The doorway between the pilots' cockpit and the crew cabin was called Station 95, an imaginary dividing line of responsibilities that was never to be crossed. Pilots and crews had to implicitly trust one another's professionalism, which made for a titanium bond.

On "that" morning in September 2001, Bravo Company had just flown an all-night training mission, ending up at a National Guard post at Camp Beauregard, Louisiana. Greg and his pilot-in-command, Dave Gross, had managed only two hours of sleep in their small quarters when Al Mack, their flight lead, started banging on the door.

"Get up! Get up! Get up! We're under attack!"

Al had a reputation as a practical joker and a cutup, so Greg and Dave cursed from under their blankets.

"Al, shut up and go away. . . . We need to sleep."

"Get up, goddamnit!"

Mack started banging on all the doors in the BOQ, until finally someone believed him and they all gathered around a small TV. How Mack had instantly decided that the first impact at the World Trade was an enemy attack, no one would ever know, but they all watched the second impact, and the Pentagon, and the black, smoking furrow in a Pennsylvania field. Their pagers began to hum and they were soon packed up and sitting aboard their birds, but for twenty-four hours national airspace was closed and no one would let them fly. At last, on the following morning, they flew back to Fort Campbell through skies that brought up images of a post–nuclear holocaust world. Nothing else moved in the air. When they stopped at a commercial airport to refuel, only their Chinooks were allowed in and out. The air traffic controllers engaged them in mournful small talk, an anomaly for the busiest men and women in the world. The controllers knew they were speaking with army aviators and wished them all good luck, and good hunting.

By the end of September things were moving very quickly. The regiment was going to war, and since Osama bin Laden made his home among the Taliban of Afghanistan, the target was assumed, while remaining unmentioned in any ops orders. While Bravo Company awaited its turn, Joe Garst trained the hell out of them, drilling them over and over again in shoot-down, emergency and survival procedures, as if he had had a vision of things to come. Garst wanted every reaction to become muscle memory, and that could be accomplished only if you drilled each procedure hundreds of times. He exhausted them. They loved him for it. Greg's deployment orders changed on a daily basis; he was going tomorrow; no, he was going the day after. He and Dana would say their final goodbyes, then he'd go off and come back again in the evening with his gear. Their two-year-old daughter didn't understand why Mommy and Daddy kept having these tearful partings, until at last it was for real and he was gone.

When Greg and his fellow pilots arrived in Uzbekistan, the unit had gone "deep black." No one back home knew where they were, no reporters were with them, they had no communications with the outside world. The helos and crews were there, already preparing to support the customers of Task Force Dagger, whose mission would be to seek out and destroy terrorist targets in the northern reaches of Afghanistan. The strip at Karshi-Kanabad was locked down, dark, empty and cold, like some Forward Operating Base on the dark side of the moon, the last stop before an invasion of Mars. You could already smell the looming war in the mixture of jet fuel fumes and frigid air.

And as happens with all armies in times of war, life at the front lines assumed its own unique character, far from the shined boots and ironed uniforms in garrison. Army Regulation 670-1, which governs uniform and grooming standards, was soon forgotten as beards and mustaches began to sprout. Black watch caps and heavy fleece jackets replaced the regulation outerwear, and leather name tags embossed with wings and ranks were torn off coveralls. In their place, the men wore only tags denoting names and blood types, the crucial information that medics like Cory Lamoreaux would need in the field: "Greg Calvert O + NKA" (No Known Allergies). If you didn't personally know a man, you couldn't tell if he was a pilot or a cook.

It wasn't long before the unique humor of the Chinook crews added "color" to the environment. The lines of perfectly ordered, charcoal helos on the deserted strip at Karshi brought up images of a pirate fleet, and soon all of Bravo Company's "vessels" had black skull-and-crossbones flags flying from the tie-down ropes. Patches with crossed cutlasses appeared on jackets and colorful bandannas hid overlong hair. The pilots began referring to the crews as "pirates" and the crews called their pilots "girlies." You could hear the occasional burst of laughter as a crew chief growled "Arrrrggh, mate!" instead of "Roger that." Greg was assigned to a Chinook that was the last Echo model that had not yet been modernized. It still had some "steam gauge" type backup instruments and electronics, and the crew had cynically named her *Queen Anne's Revenge*. It was all done in fun and as a way to lighten the psychological load, until the jokes were pocketed and they flew off into combat.

It was time to take on the Bear.

For the first few months of the war, the Chinooks of Bravo Company took off nearly every night, heading for Afghanistan to bring the fight to the enemy. Teams of customers had to be infilled to link up with the Northern Alliance, or exfilled when they had wrapped up a mission, were being tasked to another AO or had wounded among them. Some of the missions were "one way," inserting teams and coming back empty, but they all required a return trip over the Bear. Bravo Company had trained very hard for this, but nothing they'd done in the mountains of Colorado could compare to the rocketing winds and wool-thick clouds of winter in Uzbekistan.

Greg and his fellow pilots were forced to "fly the cues." Their Chinooks were outfitted with a technological wonder called Terrain Following or Multi-Mode Radar, a system that had never before been used in combat. The MMR would "paint" the terrain out in front of the helo and create a three-dimensional image on a Vertical Situation Display on the cockpit console. The pilot on the controls wouldn't look outside the windshield, but only at the VSD as he raced along, avoiding the visual "cues" of obstacles: trees, power towers, buildings and sharp thrusting peaks. It was exactly like playing a complex, very fast video game, except that you couldn't hit the pause button and take a break, or curse and turn it off if you screwed up. You would just be dead, and so would everyone else on board.

The first leg of their journey was relatively "simple," flying along at 300 and 130 knots, blacked out, using only NVGs; it was the stuff they did all the time. Then, the Bear would begin to loom in the distance, and it was as if a weather switch had been thrown somewhere. The winds picked up, heavy clouds roiled aloft from the mountain crags, frozen fog enveloped the bird and driving sleet hammered the windshield. The slabs of arching mountains were engulfed in that deadly soup, but they could not fly above it and risk being tracked by enemy radar. They had to climb the Bear, while essentially "flying inside a Ping-Pong ball" of opaque white. Greg would flex his gloved fingers, grip the cyclic and collective, lock his eyes on the VSD and announce, "I am on the cues." From that point on, the internal comms of *Queen Anne's Revenge* would grow very, very quiet. The pilot-in-command and crew were not going to disturb him. The customers in the back often slept as the winds shook the bird, and every nerve in Greg's body melded to the machine in a trancelike state, often for hours without respite.

On the far side of the Bear, they would all begin to breathe again as they broke from the storms. Yet not for long, as either Greg or his pilot-in-command would announce, "Two minutes to the border." At that point, all the customers were wide-awake, their "game faces" on. The Taliban and their Al-Qaeda terrorist comrades couldn't see the Chinooks clearly as they roared overhead, but that didn't stop them from shooting everything they had at them. Small-arms tracers threw red and orange threads across the night sky. Heavier-caliber antiaircraft guns flung "flaming basketballs" at them. On numerous occasions, shoulder-fired missiles suddenly sprang up from the black wastelands below, and the pilots would be punching chaff and flare buttons, sending out blossoms of metal tinsel or hotheaded projectiles to try to deflect the enemy warheads. They came to feel exactly like those young B-17 pilots of World War II, who took off to bomb the Axis powers each night and often never returned.

And crossing the border was, in effect, only the beginning of each mission. The Night Stalkers' objectives were often two or three hours farther downrange. Climbing over the Bear with a full load of customers would drain their fuel, and they would have to link up somewhere in the air with a MC-130 tanker. In peacetime, you could pop up to altitude and give yourself a margin of error if something went wrong, but in a war zone it had to be done just a few hundred feet off the deck at 120 knots. The huge props of the four-engined tanker buffeted the Chinook as it closed the range from behind, the helo's long refueling probe seeking out the "basket," a fixture in the shape of a badminton shuttlecock affixed to the end of an eighty-five-foot hose. As the Chinook pilots guided their "male" head into the "female" cup, that point of intercourse was actually *inside* the swath of their forward rotor blades. It was not an exercise for men with trembling fingers or eye tics.

Naturally, when at last they reached their objectives, they were often shot at even more intensely. If the weather had been unusually clear over the Bear, Blackhawk gunships called DAPs (Direct Action Penetrators) would accompany them and suppress enemy ground fire, but more often than not the weather prohibited DAP participation. It was mostly an all-Chinook show and a lonely endeavor, and the return legs were identical to the insertions.

Greg and his comrades would arrive back at Karshi-Kanabad, usually just before dawn, to find the airfield socked in and another navigational and landing challenge. Then, they would unfold themselves from their cockpits and cabins, stretch their cramped muscles, laugh over the incidents that had just nearly killed them, eat something, play some cards and collapse onto their cots. Each afternoon, they would get up and do it all again. Soon, as Coalition Forces swept through central Afghanistan, the Night Stalkers would relocate to Bagram near Kabul. It would be better to be closer to the war. . . .

IT WAS ABOUT that time, in the last days of November, that Chuck Gant arrived at Karshi-Kanabad. Chuck was a seasoned CW4 who'd been flying with the regiment for fourteen years. At forty-three years old, he was large and quiet, with pale blue pilot's eyes, bristly salt-and-pepper hair and a flat expression that completely changed whenever he smiled. In a community of hot aviators who often swaggered and denied their fears, he was not afraid to admit that he was a "reluctant warrior." Combat scared the crap out of him and he was always relieved when it was over. Of course, none of that kept him from repeating the experience.

Chuck hailed from St. Louis, Missouri, and to the best of his knowledge no one in his family had served in the military going back to before the Civil War. Just after high school in 1977, he joined the Marine Corps reserves, hoping to eventually wind up full-time in Force Recon. But the marines wouldn't make any promises, while the army was offering slots in their Ranger battalions. Chuck moved over in the fall of 1979, and by the early eighties his company was working with a classified aviation unit called Task Force 160. The idea of flying one of those fast Little Birds appealed to him; plus, he had just gotten married and thought that being an aviator would give him more time with his young wife. Infantrymen were always out in the boonies somewhere, while these hotshot pilots got to go home after work. Little did he know . . .

He graduated flight school in the fall of 1983 and went off to fly medevac Hueys in Alaska. With the goal of becoming a Night Stalker always in his mind, he racked up his hours and tuned his skills, until

assessing in the spring of 1986. By January of the following year, he
was flying Little Bird assaults with A Company. In Operation Just
Cause, the SEALs were his customers and the "Hunt for Elvis" was his
primary mission in Panama. On the morning of D-day, he and his
partner, Kevin Palush, were returning to a FARP from another frustrating "dry hole," when they spotted a plume of smoke rising from a
small marshy island. Soon the comms began to chatter with word of a
missing AH-6 that had rolled in on a PDF warehouse to support American troops calling for fire support. Chuck and Kevin flew back to the
island and discovered the flaming wreck of Sonny Owens' and John
Hunter's helo.

Chuck stayed with the Little Birds for six years, flying again in
Desert Storm, although there were hardly any missions for them during that war. He was away from the regiment and finishing up his college degree during Gothic Serpent in Somalia, and when he returned
he finally confessed his secret: He had always had a love for Chinooks.
He asked for a transition, and when he climbed into the beautiful machine for the very first time, he felt that he had finally come home. It
was "roomy" and versatile; there was a lot of interaction with the crews
and always something going on. It was more fun than he had ever had
flying, and liking your work was what kept you in the game and on
your toes. Curiously, as his hours in Chinooks began to mount, four
other former Rangers with whom he had previously served also appeared as Night Stalker pilots. Even stranger, in Afghanistan he would
discover that his customers in the back were from the Ranger Regiment, A Company, First Battalion, his old alma mater. Perhaps as he
himself had done long ago, they would envy his "easy" lifestyle as an
aviator; at least until that harrowing dawn on Takur Gar.

By the time he arrived in Uzbekistan, the weather had begun to
clear and the Bear was no longer so ominous. The "veteran" pilots at
Karshi told Chuck that he had just missed the hairiest flying of his career, and that was just fine with him. Something told him that this was
going to be a very long war, with plenty of other opportunities to get

yourself killed. The op tempo at Karshi was winding down, as most of the customer teams had already been inserted with the Northern Alliance, and they were staying out there to help the myriad warlord factions clean out Al-Qaeda and Taliban fighters. In early December, Chuck and Jason Friel were one of the first teams to take their Chinook and cross the Bear for the last time, as they headed for their new FOB at Bagram.

If Karshi-Kanabad had been like the dark side of the moon, the strip at Bagram was more like Pluto. The airfield sat upon a vast flat plain, surrounded in the distance by snowcapped peaks, from which the wind whipped down and sliced through clothing and shell holes in the bombed-out terminal buildings. The structures still standing were scorched and bullet-pocked, and the pilots took up residence in a place they called Motel Six, which had no roof. All the frozen fields surrounding the tarmac were still laced with old Soviet mines, so when the pilots walked from their aircraft to the "motel," they didn't dare deviate from a slim, marked pathway. In those early months at Bagram, a number of Coalition soldiers would wander too far afield and lose their limbs.

Yet the Wild West atmosphere at Bagram had its benefits. Customers and air crews began living and working together in very close quarters, under extreme conditions, and that dissolved formalities and welded them together. There were White and Black SOF, OGAs (Other Government Agencies), German commandos, Canadian sniper teams and sundry other foreign special operators. They ate MREs, T-rations, canned smoked oysters with Tabasco sauce and vegetables that the customers bartered off the local economy. There was no contact with home, but care packages came through and often the enclosed food that had spent a month in transit was better than what showed up in the supply chain. For latrines, the men dug slit trenches in mine-cleared areas, filled them with rock and lye and stuck four-inch-wide PVC pipes in at an angle to simulate urinals. For "heavier loads," they built ad hoc porta-potties, cut fifty-five-gallon drums in half and lowered them into the holes. The crews flipped coins each evening for the "privilege" of emptying the drums into trenches, adding oil to the mix and setting the waste aflame. The evening air at Bagram wafted with a very unusual perfume.

Eventually, the Night Stalkers moved on to better quarters: army tents with potbellied stoves and folding cots. During the daytime, if the sun appeared, the weather might warm to a balmy forty-something degrees. At night, it would drop into the twenties. Chuck discovered the temperature anomalies of flying a Chinook in mountain winter weather: The cockpit was always the warmest spot on the ship and you could fly in only your issued coveralls. Yet the possibility of being shot down on some frozen mountain was always there, so you wore your layers and dripped sweat. In the back of the bird, the heating ducts were laughable, because the crew chiefs' gun ports were open to the wind and the ramps were always cranking up and down. The crews often wore so many layers that you could see only their eyes, and after a mission they had to peel their frozen fingers from the guns.

It was almost entirely a Chinook world, and it made Chuck proud to know that he and his fellow MH-47 pilots and crews were finally making their mark. It was intense, nonstop, over-the-edge combat flying in a place where only the huge, sturdy birds could venture. They were proving their worth, penetrating the impenetrable, delivering the goods as no other machines in the inventory could do. The customers were only interested in working with their heavily armed and powerful "ships," which could get them to their targets, anywhere, anytime, in all weather. Here in this rough, hard place, with their unkempt beards and rarely washed bodies, the Chinook pilots were at last able to grin back at their Blackhawk and Little Bird brothers and say, "This one's *our* war."

As the winter slid into 2002, more of the unit flowed into Bagram, the line of Chinooks on the pierced steel planking growing longer and longer. Conventional units were arriving in-country and there were rumors of a big push in the early spring, but in the meantime there were plenty of small teams to infil and exfil. Chuck Gant and Greg Calvert began flying together and the coupling worked well. Chuck was the pilot-in-command of his aircraft, and had the additional responsibility of Flight Lead and would "run" the missions. He took Greg under his wing as Greg worked toward achieving pilot-in-command status, and although he was only slightly older than Greg, their contrasting demeanors gave the impression of a serious sibling and his wisecracking kid brother. But most of that was reserved for the tents, for when flying they were focused and intently serious. . . .

WHEN DON TABRON arrived in Bagram, he was one of the most experienced Chinook pilots the regiment had, but he knew he wouldn't be flying. At forty-five years old and holding the highest rank a warrant officer could attain in the army—CW5—his wealth of experience had taken him out of the cockpit and on to higher responsibilities as a planner, combat coordinator and battle captain. In order to fly missions you had to be "current," which meant that any substantial period out of the cockpit required a requalification process. With a war on, there wasn't time for that, so he had accepted his fate and his orders to perform other duties, albeit equally important as handling the controls.

Don was an easygoing, quiet and modest man. If you saw him in his civvies having a beer at the local bar, "special ops aviator" wouldn't likely come to mind; he was medium height, with a wiry build, short brown hair and eyes that had a somewhat Eurasian shape. He looked a decade younger than his age, except when one of his rare smiles crinkled his crow's-feet. He joined the army in 1975 as an artilleryman. While serving in the mud and snow of Korea, he saw the light and graduated from flight school as an aero-scout pilot in 1980. In eleven years of flying OH-58s he had amassed more than four thousand hours, and by 1991, as Desert Storm was about to kick off, he was the senior instructor pilot among the three scout aviators supporting Cobras in his battalion. In all his years of flying, he had never tested his skills in action and he knew this was his time. He was already packing to go when his commander called him into his office.

"You'll be staying here, Tabron."

"Excuse me, sir?"

"You're too valuable an asset. I'm deploying the other IPs."

Don was recently divorced, unattached and had no children. His fellow pilots were both married and had pairs of toddlers, and their potential loss would crush their young families.

"Sir, they've both got young wives and young kids. Send *me*. I *need* to go."

"Well, I need you here."

The hell you do, Don thought to himself and immediately applied for the 160th.

He was somewhat surprised when his assessment came up and the Night Stalkers told him he was being considered for MH-47s.

"Chinooks? You sure you got the right guy?" Don had assumed he would be assessing as a Little Bird pilot, given his record. "You know I'm a Kiowa guy, right?"

"Yes, but we're looking at you for Chinooks. Is that a problem?"

"I'll fly whatever you guys want me to." Don smiled. "I'll take your check ride. Let's go!"

He had been in a Chinook only twice before, as a passenger. His assessment pilot started it up, but then Don took over, hit his targets in plus or minus thirty seconds and flew it back to Fort Campbell. He had "air sense," and if a pilot had that overall talent you could basically move him from one helo to another without much drama. From 1989 through 1999 he flew hundreds of training missions and deployed to Haiti for Operation Uphold Democracy, and later to the Iraqi border for Operations Desert Fox and Southern Watch. His missions were primarily CSAR, and although no pilots were shot down or needed rescuing during his tours, at least no one was holding him back because he was "too valuable." He worked his way up from an

FMQ (Fully Mission Qualified) pilot, to operations officer and platoon leader, and when the events of 9/11 unfolded he was serving as a
staff officer whose task was to coordinate missions downrange. He also
had a new relationship, and a concerned family at home.

"This is our Pearl Harbor," Don told his wife when she arrived from
work that evening. He had already started packing. "I don't know
when I'm leaving, but it'll happen soon. The world has changed.
Things are different now."

"No." She shook her head, denying the inevitable. "You won't be
going anywhere."

Ten days later Don was on a flight to Saudi Arabia. He would be
working in a CAOC, Combined Air Operations Center, as part of a
team called SOLE. The Special Operations Liaison Element was
chaired by officers of the various SOF units who would be going into
action, and their function at CAOC was to advise air force elements as
to when and where their support and firepower would be needed.
From the air force's point of view, the knowledge of where the 160th
helos would be flying was crucial for de-confliction; you didn't want
American F-16s or British Tornadoes suddenly crashing into American helos—or worse, shooting one down. From Don's point of view, it
was more important not to let the scores of foreign air force officers
roaming around the CAOC know too much about the Night Stalkers'
plans, because at that point he didn't trust a damn soul. He cynically
referred to the operation as "Chaos."

The room they all worked in at CAOC was enormous, with movie
theater–size screens on the walls, a hundred workstations and a
sunken "pit" in the center where the U.S. Air Force commanding general paced and growled. As Operation Enduring Freedom spun up,
Don was constantly flipping his laptop screen down as unfamiliar
Coalition officers from six different countries passed behind his chair.
Eventually the SOLE members moved to their own secure area,
where they could work their black magic in comfort, but they were
never the air force general's favorite coworkers. CAOC utilized a

tracking system called "Grenadier Brat," which could track the move-ments of every Coalition aircraft on the huge screens glowing in the darkened steel cavern. As the helos from the 160th lifted off from Uzbekistan or their ship in the Arabian Sea, their blips crawled across the maps. Yet as soon as they crossed the Afghani borders, their transponders would be switched off and they'd disappear.

"SOLE!" the general would roar. "Where are those goddamn heli-copters?!"

"Right over here, sir," Don would call out. The blips remained on the secure SOLE laptop screens, and while the commander didn't like it, he could live with it as long as he'd be able to de-conflict.

Night after night, Don watched his friends flying into harm's way as pixilated dots on a cold flat monitor. He had the "crew cards" for each mission; he knew who was on each aircraft. He also had comms that could reach out that far, via satellites and overhead flying platforms, and at times through the crackling ether he could hear the gunfire and the clipped, tight chatter of men in combat. Sometimes it was hard to remain silent, like a father with a child in a high-stakes soccer game. But you never spoke to men in action unless you had something to offer them, such as a Hellfire missile at just the right time.

In early December, he left Saudi Arabia to spend the holidays with his family, hoping that his next deployment would not be to a desk somewhere, cheering from the sidelines. In the first week of January, he was in Karshi-Kanabad, and one month later, in Bagram.

WHEN CORY LAMOREAUX finally arrived in Bagram on the nineteenth of January, he was grinning from ear to ear. After nearly three years of training his men and nagging his commanders, his con-cept had finally been realized. His medics were flying CASEVAC on every single mission.

The first three months of the war had been personally frustrating. With the task force divided into northern and southern elements, his medical staff had been split up as well, with some deploying to Karshi-Kanabad and the rest, including Cory, sitting aboard an aircraft carrier in the Arabian Sea. The helos and customers were lifting off the deck every night on missions, but his commanders still weren't letting the Night Stalker medics fly. Both the Black and White SOF teams had their own embedded medics, so it made no sense to take another doc if you could squeeze an additional shooter on board. Special Forces, Rangers, marines and SEALs were vying for a chance to "go get some," so Cory and his people were mostly left behind, twiddling their thumbs. He talked his way onto a couple of CSAR and DART missions when Coalition aircraft went down in the wilds, but that was about it. In December he rotated back to Fort Campbell for the holidays, where he heard that things were decidedly different for his people in the northern war. He was thrilled to spend Christmas and New Year's with Laura, Bailee and Hunter, but he had one eye cocked on the calendar.

In the second week of January, he swung through Karshi-Kanabad on his way to Bagram, where he found out it was true. His medics told him that as soon as the Chinooks returned from their first missions over the Bear, with their crews half-frozen and bullet holes in the fuselages, Joe Garst had said, "Put the medics on the airplanes. That's why they're here!" Cory nearly danced a victory jig when he heard that.

It was already nine o'clock at night when he flew into Bagram aboard one of the last Chinooks to abandon Karshi-Kanabad. His medics greeted him with whoops and hollers, and sarcastic remarks about how he was only showing up because he thought the war was over. His flight surgeon, Dr. Kyle Remick, was there as well, and they all stayed up chin-wagging until one in the morning, when they finally crashed at Motel Six. Two hours later, Cory and Remick were suddenly poked awake. A CH-53 heavy lift helo had crashed in the mountains somewhere and a Quick Reaction Force was being launched. The two men hustled their enormous aid bags out to the Chinooks.

The flight was short, less than half an hour. Dawn was breaking and the skies were clear. As the pair of Chinooks circled the crash site, their crew chiefs peering over their miniguns for enemy combatants, Cory spotted the crashed 53. There was nothing left of it but the tail and a huge charred hulk where the fuselage had been, sitting there smoking in a bowl of blinding snow, at an altitude of nine thousand feet. The birds flared and settled, kicking up a curtain of swirling white, and through it Cory could see injured men lying everywhere, like mock-casualties at a disaster drill. One man was still on his feet, waving them in, yet as the ramps dropped down the QRF men sprinted off to form a defensive perimeter, and no one was going for the patients. It wasn't Cory's job to leave the aircraft, but he grabbed his aid bag and told Remick, "I'm getting off."

He started to triage the men. They were marines and they'd been lying there for three hours in the freezing cold. One of their crew hadn't made it out of the burning wreck at all; another had crawled away to die. The rest were all injured, one with an open femur fracture that had swelled his leg to two times its normal size. The only man still on his feet was the aircraft commander, his head bruised and swollen from an impact with his console. None of them seemed to know exactly what had happened, but Cory assumed enemy action and wanted to get them all out of there fast. He yelled out to members of the QRF to haul his litters as he raced from man to man through the knee-deep snow, and when the last one was finally aboard the bird, he crawled up the ramp and vomited up his past two meals.

He realized then that he had AMS, Acute Mountain Sickness. Bagram was at an elevation of five thousand feet and he certainly had not had the time to acclimate, let alone work feverishly at nearly twice that altitude. As the helo banked away, he crashed onto his back, avoiding his regurgitated chunks as his searing lungs refilled with oxygen. Then he smiled, got himself up and went to work with Remick. He hadn't been in-country twelve hours yet, and he had just flown his first CASEVAC.

By nine o'clock that morning, Cory and the doc had finished delivering their Marine Corps patients to the 274th Forward Surgical Team, which had set up its operating room in the base of Bagram's old control tower. He and his Night Stalker medics discovered that a mobile PX had erected a temporary tent outside Motel Six, so they got in line and zigzagged through the stacks of Mountain Dew and Power Bars until they spotted a box of Macanudo cigars and grinned at one another, all thinking the same thing. They climbed onto the roof of the motel and sat out in the early sun, puffing and joking, and they got someone to come up and take a picture of them holding up a flag. Two of them would depart that day, leaving Cory and Rob Kiely as the only two medics with Bravo Company. It would be their last moments of lull and reflection for a long time.

After that, Cory would come to regard the days and nights of nonstop operations as "just crazy." He and Kiely were rotating on missions, at least one of them flying nearly every night. During the next six weeks, Cory's combat hours ticked up over one hundred, which meant that he was flying scores of missions because they were of relatively short duration compared to the previous long-range excursions from Karshi-Kanabad. Bagram was much closer to the action. You could be landing at a safe house in Gardez after only forty-five minutes, pick up a load of customers and be infilling them an hour or two later. And nothing was mundane, nothing routine. They were shot at every night. The Al-Qaeda and Taliban would hear the helos coming, searchlights would flash up from the valleys below, RPGs would start whooshing up at the helos, bullets would whistle through the rotors and fuselages. At times the missions went from right down on the deck to over twelve thousand feet in half an hour, and the crews would be quaking with cold inside their "mustang" suits and wearing oxygen masks. At times the rides would be nice and smooth, because the Chinooks were very steady birds and the crews in the back could sit comfortably or stand up and look out the windows. Then, the dance of the RPGs and flaming basketballs would begin; the pilots would go evasive and the crews would be hanging on for dear life and banging around the cabins like passengers in a runaway subway car. After a few such missions, "crazy" became the norm. When Operation Anaconda started spooling up toward the end of February, nobody thought it was going to be anything unusual.

It had been three months since the Taliban and their Al-Qaeda allies had been driven from power in Afghanistan's major cities, but now their remnants had retreated a hundred miles south of Kabul to the Paktika Province. In a brace of rough peaks looming above the Shahikot Valley, they were ensconced in networks of deep caves and mountaintop redoubts. Arab jihadists from twenty-odd countries had joined them, along with Chechens, Uzbekis and even Pakistani cohorts, all of whom were suspected of harboring their "queen bee," Osama bin Laden, perhaps somewhere within those frozen crevasses. The plan for Anaconda was to have the Northern Alliance, advised and guided by Special Forces, attack from the north and drive them into the Shahikot. Simultaneously, Coalition Forces from the U.S. Army's 101st Airborne Division and the Tenth Mountain Division would strike into the valley in lightning ground and air assaults. Canada's light infantry would also take part, along with Australia's and New Zealand's SAS and German commandos. France, Norway and Denmark would also be participating. It was a time when even America's most reticent allies still cared about what had happened to her on September eleventh, and were prepared to show it.

It was to be a complex operation, with Special Operations forces from Task Forces Hammer and Anvil and the paratroopers and Rangers of Task Force Rakkasan. There would be axes of assault called Iron, Metal and Steel, and blocking forces to kill or capture the fleeing enemy called Chevy, Ford, Oldsmobile and Jeep. They would all be covered from the air by B-52s, B-1 and B-2 bombers, AC-130 gunships, F-15s, F-16s and Apache helicopters. Predator drones and P-3 Orions would be televising all of it live to Tactical Operations Centers far away. All of those red and blue arrows representing the coiling snake of Anaconda looked very promising on the tactical maps, but they represented men who would be breathing very hard in that thin mountain air, while they killed and tried not to be killed.

Yet all of that was the "big picture," into which the Night Stalker pilots and crews didn't delve very deeply. Their missions were close focus: getting their black or white SOF teams into the mountains to hunt for high-value targets and do the toughest of the advance, recon and OP work for the upcoming battle. It was get them in, get them out or move them to a better place. Someone in the TOC and much higher up, maybe at USSOCOM in Tampa, would be making those decisions about when, where and why. The Night Stalker mission was to do or die.

Don Tabron was now serving as the AMC, air mission commander, for many of those lift operations. As such, he would not be in the cockpit, but sitting in a collapsible jump seat on the threshold of Station 95, just behind the pilots of whichever bird was designated as Chalk One. As AMC, it was his task to interface with the customers who'd be climbing aboard. When he first arrived in Bagram, the incoming customers who hadn't worked a lot with the 160th had to be shepherded through the process and had difficulty understanding the limitations. Don would have to explain to them that altitude, range and gross weight were the factors that determined how many men could participate and what they could carry. But the customers who were Night Stalker "regulars" already knew the drill. They would give Don a target, and, working with the flight lead, he would calculate the round-trip range, fuel requirements, weather projections and altitude factors, and return to them with a load allowance. "All right," he would say to a Ranger platoon leader, "you can bring eighteen hundred pounds." That officer would then immediately know how many men, machine guns, ammunition and grenades he could herd into the bird. After a bit of patient coaching, they all got it and it ran like clockwork.

In the few days before Anaconda kicked off, the commanders of the operation halted all air missions so that aircraft maintenance crews could catch up and all energies could be focused on the upcoming assault. But the Night Stalkers still had customer teams downrange who needed to be resupplied, moved to better positions or replaced by fresh operators. Missions were beginning to stack up, so the Bravo Chinooks found themselves suddenly working at a breakneck pace.

On the night of March 3, Anaconda had been running for two full days. Chuck and Greg were flying as Razor Zero One, their call sign no matter which bird they were actually using. Chuck was flight lead and pilot-in-command, Greg to his right as copilot. Don was in his position in the jump seat. They had been grounded for a few days, hanging back as the Quick Reaction Force with a platoon of Rangers, in case someone needed emergency support. But nothing like that had happened, so Chuck had gone into the TOC to see Joe Garst.

"Captain, my guys need to fly," Chuck said. "Can you swap us around, put us on some of the infils?"

"Don't see why not," Garst said. He took them off the QRF and gave them enough infil, exfil, and resupply missions to keep them busy.

RAZOR ZERO ONE lifted off from Bagram, with Razor Zero Two close behind. Randy Olson and Ray Smiley were piloting Zero Two and both helos had customers aboard: Canadian Strategic Recon teams that had to be infilled to help cover the valley. Another White team far up in the peaks needed to be resupplied, and then two German SR teams had to be pulled out, because their vantage points weren't good enough to be valuable. It would be five missions rolled into one, a long, freezing night of hopping from peak to ridge. Altitudes were up above eleven thousand feet and the mountains were slippery with wet, fresh snow. But it was nothing unusual for a Bravo Company team, and by two o'clock in the morning they were back at Bagram and taxiing toward the FARP, when a call reached out from the TOC.

"Zero One, we've got a broken aircraft out at Gardez. Need you to refuel, take your flight out to them and swap helos so they can complete their mission. Bring their busted bird back here."

"Roger," Chuck answered. Don Tabron had to quickly gather intel on the intended mission of the broken bird and determine exactly how much fuel they would need when replaced. Then they filled Zero One up to the proper level and took off with Zero Two for Gardez.

The broken Chinook was Razor Zero Three, piloted by Al Mack. He and Razor Zero Four, piloted by Jason Friel, had Black teams on board, SEALs who were supposed to be infilled into two separate locations. Al's customers were to be dropped at the base of a mountain called Takur Gar, and then climb to their OP on top. Cory Lamoreaux was aboard Al's aircraft; Al sort of regarded Cory as his "good luck charm" and liked having him around whenever he flew. They had landed briefly near a safe house in Gardez to pick up some additional SEALs and were ten minutes out from the target when the AC-130 circling above ran low on fuel and had to pull off station. Overhead platforms had reported no activity on the objective, but Al was no fool; he wasn't taking his men in there without some decent firepower overhead. He and Razor Zero Four flew back to Gardez to wait for a fresh AC-130 to come on station, running the engines down halfway to conserve fuel, and then shutting them and running on only APU power. Then they had to wait some more while a flight of B-52s started working the enemy ridgelines. At last they got the "go," but when Al went to fire his engines back up, he had a "runaway" on Number Two; flames shot out of the exhaust, essentially burning it up.

When missions were running back-to-back and a bird broke down, the Night Stalkers would only swap "front enders." The new helo would fly in and only the pilots and air mission commander would disembark and offer up their seats, leaving the cabin crew in place. Then, the pilots of the broken bird and their customers would jump into the mechanically sound replacement. It wasn't optimal, because you might have pilots and cabin crews that had been working together for an extended period of time and already had "symmetry," yet with the op tempo so high you didn't want to take the time to switch over all those personnel and gear. Al Mack wanted Cory to come over with him to the new bird being delivered by Chuck and Greg, but there was already a Night Stalker medic on board that aircraft. It was Kevin Zites, a fine regimental medic who had come into Bagram to replace Cory, who in turn was scheduled to be back at Fort Bragg for his SOF medic refresher by March 10. Cory told Al over the ICS that it would take too much time for him and Zites to switch out all their gear.

Al Mack, his copilot and his SEAL customers hustled through the darkness to the aircraft Chuck and Greg had just brought in, which now became Razor Zero Three. They soon lifted off for their mission, with Razor Zero Four peeling away toward its own objective. Chuck and a maintenance pilot and crew members were going to nurse the broken bird back to Bagram, empty. Everyone else climbed aboard Randy Olson's Razor Zero Two. Cory found himself making runs back and forth from his two-hundred-and-fifty-pound pile of equipment to Randy's helo, realizing that he was humping his gear across an open field in one of the most heavily mined pieces of real estate on earth. When the crew of Zero Two saw him sweating and huffing steam, they thumbed their noses at him.

"Oh, so *now* you want to fly with us, Lamoreaux? Now that your bird's all busted, huh?"

"Shut up and help me," Cory grunted.

In the short period of time it took for the broken bird and Zero Two to return to Bagram, Al Mack and his customers encountered the first taste of hell on Takur Gar. Hours had been burned up due to the malfunction and now there wasn't time for the SEALs to land somewhere else and make the vertical climb. Al would put them right on top. He was already flaring for his landing, his SEALs poised on the open ramp, when they came under a hail of murderous machine-gun fire that punched through the electrical systems and hydraulics. An RPG rocketed into the cargo cabin, slamming the crew to the steel floor as a ramp man yelled for Al to abort. His controls weren't responding; it felt like he had one engine out, and the Chinook was bucking like a mechanical bull. He dove over the cliff side to try to gain some airspeed and bounced into a hard landing on the valley floor, seven kilometers from the peak. But the SEALs in the back were going nuts. They kept taking and repeating a head count. They had *lost* one man. Navy Petty Officer Neil Roberts had fallen off the ramp into the snows of Takur Gar. He was alone up there, with only his Squad Automatic Weapon and his wits, surrounded by scores of enemy fighters that no one had anticipated and no overhead platform had spotted.

As Chuck and Randy were landing their two birds at Bagram, a call came from the TOC informing them that they would have to go out again. A helo had gone down somewhere in the valley. They knew that it could only be a 160th bird. Greg was instructed to move from the back end of Razor Zero Two to rejoin Chuck in a "new" aircraft. The new Razor Zero One would be MH-47E, Number 475. Sergeant Phil Svitak, an experienced and highly respected flight engineer and crew chief, was already over on the flight line, opening up the bird. Phil was thirty-one years old, with the wide, rugged face of a light-bearded lumberjack. He was a quiet type with a shy smile, but he really knew his business. His fellow door gunner and crew chief was Dave Dube ("Doo-bee"), a man of nearly equal experience, and in the back on the rear ramp would be Sean Ludwig and Brian "Jed" Wilson. Sean and Jed were younger Night Stalkers in their early twenties; Sean was medium height, dark-haired and muscular, while Jed was a lanky redhead with a wide grin. In addition to their air crew skills, they were all paratroopers and well-trained ground combatants.

"What the hell's going on?" Cory asked Rob Kiely as the medic came over to Razor Zero Two to help his boss offload his gear.

"Not sure. Looks like something bad, though."

Blades were whipping around the helos in the freezing night. The urgent voices of commanders under pressure crackled from radio speakers inside the bombed-out TOC next to the tower. It would have been SOP for Cory to now stay behind as Kiely took on this new mission, because Kiely was "sitting on" the QRF in case something like this happened, but someone in the TOC knew that a desperate situation was developing rapidly and wanted a senior medic out there.

"They told me to stay here," Kiely said as he started hauling Cory's gear over to the bird that Phil Svitak was opening up; the Night Stalker medics were always aboard Chalk One of any mission. Chuck Gant was already in the pilot's seat, running up the nav systems and the APU.

"They did?" Cory shouted above the whining generator.

"Yup."

There wasn't time for the two medics to go to the TOC and straighten things out, so they loaded up the CASEVAC gear and got it set up.

Chuck, Randy and Don remained in their helos. They had been told by their commanders to spin up, await orders and prepare for immediate launch. They were going to launch as a QRF package now. Captain Nate Self, the Ranger commander of the Quick Reaction Force, showed up with his nineteen men, including his TAC (Tactical Air Controllers), who were embedded with the Ranger teams to call in fire support. Self started dividing them all up into the two birds. He was a twenty-five-year-old West Point graduate and a quickly rising star in the Ranger Regiment. He and his platoon had been in-country for two months and hadn't yet fired a shot.

Meanwhile, things were getting worse in the valley below Takur Gar. Al Mack's bird was done for the night, all shot up, his radios shattered, and he had failed to make his rendezvous back at Gardez with Razor Zero Four. Jason Friel, the pilot-in-command of Zero Four, finally heard from an AC-130 on station that Al and his crew were down but seemed to be okay, and the air force pilot relayed the coordinates. Friel flew to the crash site and got everyone aboard, only to hear of the worst nightmare a special operator can envision: a man lost and inadvertently left behind. That wasn't something you let stand for very long. Razor Four would be going back in.

Friel didn't need further urging from the pumped-up SEALs, but they couldn't lose their heads; they would have to come up with a quick plan elsewhere. The air force Spectre pilot was telling them to get the hell out of there, because enemy combatants were closing fast on the crash site. Friel hauled Razor Four back to Gardez and set down, calculating the fuel he had left in his tanks, how far they would have to go and how high. He was almost dry. There was no FARP at Gardez and he had just enough to make it to the top of that peak and then he'd be done. He ordered everyone off the bird but his crew, the SEALs and their air force combat controller, Tech Sergeant John Chapman, and then he pulled power.

Half an hour later, he was peeling away from the peak, his bird peppered with machine-gun holes. He had successfully inserted the SEAL team, but they had charged headlong into a brutal firefight. Takur Gar was crawling with enemy fighters. They were holed up in a bunker and a warren of slit trenches, and they had multiple heavy machine-gun positions, recoilless rifles and RPGs. The SEALs failed to find Roberts, but they fought a horrendous close-quarters battle for another thirty minutes. John Chapman was killed at point-blank range, and with him went their air cover. Half the remaining men were wounded, one with a leg nearly shot off. They had no choice but to withdraw or all die up there, and they half climbed and half fell down the face of the mountain.

Not very much of this detail was coming over to the pilots of Razor Zero One or Two back at Bagram. Randy Olson called over to Chuck on the radio and told him to switch frequencies and pick up some satellite comms. The transmissions that night were intermittent and garbled, crossing over one another, fading in and out. Atmospheric conditions could wreak havoc with the radios in those mountains, no matter the sophisticated technology. In addition to that, White and Black organizations had different "fills," sets of secure frequencies depending on their mission profiles. Chuck and Greg struggled to track what was going on as Don finished sorting out the QRF package and climbed into his jump seat in the companionway.

"This is Toolbox. . . . Yep, he's out of there. . . . Looks like they got him. . . . Aircraft is shot up. . . . Looks like they landed okay. . . ."

Whooaaa, Chuck thought. He turned to Tabron. "Hey, Don, looks like we're holding here for a bit. Why don't you go over the TOC and see if you can get some more info for us."

Don hopped out of Zero One and ran into the TOC.

"You need to get back out there, Tabron," his commanders immediately snapped at him. "Prepare for launch. We'll sort it out when you get to Gardez."

Don ran back to the bird and strapped in. Over in Zero Two, the ground crews were trying to configure an eight-hundred-gallon Robertson tank and haul it into the Chinook. Someone at Gardez was definitely going to need gas at some point, but it just wasn't happening fast enough. The TOC called periodically to check the status of the aircraft. Forty-five minutes had elapsed since notification, and it was now approaching 5:00 A.M.

They all knew what that meant. Even if they launched that very minute, it would be dawn by the time they reached the objective. Chuck called the TOC.

"We need to *go*. It's gonna be daylight."

The TOC responded with instructions to go ahead and launch, without the Robertson fuel tank configured. Chuck alerted the cabin crew, pulled power and thundered off the planking, with Randy on his tail. . . .

THROUGH THE LAST of what remained of the night, the two birds swept toward Gardez, flying low and fast. All the pilots were using their NVGs, but they wouldn't need them for long. Streaks of gray were already painting the purple curtains behind the distant peaks, and the distinctions between black and green terrain features inside their eyepieces were beginning to blur. In Razor Zero One, Chuck was in the left seat, trying to sort out his mission as he flipped through his frequency selector, keyed his mike to ask questions and listened. He had turned the controls over to Greg, who was going to fly the infil. Don perched behind them, up center in his seat. He wasn't piloting the bird, so he would keep his peace unless he discerned something through the incoming transmissions that might be worth discussing. In the back, Cory was wearing an air crew helmet, attached to the comms by a long, curled cord. He was no more than a passenger now, albeit an important one if things went sour. It was the third bird he'd flown on that night and he hadn't been able to get all his gear from one to the other, which didn't please him. But he had his main aid bag, a second hanging bag with more supplies, his electronic vital signs monitor plus blankets and oxygen, which would do the job, barring a major fiasco. Phil Svitak and Dave Dube were gripping their miniguns on the right and left forward doors. Sean Ludwig and Jed Wilson had their fingers on the triggers of their older M-60 machine guns in the rear. The Rangers and PJs were hunkered down on the floor. Nate Self, as always, was on his feet, peering out the small side bubble windows.

No one aboard knew exactly where they were going yet, but both helos pushed on for Gardez, a good interim spot close to the action if they had to hold somewhere. Secure traffic confirmed that Razor Zero Three had tried to insert a Black team, had lost one man and been shot down. Now they were hearing that Razor Zero Four had rescued that crew and their customers, dropped the crew at Gardez and returned to the objective. But they had also sustained battle damage and had to put down somewhere else, out of action. Suddenly, a heated discussion ensued between the air force pilot of the AC-130 gunship that was now covering the AO and the overall ground commanders controlling his flight. Apparently some sort of missile had been fired at the Spectre, but the pilot was heroically refusing to leave his post.

"We want you off station immediately," Ground was insisting.

"Copy. Negative. I am not leaving these personnel without cover."

"You need to leave *now*. You've had a SAM fired at you, it's almost daylight and we don't want you orbiting at that altitude. Leave."

"Copy. Negative. I am remaining on station."

With that, the ground commanders began shouting and threatening. The Spectre had a full load of eleven air crew and gunners aboard. If it took a heavy hit, it couldn't hope to auto-rotate into a semisafe landing like a helo. It would just slam into a mountainside and explode.

"All right," the AC-130 pilot finally complied. "But I want it clear that I am leaving here under duress."

Chuck and Greg looked at each other. The hairs on the back of their necks were starting to tingle with that unpleasant electrical sensation that warns all mammals to tread no further. As the flight approached Gardez, Chuck called the TOC, relayed his location and asked for further instructions. The TOC called back and told him they were committing his QRF package. He would now be turned over to another aerial platform flying much higher above, which had eyes on his target. He switched frequencies and began talking to a P-3 Orion.

"This is Razor Zero One. Confirm these coordinates." He read the number sequence off.

"Roger, that is correct."

"What else do you have for me?"

"Four to six movers on the objective." The P-3 observer was talking about people moving around on top of Takur Gar, who appeared as small "hot spots" in his FLIR screen.

"What's the status?" Chuck asked him. "Friendly or enemy?"

"That is unknown."

Terrific, Chuck thought. He tried to reach out to the AC-130 that had gone off station, to perhaps get more concrete intel from a guy who'd just been there, but all that popped in his headset was a breaking squelch. He told Greg to move into a holding pattern above the valleys while he checked the coordinates again on his digital map, and when they came around again full circle, there was no doubt. There it was: a single, lonely, visually stunning peak less than ten miles dead ahead. Its cap shimmered with fresh snow. The skies enveloping it were going from slate gray to Pacific blue. All he really knew about it was that it was a hot LZ. He had no idea that the bodies of Neil Roberts and John Chapman had already been dragged into an enemy bunker atop that peak, or that the terrorists who had killed them were now hunkered down behind cold rocks, waiting for the next batch of heroically foolish Americans. No one could tell him that the half-decimated SEAL team was crawling and bleeding into a crevice down the mountainside, because no one knew. You didn't want to set a helo down on a place like that unless there was nowhere nearby to infil your customers. There was no such alternative in sight. He heard a staticky whisper over the comms, someone discussing the fate of the lost man.

"Listen, it's getting close to full daylight. If we don't get him now, we're gonna lose him forever. . . ."

Chuck took a breath. Many men would be making decisions that day—some good, some bad, some carefully considered, some instinctive. Later on, with the comfort of armchair analysis, some would call the events on Takur Gar a mishap, a tragedy or a fiasco. They would blame poor planning, miscommunications and faulty equipment. But it was none of those things. It was just war, and incidents of war often take place in very close quarters, and with as much time to consider one's responses as in an unprovoked bar fight.

Chuck Gant was bombarded that dawn with bits and pieces of incomplete information, but he knew one thing for certain: There was an American soldier up there on that peak, all alone, perhaps wounded and dying. They were going to get him out, or die trying. He called Randy Olson in Razor Zero Two.

"Zero Two, I want you to pick up a separation."

Chuck was ordering Randy to peel away and hang back, and Randy knew why. All of their skins were crawling at that point, and Chuck wasn't going to give the enemy *two* fat targets to shoot at. Randy could have argued the point, but they didn't do things that way in the regiment.

"Roger."

"You can go back to Gardez," Chuck said. "I'll call you if I need you."

Randy didn't answer. A standard separation would be about one minute, two miles in range behind Chalk One. But where he held exactly was up to him, and he wasn't going all the way back to Gardez. He banked off his flight path but orbited just over the valley and watched.

"All right," Chuck said to Greg. "Let's make a high-speed pass."

"Roger."

Chuck wanted one good look at the LZ before they made their final commitment. They were climbing straight up the face of the mountain now, the summit looming above, and it was as if the rest of the world were falling away and there was nothing left but that peak. Phil Svitak's voice came from the right side of the helo.

"I've got a bird down there on the valley floor. Must be Zero Three, but he's about four miles away."

Four miles? That made no sense to any of them. They had assumed that Al Mack had gone down close to the objective, so maybe this was the *wrong* objective. Chuck called the P-3 one more time to double-check his coordinates.

"That is *correct.*" The P-3 guy was sounding exasperated now, which was a luxury he could afford since he was out of harm's way. "And you've got a Triple-A site up there, too. No one's on it."

A *Triple-A site?* There was a heavy-caliber antiaircraft gun up there.

"No one's on it at the *moment,*" Greg said to himself. The Chinook's two engines were pumping out everything they had, and then he popped it up to the left of the narrow mountain cap and banked hard to the right, doing 120 knots as Chuck spoke to the crew.

"Okay, everybody, look for anything you can see. Enemy positions. Friendlies."

No one in the back reported anything that Chuck and Greg couldn't see themselves. It was broad daylight now and their NVGs were pushed up over their helmet visors; some trees, rocky outcroppings and a single thick bunker at the very top, with a narrow firing slit that was blackened and looked like it had taken a direct hit, probably from one of the

AC-130s. The only possible LZ was a narrow slope about a hundred meters long, which led down from that bunker to a fist of rocks and a sharp drop-off. Chuck called the P-3 to report the bunker and asked one more time to confirm the coordinates. The P-3 confirmed. Chuck pressed his ICS switch again.

"All right. We are turning inbound."

Greg took the helo back down below the peak, making a long, wide circle through the valley. He would take the Chinook straight up the wall again, hugging it tightly so if there were enemy fighters up there, they wouldn't see him until he roared into the LZ. But the sun was already up there with them now. They would look like a huge black boot stomping down from the sky.

"Six minutes," Chuck warned over the intercom.

"Six minutes!" Nate Self turned and shouted to his men as he held up one full hand and an extra finger. His Rangers struggled to their feet, gripping the steel handrails mounted above the small portholes.

"Listen up," Chuck said to his crew, "hold your fire. We don't know where any friendlies are up here. Phil, that bunker's on the right side. Keep your gun on it. I'm not sure what's up with that."

"Roger."

Electrical power was surging into Phil's and Dave's miniguns now, their gloved fingers twitching over the triggers. A knife-like wind was whipping past their barrels and into their faces. On numerous missions in the past, Cory would nudge up close to Phil and peer over his shoulder, helping him spot any potential targets. As he moved into that position now, Phil keyed his mike and spoke to him.

"Doc, move back."

Cory shrugged inwardly and complied. He retreated five feet, gripped a side rail and peered out a bubble window. They were on short final. The ramp was halfway down. The bird was tilting nose up. Spirals of snow were swirling up from the rotor wash.

Greg was committing. He had picked out his landing area. He was flaring, descending . . . sixty feet . . . fifty . . . And then the world suddenly opened up. The windshield splintered and completely shattered as bullets punched across the console and slammed into his body armor. He heard Phil call out, "Fire from two o'clock!" and then he heard Phil's gun start to roar and Dave's gun, too, from the left side. He had to finish the approach, yet when he glanced down at his instruments they were all gone. Don Tabron's boots flew up past his face as the AMC hurled himself backward out of his seat. He heard Chuck's voice, as if coaching a novice flight student, "Forward and down, forward and down." Something exploded. The left engine started to scream, so he knew the right one was out. The thought flashed through his mind to abort and take it right over that pinnacle in front of the bird and then dive down and pick up airspeed, but he knew the ship wouldn't make it. She had only one landing left in her and this was it.

Chuck had been hit in his left leg. A heavy-caliber bullet had pierced his side door and center punched through his femur, taking out two inches of bone. Yet even with that sledgehammer impact, he was still focused on the landing, and as he realized that the LZ was upslope to the nose and slightly down to the right he called out to Greg, "Watch the slope," and grabbed for the controls. But Greg had it, he had seen it, too, and he stuck the left wheels into the snow and held the cyclic to the left so they wouldn't roll over. The Chinook slammed down hard and Chuck knew they were done. He reached up and yanked the ECLs back to kill the engines. The miniguns had stopped firing, but enemy bullets were banging into the cockpit from everywhere. He turned to the right to climb through the companionway, but only the top half of his leg followed. He looked down. The rest of it was still attached, but hanging in the bottom of his coverall like a bag of ground meat.

He reached up, hit the jettison handle on his door, grabbed his M-4 from the circuit panel and hurled himself into space.

Greg's head snapped to the left. Something had smacked his helmet. He looked to the right. It was so hot in the cockpit when they flew that he always kept his "Dairy Queen" window open, and through it now he could see three men starting to come over a rock, at his two o'clock and not fifty meters away. He grabbed the cyclic with his left, snatched up his M-4, stuck it out the window, flicked the safety off and opened fire. The bird felt steady enough now. *Time to get the hell out of here.* He reached for the yellow-and-black handle, twisted it and kicked at the emergency door, and as it popped away from the cockpit his hand suddenly flew from the door. They were shooting at him again and he wanted to shoot back, but when he tried to grab the stock of his M-4 again he froze and stared; bullets had torn through the webs between his fingers and completely blown out his wrist. His glove was flipped off and turned inside out and the hand was just hanging by the ulnar bone and a few tendons. A tracer bullet was lodged in the diced-up flesh, glowing and smoking, and his arterial blood was squirting all over the cockpit.

Cory woke up. He was lying flat on his back halfway down the cabin and he knew he'd been knocked out. He remembered the storm of gunfire just before the helo's wheels pounded into the snow, and men and equipment bouncing off the walls and ceiling like in one of those zero-gravity planes the astronauts trained in. An incredible amount of gunfire was still raking the helo, bullets lancing in through one side and out the other. The fuselage was lined with quilted sound-proofing and it was disintegrating and floating down like confetti. Sparks were spitting and flying, men were yelling. The Rangers were charging off the ramp into a blinding white square that swallowed them up. Don Tabron flew by with his M-4 in his hand, following them. Cory reached for his face and wiped away a pool of blood that had settled in his left eye. Three bullets had struck his crew helmet just above the lip where his visor was mounted. One had entered far enough to lacerate his brow, but that was all. He shook his head and realized he was "alert and oriented."

Holy cow, I'm okay!

He rolled over onto his belly as he focused hard and his training took over. *Time to go to work.* He had to identify and treat the most life-threatening injuries, anything that was going to kill someone right now, and move on to the next. Then he would get his patients to safety. He looked up forward. The cockpit was just coming apart as bullets hammered into it, but he couldn't see anyone in there. On the right, Phil Svitak was lying on his back just below his silent minigun. On the left, Dave Dube was sitting up against the cockpit bulkhead, pale and ashen and obviously hurt. He turned his head and looked back past his boots. One of the Rangers was lying on his back near the rear of the cabin. Jason Cunningham, the air force PJ, was crawling toward him. Sean and Jed were lying on their bellies next to their M-60s, alive. Two more Rangers were sprawled on the ramp.

Cory turned forward and started low-crawling toward Phil. He yelled his name over and over; no response. He checked his carotid pulse. It was there but very weak, and then he tried to find the crew chief's wounds, but there was no blood anywhere on his winter mustang suit. He checked his pulse again. Nothing. Phil Svitak's final acts had been to move Cory out of the line of fire, which had most certainly saved his life, and then to spray the enemy bunker with his minigun until he himself was killed, which had kept the helo from being blown out of the sky. A single heavy-caliber round had found him just below his body armor.

Cory hung his head for just a moment, then Jason called out to him that the three fallen Rangers were all KIAs. He had taken their dog tags: Crose, Bradley S.; Commons, Matthew A.; Anderson, Marc A. Cory nodded and began to move on.

Greg knew he was in trouble. He was still in shock and his mangled hand and wrist weren't hurting yet, but he had been a medic himself and an arterial hemorrhage could bleed you out in no time. He dropped his M-4 on the center console, rolled onto his stomach, gripped his wrist with four fingers and pushed his boots against the shattered instruments, trying to launch himself though the companionway. But Don hadn't had the time to lower his AMC seat when he flipped him-

self backward, so Greg was jammed right there in the opening, hanging halfway into the crew cabin. He looked down at Dave Dube, who
was trying to put a tourniquet on his own thigh. A bullet had smashed
into his knife scabbard and driven splinters of the blade into his leg.

"Dave!"

Dube looked up and mouthed something, but Greg couldn't hear
a word.

"Dave!" he yelled again.

"Take your fucking helmet off!"

That Greg heard, and he reached back and flipped his crew helmet
off over his head.

"Dave, are you okay?"

"I'm hit."

Greg spotted Cory and screamed for some help. His flight vest and
"bat belt" were snagged between Don's seat and the door frame and he
couldn't move any further. He looked down at Phil and saw him lying
there lifeless, half covered by shredded soundproofing. He yelled
Phil's name and got no response. An RPG round suddenly split
through the nose of the helo and exploded inside the cockpit, shrapnel tearing through Greg's flight suit and into his legs, and then he
found himself on the floor, just a foot in front of Cory's face. His blood
was pulsing out in streams all over the cabin, and Cory immediately
reached inside his vest for a tourniquet.

"I'm hit, Cory!" Greg yelled.

"I can see that." Cory had to make a quick decision. A glance at
Greg's skewered hand told him the pilot was going to lose it, but if he
placed the tourniquet below the elbow and squeezed the shattered
bones against the artery, maybe he could save the joint.

"I'm hit," Greg groaned again, as if pointing that out repeatedly
might make Cory care more.

"Well, shut up and suck it up, 'cause we gotta *do* this."

There were all sorts of newfangled tourniquets coming out of pro-
curement, but Cory preferred his tried-and-true cravat, wooden dowel

and zip-tie. As he finished setting it up, Greg plucked the remains of a bullet from his bloody flesh and stuck it inside his shoulder pocket, as if he'd need the forensic evidence to prove he'd been shot. Cory was ready.

"This is gonna hurt," he warned.

Greg nodded. Cory started twisting the dowel down. Greg screamed.

"Fire!" someone yelled from the back. "Fire!"

Cory looked up. Hot shrapnel from the RPG's warhead had struck the oxygen console just above Dave Dube's head. Flames were licking up along the soundproofing and starting to crawl along the ceiling. *One damn thing at a time.* He pulled a role of Kerlix from his aid bag, a cotton-like material, and started stuffing it into Greg's open wound. It just kept on going and going, like some magician's handkerchief act in reverse. Then, Sean Ludwig was beside him, offering bandages from Cory's kit. Sean's knee had been smashed during the crash and he couldn't do much more than slither.

"We gotta put that damn fire out!" Sean yelled above the racket of bullets that kept striking above. Greg was just trying to breathe through the incredible pain as he lay there and watched the fuselage filling with slim spears of light from fresh bullet holes. Cory slapped a large triangular muslin bandage around Greg's forearm and cinched it down. *Next problem.*

The cabin was starting to fill with smoke, but the forward fire extinguisher was gone from its mount. Sean had crawled toward the rear for the other red canister and he slid it forward and Cory grabbed it. Cory pulled the pin and looked up. *Now how the hell am I going to do this?* To reach the fire, he would have to stand up, right in front of Phil's open gun door.

He leaped to his feet and charged at the flames, spewing a cone of white chemical spray as a bullet struck his back plate dead center. Then he slammed himself back down on the floor as the fire sputtered and died. He lay there for a moment, trying to decide if they would all be better off outside the helo or inside, when they heard the sweet sound of the Rangers' guns roaring back at the bad guys out there in the snow.

"Where the hell is Chuck?" Greg yelled.

Chuck was lying on his back in two feet of wet snow, just outside the left cockpit door. He had fallen through the air and thumped down hard, and his left leg had just flopped to the side at a thirty-degree angle. He assumed it was severed below the thigh and only his coverall was keeping it there, but so far it was just a dull ache. At the moment, all he wanted to do was hear what was going on, so he tore his helmet off along with his CEPs, the small earpieces inside the cushioned cups. What he heard was mayhem: men screaming inside the Chinook's body where it loomed above him, enemy machine guns howling from the far side of the airplane, the horrific sound of screeching metal as bullets chewed up the fuselage, and above all of that, the steady *chew, chew, chew* of the rotor blades as they slowly coasted to a stop. The bird's belly was above the snow, canted at a weird angle over its wheels, and he looked at the drainage plugs where some sort of dark liquid was fauceting out and steaming as it splashed. He didn't want to think about what it might be, but the image was like a huge, majestic elephant being slaughtered by poachers.

The enemy fighters who had shot him from the left side were gone now. He knew that Dave Dube had raked them with gunfire just before the helo hit, but they might be back. He reached for his M-4, jacked a round in the chamber and flicked the selector to semi. Now he had to do something about his leg or he was going to bleed to death. His kneeboard, the small clipboard with his checklist and mission codes, was still strapped around his upper thigh above the wound. He reached down and twisted it three times to the right, ignoring the pain that came with the cinch as he held it and pressed his fingers into his femoral artery. He looked under the belly of the helo and could see a Ranger on the far side, standing fully erect behind a rock and calmly firing his weapon as if he were down at the ranges at Benning, having a little target practice.

"Hey!" Chuck called out. "I need a medic over here!"

The Ranger's head turned. "Just hold whatcha got. Can't get to you right now. Just cover the left side of the helo."

"Okay," Chuck called back. "I'll do that."

He rolled onto his side and peered to the left, gripping his wound with one hand and his M-4 with the other. But he was in a small defilade and could see only about fifteen feet. If they came back from that flank, it would just be him and them, at point-blank range.

"Mayday! Mayday!" It was Greg's voice from inside the helo, using a PRC 112 survival radio. "Razor Zero One, taking fire from all sides!"

Chuck thought that was sort of ironic. The men receiving Greg's transmission were probably in that P-3 overhead, and they were watching the slaughter real-time on their surveillance screens. It seemed like another full ten minutes passed before he called out again to the Ranger.

"Hey, I need a medic up here. I need a tourniquet!"

"We can't get to you right now. Keep on covering the left side."

"Okay. Roger."

Shit. If someone didn't get to him soon, they could forget about the tourniquet. A pool of blood was slowly staining the snow beneath his leg.

Don Tabron was on his belly in the snow, just outside the cargo ramp, covering the back of the helo with his M-4. He had charged after the Rangers when they hauled ass out of the bird, because he could see immediately that they had three men down already and would need help. Right away, they had found light cover behind some rocks and started double-tapping rounds, conserving their ammunition and tossing grenades. Don had tucked up next to them and shouted, "What do you need me to do?"

A Ranger pointed at the downed helo. "Provide security on the left side."

"Roger."

Don jumped up, ran, flopped down and flicked his selector to full auto. He had seven magazines of thirty rounds apiece in his vest, and no idea that he was going to be there fighting all day long. Yet of all the men aboard the aircraft, he was the most appropriately dressed. The AMC seat was the coldest spot in the helo, so he was wearing long johns, his desert flight suit, a fleece jacket and his GORE-TEX jacket over that. He had his flight gloves on and his insulated desert boots, but the only thing on his head was a black watch cap. A bullet had taken off the tip of one of his fingers, but he was ignoring the wound.

Jed Wilson, the redheaded ramp gunner, came out of the helo and thumped down next to Don with his M-4.

"What d'ya need, sir?"

"I'll cover six to nine o'clock, you take eight-thirty to twelve."

"Okay." Jed shifted his position.

Just then, the Ranger that Chuck had been calling to sprinted back to the right side of the Chinook and yelled inside, "Hey! You got one of your pilots down on the left side."

Cary Miller, another air force PJ who was working with Jason Cunningham, came out the back, and he and Don trudged through the snow up the left side and found Chuck. They looked at his shattered leg and the spreading pool of blood.

"You all right?" Don asked him.

"I'm on my knees," Chuck said, "but just do what you have to do."

They grabbed him by his vest and started dragging him back toward the ramp. En route, Don saw Chuck flip his M-4 selector to "safe." He reached down and flicked it back to "full auto." Chuck flicked it back again.

"You're worried about firearms safety out here?" Don nearly laughed. "I want that bad boy ready to go!"

Cory had decided that at least for the moment, the interior of the Chinook was the safest place for his wounded men. There was absolutely no cover outside, and at least if they all stayed below the level of the ballistic fuel tanks, which were two feet high and ran the entire length of the cabin, they'd be all right unless the whole damn thing exploded. Cary Miller had put a tourniquet on Chuck's leg, and he called for Cory to check his work. Cory low crawled down the ramp and out into the snow. It was freezing cold out there, yet he hardly noticed it. An RPG came in from somewhere and exploded above his head against the helo's rotor pylon, but he ignored it. He checked Chuck's bandage and then had Don and Cary drag the pilot behind the helo.

"He's mine now," he said to Cary rather proprietarily.

But Cory was worried mostly about Greg. He had already lost a lot of blood and he was fading in and out. He and Jason started an IV line on Greg and pushed the bag under his body, so the weight would keep the Hespan flowing. Hespan was a "volume expander" and good for massive blood loss, but it ran out quickly and he switched to a crystalloid IV solution. Jason was trying to clip an oxygen monitor on Greg's finger to get a reading; he was a brand-new PJ and had only recently finished up his training, so he was determined to use every tool in the book. Greg lifted his arm up; the oxymeter's wires had been shot clean through. Cory quickly used up the single oxygen bottle he had on Greg. There was plenty of O_2 left in the aft console of the helo, but he didn't know how to work it. Sean Ludwig coached him through it and he placed a standard pilot's mask on Greg and felt better about that.

"Let's pack 'em all up," Cory said to Jason, "in case we have to move 'em."

Jason started unfolding litters for Greg and Chuck.

At this point, Don was on his knees out in the snow, just trying to catch one good breath. The Rangers had been calling out for more ammunition as they slugged it out with the hunkered-down bad guys, and someone had to get it for them. There was still plenty of ammo in the helo, and he had started running it back and forth to Nate Self and his men. All the Night Stalkers were in fine physical shape, from the youngest ground crew members to the oldest pilots. At sea level the constant sprints would have been nothing to Don, but at more than ten thousand feet, he had to collapse and just breathe for a good four minutes before being able to get up and make another run. At first, he had hauled the ammo cans on his feet, but the terrorists up top really enjoyed that; they fired at him as if trying to win themselves a prize stuffed animal at a carnival. After that, he just hugged the ammo and his weapon to his chest and rolled back and forth—across the hill to the Rangers, back across the hill to the helo, and across the hill again. The combat air controller up above with Nate Self had started calling in fast movers to strafe and bomb the bunker. Five-hundred-pounders were hitting "danger close," lifting Don almost clear of the snow as they impacted, but having little effect on the enemy. He saw an F-16 making a gun run and the cannon sounded like someone rolling a bowling ball over bubble wrap, but that didn't seem to do much either. Jed had been helping Don deliver ammo, but the Rangers had lost their M240 assistant gunner on the ramp and needed someone to feed their machine gunner. Jed had volunteered and gone up there into the fight. He had no helmet.

Don was finally so spent that he had taken to rolling up toward them as far as he could and then tossing the ammunition over to them.

"Hey!" he called out at one point as he gripped a bandolier of M203 projectiles. The M203 was a grenade launcher slung beneath the barrel of one Ranger's M-4. "Is it all right if I throw these?" They looked like huge, fat bullets the size of small coffee mugs.

"What are they?" a Ranger called back to him.

"M203 grenades."

"Hell, no! Don't throw *those!*"

Shit. Don had to get up again and zigzag through the gunfire as it chewed up the snow at his heels.

With only six Rangers, their combat air controller and Jed as an assistant gunner, there weren't enough of them up there to successfully assault the trench complex and the bunker, but Self and his men were definitely holding their own behind some outcroppings of sturdy rocks on the helo's forward right flank. The enemy fighters must have known that they couldn't take this team of aggressive young Americans, so they focused on the downed Chinook. It was just a flak magnet and it kept on bucking under bursts of machine-gun fire and RPGs flying across the flat, bright snow. During one of Don's ammo crawls, Self called him over and told him to relay to Cory to start moving the wounded off the helo. Just off the ramp, on the helo's right flank, was a fairly wide saddle, a depression in defilade that would keep them out of harm's way from above.

Cory didn't question Captain Self's decision. The man was an infantry expert and could read the situation on the ground better than any of them. He and Jason strapped Greg and Chuck to litters, and then Don, Cary and Sean pitched in to help the two Night Stalker medics haul the pilots off the ramp and through knee-high snow. It took a long time. All of them were suffering from AMS by now, and Cory would take short breaks only to vomit and carry on. Dave Dube had been moved onto a Skedco, a plastic cocoon designed for dragging wounded personnel, but as the men were leaning back on the handles and easing him down the saddle, they lost their grip. He started to slide. They yelled and tried to chase after him. The Skedco picked up speed, heading straight for the southern lip of the mountain and nothing below but clear air and certain death for Dave if he went over the edge. By some miracle, he slammed into Chuck's litter and Chuck reached out and grabbed him. They all fell to their knees, gasping as someone said, "Holy *shit*. Can we *please* not do that again?"

It was Chuck who first heard the distant thunder of Razor Zero Two. It was eight-thirty in the morning and there had been constant gunfire, bombing and strafing runs for more than two hours, but this was a sound like no other. He, Greg and Dave were lying close together in the snow of the saddle, covered up with "space" blankets while Cory, Jason and Cary constantly mothered them. Don was still making his ammo crawls back and forth to the Rangers, and Jed was up there with them, too, as they continued their Mexican standoff. Sean Ludwig had just crawled over to Chuck, raised himself on his elbows and grinned.

"You don't know who I am, do you?"

Chuck actually felt himself blush. He did not, in fact, know Sean's name and he was embarrassed. He always made it a point before any mission to personally brief his crew and introduce himself to anyone he hadn't met before. But this whole thing had happened so fast, and they had switched crews.

"I'm sorry to say, I don't," Chuck said.

"S'okay," Sean said. "I'm new." He extended a hand and gripped Chuck's glove. "Sean Ludwig."

"Chuck Gant."

"Nice to meet ya," Sean said, then he, too, turned his head to the rising sound of heavy rotors in the valley below.

From the cockpit of Zero Two, Randy Olson had indeed seen and heard everything that was happening atop Takur Gar. Hanging back as he had been ordered to do by Chuck, he had witnessed the crash and been immediately ordered by Task Force Mountain to get the hell out of there, go back to Gardez and await further orders. It was certainly hell in a very small place for the men atop the mountain, but it may have been worse for Randy and Ray Smiley as they listened helplessly to the Mayday calls from Greg and the incoming reports of more dead, more wounded. In the back of the helicopter, the remaining ten Rangers of Self's QRF were beside themselves, like German shepherds trapped in a cage while their beloved masters were outside being mauled. They desperately wanted to get onto that peak, but no more than Randy wanted to, yet the pilot knew that no one would give him clearance for that. He worked out a compromise with headquarters: He would put the Rangers into an LZ below the peak, and they would climb to the top. As Zero Two lifted off from Gardez and closed the range to the LZ, the two Ranger staff sergeants in the back of the bird were at last able to talk to Nate Self. Word was passed from Ranger to Ranger that Crose, Commons and Anderson were dead, and their jaws set hard with fury and determination.

The LZ that had been chosen for Randy was a full two thousand feet below the peak. He back-ended it and dropped the ramp, with his rotor blades just barely missing granite. The ten Rangers scrambled off, looked up and started to climb. Almost immediately they came under fire from enemy positions on the nearby ridges.

It is hard to imagine that any but this minion of angry young men would have been able to make that climb—at eight thousand feet, in the dead of a Far Eastern winter, frigid air knifing your lungs, an altitude at which a mild toothache becomes a raging fire inside your mouth. It was straight up, vertical, each of them with a hundred pounds of weapon, ammo, grenades, knife, helmet, body armor, boots and buckles. Mortars were exploding among the rocks, shearing off branches of flimsy pines. Sniper fire was cracking across the valley and chipping up shale. It would have challenged a Sherpa guide. Perhaps they were only able to do it because they were Rangers with comrades in peril.

It was less than two hours later when Cory saw the first of the Rangers cresting the mountaintop from the south. It was hard to believe, but there they were, and more of them coming on. He didn't know how far they'd climbed, but he knew how he himself felt just being up there with the waves of adrenaline and dearth of oxygen trembling his limbs. They were trotting up the slope now toward their commander, and while they glanced at the wounded and nodded at him tersely, they had a job to do. The last man was their medic, Matt LaFrenz, and he walked over to Cory's Casualty Collection Point.

"Are you the 160th medic?" he asked Cory.

"Yeah. Are you the Ranger medic?"

"Yup." They shook hands. "I'll be back in a minute to help you out," LaFrenz said. "We're gonna go assault that bunker."

"All right, dude. Good." Cory shot him a thumbs-up. "See you in a minute."

LaFrenz went up the hill to join the rest of his team, and then the Tactical Air Controller started calling in some heavy stuff to soften up the bunker before the assault. "Five-hundred-pounder comin' in!" he yelled, and to all the men at the CCP it looked like those huge black bombs were going to land right on them as the F-16s screamed in and banked away, dropping their payloads. They covered their heads as the earth belched with the impacts, tossing them up off the snow, and shards of shrapnel and rocks and tree limbs sailed overhead. But the bombs and cannons weren't doing enough damage for Nate Self's satisfaction.

"Has that Predator up there got a Hellfire on it?" Self called out to his TAC.

"What?" Air Force Staff Sergeant Kevin Vance knew there was a Predator drone circling above, but he didn't know if it was one of the newest armed versions.

"Just ask 'em if it's got a missile on it."

It did indeed happen to have a Hellfire hanging from its wing, and soon Vance called out to everyone, "Hellfire inbound!"

The sky seemed to tear open as the missile streaked straight down from somewhere above and pierced the cap of the rocky bunker dead center. The explosion was deafening, and then Cory raised his head in time to watch Nate Self and his men jump up from their cover and charge over the crest. They were shouting to one another, firing their weapons as they streamed through the slit trenches and wiped out the rest of the enemy combatants. Within a few minutes it was over. The last of the gunfire had died away and the Rangers were back atop the crest, slapping one another's backs like a winning football team, laughing with relief. Cory heard his fellow Night Stalkers hissing out sighs. "All right! Finally! Shit!"

Nate Self called down to Cory from up above. "Lamoreaux, we're going to set up our new perimeter up here."

Cory waved in acknowledgment and struggled to his feet. It felt so great to be able to stand up after four and a half hours of crawling. The sun was sliding up high toward noon, and if you weren't being shot at every other minute you could finally catch a good breath. Don had found a couple of Power Bars in the helo and they were passing them around, taking small bites. Without discussing it, all the Night Stalkers knew that despite the Rangers' victory, no other helo would be landing to rescue them until dark. There were still too many bad guys in the area. Cory wasn't too concerned about Chuck or Dave; they would make it. He wasn't so sure about Greg. Each of the pilots and crew had a morphine tubex tucked in a sleeve pocket, and Cory had some more in his aid bag. He hadn't used any of them yet, and wouldn't unless someone started screaming.

"Let's move the CCP up there," he said to Jason. He tried not to think about Phil or the three dead Rangers in the helo. He had taken Phil's wedding ring from his cold hand and clipped it to his body armor. Eventually, they would have to be moved up as well, but the living had priority. He chose to move Dave first, because the Skedco could be dragged, and along with Don and Jason they had progressed ten meters up the hill when a stream of bullets raked across the saddle.

What the hell?!

The gunfire was coming from a completely new direction, south of the Chinook's tail as opposed to north of the nose where the bunker had been. Two hundred meters aft of the cargo ramp was a tweny-foot-high cluster of rocks at the very edge of the peak. Somehow, an entire squad of Al-Qaeda and Taliban had worked their way up there. They were popping up and firing long bursts from their AK-47s, shouting and cackling in some unintelligible tongue, but "Gotcha now, you American bastards" sounds the same in any language.

Where the depression of the snow saddle had shielded Cory and his comrades before, now it was nothing but a huge white target with a bull's-eye of totally exposed wounded men and their medics. Everyone slammed into the snow as geysers of white spit up all around them. Almost simultaneously, Jed, Cory, Jason and Don rolled onto their backs, sat up with their boots downhill, unslung their M-4s and returned fire.

Above them on the crest, the Rangers leaped to the opposite sides of the rocks they had spent most of the morning behind, and started pouring fire down at the new enemy position. But the enemy combatants had chosen a perfect position; they were up high, had tons of granite cover and were firing straight across an uphill grade into targets who couldn't go anywhere, because Cory, Don, Jason, Jed and Sean were *not* going to leave their wounded friends.

Don's weapon had malfunctioned earlier in the day, so he had taken Chuck's from him. The short-barreled M-4 has a particularly loud report, and Don's barrel was barely a foot from Chuck's head as he repeatedly fired bursts at the thickly robed figures popping up from the rocks.

"Ow! Dammit!" Chuck yelled every time the weapon pounded his eardrums and hot shells bounced off his face.

Don ignored Chuck's protests. *What do you want me to do? Stop shooting?*

"We gotta get my guys outta here!" Cory yelled up to the Rangers as he changed magazines and kept on firing. He and Jason had slithered down to protect Chuck and Greg.

"Hold on!" someone called back to him above the din. "We've got air inbound!"

Well, it better get here goddamn fast, Cory thought. They couldn't possibly survive this onslaught for very long. Then it got worse, as from somewhere else mortar rounds started impacting on the peak. They could hear the hollow *thunk* of the tubes echoing beyond the cap, but because the snow was so deep the projectiles were being swallowed up as they detonated and were mostly spraying snow and dirt. *That ain't shit,* Cory thought. *It's those assholes behind the rocks I'm worried about.*

Farther up the hillside, Jed was covering Dave on his Skedco, firing over Cory's head. Don kept calling for the Rangers to come down and help them move the litters, but the firefight was so horrendous now that no one could hear him. He and Cory and Jason decided to go it alone, but they couldn't lift Chuck's litter. The only strength left in them was in their trigger fingers. It seemed like half an hour had gone by already. Where the hell was that air cover? Cory was on his seventh magazine, and he only had eight in his kit.

"All right," Don finally said, "I'm gonna go up there and grab a couple of those guys to help us."

"Okay, man," Cory said. "Go ahead."

Chuck reached out and grabbed Don's jacket, addressing him by his call sign.

"Don't forget about us, Dragon."

"Chuck, I'll be *right* back," Don promised. He turned to Cory as he got to his knees. "See ya in a minute."

"Okay. Good."

Neither man really expected to see the other alive again. As Don sprinted away up the hill, the fire intensified, coming closer, ranging in, kicking up geysers of snow all around them. Chuck and Greg turned their faces uphill. They didn't want to see the AK-47s firing at them anymore. It was just Cory, Jason and Sean with Chuck and Greg now. Cory didn't know where Cary Miller had gone, but he wasn't there any longer. Maybe he had charged off with Don to get help. It didn't matter. If Cory was going to die, it would be right there with his pilots. That was the Night Stalker way.

Cory and Jason decided together to crawl a few feet higher and draw the fire away from their patients. At twenty-six years old and a young father of two, Jason was one of the best natural combat medics Cory had ever met, air force or not. As they both sat up now and started shooting again, a burst of automatic fire scythed across their midsections. Three rounds smacked into Cory's belt buckle and bat belt, one glancing off metal, another setting off a 9mm round in his pistol magazine, and the third slicing up under his body armor and piercing his bladder. As he grunted hard and curled up, another pierced his buttocks. Bullets from the same burst cut through Jason's abdomen and exited through his pelvis.

"I'm shot in the gut," Jason rasped.

"Yeah, me too," Cory moaned.

They both knew what that meant. With those kinds of wounds, they could bleed out internally and no one would know it was happening until it was too late. Surgery was required, and that wasn't going to happen anytime soon.

This is really gonna suck for Laura and the kids. . . .

And that was when Cory started to think about his dad, and pulled himself together, got to his knees and started to check himself out. He still had patients on that mountain and he wasn't dead just yet. He pulled off his gloves and threw off the helmet he'd borrowed from one of the dead Rangers on the ramp. He steeled himself and stuck his fingers up under his body armor. They came away wet, but it wasn't blood. Someone was calling for the Ranger medic. Matt LaFrenz slid into the snow beside Cory.

"Get this damn body armor off me," Cory grunted. "I'm tired of wearing this shit."

LaFrenz tore open the Velcro straps and pulled the armor over Cory's head. He reached down to inspect Cory's stomach wound.

"What's it look like?" Cory asked.

"Doesn't look too bad."

"It's real wet down there."

"Yeah, I think it might be urine."

Well, a bladder wound's better than a stomach wound.

"Go check on Jason," Cory said.

LaFrenz moved over to inspect Jason's injuries.

"Incoming!" the combat air controller warned from atop the peak. "JDAM inbound!"

Everyone on the hill made a hole for himself. The JDAM was a massive, two-thousand-pound, GPS-guided bomb, being launched from an invisible B-52. The gleeful enemy fighters were still laughing and popping off rounds at the wounded Americans when their rocky cover disappeared in a huge black plume. The chunks of earthen debris and bone that rained down were very small, and then the sounds atop the mountain receded to an unearthly quiet. . . .

FROM HIGH NOON till sunset is a long time to wait, especially if you are cold, hungry, exhausted and badly injured. Many of the Rangers who had fought the battle on Takur Gar were wounded, including Nate Self, but none of them as badly as the Night Stalkers or their air force PJ, Jason Cunningham. All of the wounded were carried on their litters to the craggy cap of the summit and arrayed close together in the snow, while the Rangers devised a defensive perimeter to protect them. Self's orders were simple: No one was going to penetrate that cordon of young warriors, no matter how long it took for the rescue helos to arrive. There were long bouts of supreme silence, broken occasionally by some desultory mortar rounds or inaccurate sniper fire from nearby ridges, and during those lulls Self asked for extraction. He had seriously wounded men up there. He had fallen men who needed to go home. Yet the Nights Stalkers who lay there knew what the answer would be: Wait until dark. They understood it and they wanted it that way. Chuck and Don summoned a Ranger and told him to pass a message to Captain Self: "Do not bring anyone in here by daylight." They did not want to be rescued if it meant that more of their comrades might die.

For all those hours, Matt LaFrenz managed the care of the wounded, moving from litter to litter, checking vital signs, changing bandages, monitoring infusions. Don helped LaFrenz, all the while being coached by Cory, who could do little more than talk. "Go get my aid bag, Don. In the bottom right pouch you'll find a such-and-such. Take that out and do this with it." Don was amazed that Cory's head was still in the game, especially given his wounds and condition. Some of the Rangers would look at Cory and Jason, then turn their heads and speak in low tones. In the midafternoon, task force commanders came over the comms, asking to speak to the Ranger medic.

LaFrenz moved off to take the call, and when he answered simply, "Two," Cory knew he had been asked how many of the wounded might die if a helo did not come immediately. He assumed he was one of those two, but he had no intention of dying.

"Don, you need to go down there and get Phil's wedding ring."

Cory had taken Phil's dog tags and stuffed them into his pocket, but the ring was still clipped to his body armor, which was now far away in the snow below the helo. Occasional bullets were still plucking at that area from somewhere. Don and Jed had been running back and forth to the bird and stripping her of secure equipment in anticipation of the eventual rescue. They were also bringing back more ammunition and water, and tearing down soundproofing to use as blankets for the wounded. Don was far past exhaustion at that point.

"It's still pretty hot down there, Cory. I'm not sure it's worth risking someone's life to go get a wedding ring. His wife will understand."

"You *gotta* get his ring, Don."

"Okay, Cory." He had already risked his life a hundred times that day, so he figured he had one more sprint left in him. He got Phil's ring.

Dave Dube was worried that they were going to lose Greg. The two were next to each other not far from the demolished bunker, and Greg kept losing consciousness, then suddenly waking when a bullet would snap overhead. His bandages were completely soaked in blood, and LaFrenz had cinched his tourniquet down tighter. Dave kept engaging Greg in ridiculous conversations about home, food and women, and whenever the pilot's eyes would start to roll back in his head, Dave would throw snowballs at him. In addition to his shattered wrist and the shrapnel in his legs, Greg's face had been badly burned from the explosions in the cockpit. The freezing snow hurt like hell on his raw cheeks, but he knew that if you were hurting, you were alive.

Chuck pitched in to keep Greg alert and oriented, but there were also stretches of time when he lay there looking at the clear blue sky and the magnificent view across the mountains. He was thinking a lot about the mission and wondering if he had made the right decisions.

At a distance from the casualty collection point, the Rangers had now gathered up all of the dead, who lay like snow angels, their boots pointed up. He turned his head toward the bunker. Self's men were using ropes to recover the bodies of the two men they'd all come up there to find, because no one was sure if they might have been booby-trapped. Yet nothing exploded, and the SEAL and the air force combat controller joined their fallen comrades. Chuck did not yet know their names, but Neil Roberts and John Chapman would be going home, too. He closed his eyes.

Late in the day, as the sun was at last beginning to descend, Jason Cunningham began to grow weaker. They had all been taking turns keeping the pressure on his bandages, yet there was nothing they could do for his internal bleeding. Don had spent nearly an hour on his knees next to Jason, pressing a bloody bandage against his pelvis. Jason spoke to him, his voice thin and far away.

"Hey, Don, make sure you tell my wife and kids that I love 'em and miss 'em, okay?"

"Bullshit, Jason. You tell them yourself."

"Don, just please tell 'em."

"No, Jason. *You're* gonna tell them."

It was only an hour before dark when Jason died. It had begun to grow very cold on the peak. Matt LaFrenz and Cary Miller gave Jason CPR, and Cory coached Don into pulling out everything he could think of from his aid bag, but nothing worked. They lost him. Don would have to tell Jason's wife and children how much he had loved them. For all of the Night Stalkers, it was the hardest moment on Takur Gar.

It was a blessed darkness that finally cloaked the peak. Soon after that, the men heard the buzz saw hums of Spectre engines as the gunships began to pound enemy positions surrounding the mountain. Yet it was the familiar thunder of approaching Chinooks that really lifted their spirits. Chuck's and Greg's and Dave's and Cory's wounded bodies surged with energy long faded. Their hearts hammered. They were going to make it.

The first bird in was Razor Zero Two, its rotors kicking up a hurricane of frozen snow. A team of SEALs charged off the ramp to set up security, but no one really needed that now. What they needed was help to carry the wounded, yet that would be left to the Rangers and Night Stalkers who were still able to walk, even though they were far beyond exhaustion. It took them a long time to carry all the wounded into Randy's bird, yet at last it was spinning up, getting light on its wheels. Dave Dube lay on his litter, smiling. Chuck and Greg were next to each other in the center of the cabin. Greg's good hand reached out and Chuck gripped it hard. Cory was the last casualty aboard, in the rear by the ramp. He raised his head, searching desperately for one of his medics, but none of them were aboard. There were only three PJs, sitting on the benches, talking to one another, and none of them even looked at the patients. He was furious. *They don't know shit about CASEVAC.* The helo rose into the night and slipped away from the peak.

Three more Night Stalker Chinooks came in shortly thereafter; one for the dead, one for the security team and the remaining Rangers, and one for the SEALs who had been trapped all day down the side of the mountain.

Don Tabron flew with the dead. He could have gone aboard Randy's bird with the wounded, but it just wasn't right. He wasn't badly injured, and someone had to ride with the fallen and honor them. They were all there, neatly arranged on the cold cabin floor, some on litters, some without. Phil was there, and Jason, and the SEAL and the combat controller whose names he did not know. The Rangers who had died at dawn were back near the ramp, and that's where Don was, too, slumped against the fuselage because he hadn't the strength to go farther. Comms crackled from the cockpit, the crew chiefs hugged their guns, and then it went dark and the bird lifted off.

Don looked down and saw the arm of one of the Rangers, lying stretched out and alone. He reached down and folded it over the young man's chest, and then he held it, and he wept. . . .

THE NIGHT STALKERS swear, with good reason, that no other unit in the U.S. military cares for its wounded, fallen and families the way they do. In concert with that ironclad tradition, while the events of Takur Gar were a tragedy for many and a victory for some, its aftermath was also a point of pride for the 160th. Within minutes of touching down at Gardez, Cory, Chuck, Greg and Dave were all being treated by the doctors of a Joint Medical Augmentation Unit. Once at Bagram, they were rushed into the operating theater at the base of the old control tower, where all but Don underwent emergency surgery. From there, they would all be flown to a CASH at Karshi-Kanabad, then to the American military hospitals in Turkey and at Landstuhl, Germany, and finally to Walter Reed. Yet even before being medevaced out of Bagram, half a world away the unit's casualty assistance officers were gently informing their wives that they were wounded but alive.

Well, actually a Night Stalker officer and NCO made the mistake of showing up at Greg's home without calling first. Dana Calvert and many of the other wives had been huddled together all day long, after hearing on CNN that an MH-47 had been shot down on a mountaintop in Afghanistan. The women knew there was only one unit flying those kinds of helicopters over there, but by 10:30 at night they had all gone home, leaving Dana alone. When the doorbell rang and she saw the uniforms through the windows, she fell to her knees. The door swung open and a neighbor, who happened to be the wife of a Night Stalker major, shoved the soldiers aside and hugged her close. "He's all right, Dana! He's just wounded!" Greg would not let those men soon forget their blunder. Cory's and Chuck's and Dave's families were informed with more aplomb. Cory's wife had to actually bring in

help to handle the telephone, because the comfort calls were too numerous for her to answer them all. At Chuck's house it was the same,
and at Don's as well.

At the home of Phil Svitak, there was no such joyous news. There
was little the unit could do for Phil's family but help them grieve, support them financially and emotionally, and never forget what they had
sacrificed. He would be buried with full military honors, and his wife
would be sadly welcomed into the Gold Star Wives Club. His children would never want for anything they needed, and Phil's comrades
would be visiting often, to remind the Svitaks of the things he had
done for his friends and his country. The Night Stalkers have a wealth
of experience in these things.

From Bagram to Germany, nearly every doctor who examined Greg's
hand recommended amputation. It had swelled to five times its normal size, his arm above the tourniquet was entirely purple and black,
and an infection had set in. Greg refused treatment. He wanted to wait
to see the hand specialists at Walter Reed, where he and Chuck and
Dave would occupy the same room for a month. They were not the
most cooperative of patients, but they were grateful to be together and
they hardly spoke about Takur Gar. The Night Stalker Association
paid for all of their wives' air tickets to visit them in Washington. Dana
Calvert was pregnant again; apparently all those endless goodbyes had
paid off. Nine separate surgeries were required to repair the damaged
tendons, nerves and blood vessels in Greg's arm. There were further
operations to cure the shrapnel damage to his leg, and he would wear
a brace for some time and undergo many rounds of physical therapy.
Eighteen months after the events of Takur Gar, he would be flying
again. Sometime later, someone would ask him why he had never
shown symptoms of post-traumatic stress disorder, given his horrific experience in Afghanistan. "I guess I never had PTSD"—Greg smiled—
"because I had NSDQ."

Chuck's leg also required a number of surgeries, including having an
orthopedic plate bolted to his femur to hold the severed ends together.

The bones would eventually merge and heal, but the plate would stay forever. He and Dave had similar wounds from which they both would recover, and Chuck would be flying again within a year. For a long time after the events of Takur Gar, newspaper and magazine reporters would flock to Fort Campbell to hear the story from those who had been there, and Chuck would politely decline the interviews. He had decided it wasn't fair that heroes like Phil Svitak were unable to tell their stories, while there were those outside the Night Stalker community who hadn't been there at all, yet judged the actions and decisions of that fateful day. He would let God judge what he had done or not done, and that would be enough.

Don's wounds were not overtly serious. He had sustained a number of contusions during the shoot down, huge bruises and welts that he hadn't even noticed until the doctors at Bagram cut his uniform away. Yet his fingertip had been severed and that was enough to allow him the choice of his medevac route. After having watched over his wounded brothers for so many hours on that peak, he chose to remain with them until they all got to Walter Reed, and then he went home. Externally, he healed quickly. Internally, he had been wounded by what he had done and seen up there. Takur Gar would stay with him for a very long time: nights of flashbacks, cold sweats and scant sleep, until he would finally drift off, then wake to the sounds of gunfire that wasn't there. He made sure that Phil's ring was returned to his wife, and he went back to Afghanistan for three more tours.

For their actions that day on Takur Gar, which would soon become known as "Robert's Ridge," all the men of Razor Zero One were formally awarded. Phil received the Distinguished Flying Cross. Don and Jed received the Silver Star, for the things they had done at their own peril; things they didn't have to do. Dave and Greg received the Bronze Star. All but Phil stood proudly at attention as those awards were pinned, but then they tucked them away and went back to work. They were not the kinds of men to voluntarily speak of their reams of commendations or their Purple Hearts. You would have to ask them.

Cory took a turn for the worse in Turkey. The doctors in Bagram had performed an exploratory laparotomy, filleting him open from his pelvis to his breastbone so they could pluck out the bullet shards, repair his bladder and put him back together. By the next leg of his journey he wasn't doing well and spent some days in Intensive Care, while his friends from Razor Zero One moved on to Landstuhl. Cory was angry and frustrated that he wouldn't be able to accompany them. The bonds they had forged on Takur Gar were so strong that he felt like a brother being torn from his family.

Finally, his condition improved enough to transfer him to Germany. Laura wanted very much to fly over there and be with him, but she didn't have a passport. In the span of a single day, a unit personnel officer came to Cory's house, retrieved Laura's birth certificate, drove to Nashville, flew to Washington, made the return trip and handed her the travel document. She was packing to leave when she got word that Cory would shortly be medevaced home and would finish up his recovery at the Fort Campbell post hospital.

At Andrews Air Force Base, a Night Stalker major stomped aboard Cory's C-141 as the ramp was still descending and shouted, "Where the hell is Lamoreaux?" He handed Cory a bottle of Jack Daniel's with "Night Stalkers Don't Quit" penned across the label, and welcomed him home. A Night Stalker fixed-wing airplane flew him back to Campbell, where his medics, friends and family were waiting with gifts and tears and welcome posters from the unit. At the post hospital, the army surgeon wanted to admit Cory for an extended stay.

"Look, sir," Cory said, "why do we need to do that?"

"Well, you've got dressings and a catheter that'll need changing."

"I'm the unit's senior medic, sir," Cory said. "I can do that stuff myself, at home."

He went home on the fourteenth of March, eleven days after the shoot down. In the middle of April he went back to work. By the end of May, he was fast-roping for a Night Stalker anniversary exhibition. He, too, would receive the Silver Star and Purple Heart. There were many who thought he deserved the Congressional Medal of Honor, but Cory didn't care about the medals; the lives he saved were his treasures. Less than a year later, he would deploy to Iraq for the first of numerous tours.

Cory never dwelled on the events of Takur Gar, or question the actions or decisions that any of them made that day. He was incredibly proud of the 160th and the men who'd battled and died beside him. Greg had flown and fought until he could fight no more, and so had Dave. Chuck's choices had been the right ones for all of them. Don, who in some ways had been along that night as a passenger, had saved an uncountable number of lives. Jed had rushed headlong into combat without a second thought. Phil and Jason had given everything they had, or would ever have.

It wasn't that Cory didn't think about Takur Gar. He would always remember it vividly, but those thoughts would never slow him down or stop him from wanting to fly CASEVAC. His insistence on that procedure would never be opposed by anyone again. Once, just once, as he was flying aboard a Chinook on a training mission in the States, an unfamiliar sound thumped from the engines above. For a moment, his fists balled and his knuckles whitened, and then the familiar droning sounds returned and he smiled at himself, stretched his legs and relaxed.

He was not about to get shot down again.

Not today.

THE GHOSTS
OF HEROES

THEY CAME OUT of the darkness, through a mist of swirling dust.

There was no moon that night, and only the strongest stars winked between the curtains of grit blowing eastward out of Syria. To the naked eye, their shapes were indiscernible, perhaps mirages, perhaps nocturnal ravens on the wing. No points of light issued from their black bodies, no glints of metal sufficient enough to define their silhouettes. Yet as they quickly loomed, low growls hummed from their throats, and the desert falcons that usually ruled this barren swath of desert retreated wisely, for larger prey was in the air.

First were the Little Birds, a tight formation of four. In the lead, a pair of AH-6s were slung with rockets and miniguns, while close behind followed two more MH-6s, with cold-eyed Special Forces shooters perched on their pods. They raced so low over the sun-cracked wadis and flicked away so quickly that grazing goats were barely startled and only raised their eyes as they chewed dry sage.

The Blackhawks were next, a deeper sound, a palpable thunder. There were six of them. The first four were MH-60 "Kilos," heavy with Rangers, their armored bellies bloated from having freshly sapped the fuel from a C-130 Combat Shadow tanker. Yet they were fast as well, steady and sturdy, buttressed less by the wind and weather than their Little Bird brothers. Behind the four, two more Blackhawk DAPs flew sentry. They had no customers aboard, only crew chiefs to service the weapons, their cabins stuffed with many rounds for their flank-mounted 30mm chain guns, to complement their beehives of rocket pods.

And last were the Chinooks, four of the heavy beasts, and their thundering passage left its mark on every patch they passed below. Sand coiled up in rushes toward their massive, spinning rotors. Small rocks trembled as if giants stomped the earth. The two lead birds were filled with secret men—unnamed, no clear distinction between officers and noncoms. They would be last into the target yet most intent, professional and deadly. Behind them, the final pair of MH-47Es flew shotgun for the armada, packed with Quick Reaction Forces and CSAR teams, all believers in Murphy's Law.

By this time, peasant farmers had ventured from their huts to stare, Bedouins from their tents. Their faces rose and turned, eyes squinting in the painful wash, the echoes of many engines fading in their ears. Yet there was no one they could summon, no alarm to raise. They did not know where these machines were heading, but they were grateful not to be there.

It was a place called Al Qadisiyah, seemingly a sleepy town on the southern shores of a lush reservoir, where herons plucked fish from blue waters and ancient dhows still trolled. It was far from any of Iraq's major cities, an hour's difficult drive north of the Haditha Dam, in the northwest regions where smugglers and brigands scoffed at the nearby Syrian border. There had been a secret chemical and biological weapons research center at Al Qadisiyah, a split compound constructed without regard for the local citizens, and so remote and dangerous that the United Nations Special Commission on Iraq had not even thought to venture there. It appeared on no inspector's list, but was whispered of by scientist defectors. Only two days prior to this night, U.S. Army Special Operations Command had been tasked with the mission: assault Al Qadisiyah and collect intelligence. The first flash message had gone out to the Night Stalkers. By this time, it was widely assumed that Saddam Hussein had "donated" the treasures of his weapons programs to Syria's Bashir Assad, yet some evidence might still remain.

If there was nothing at Al Qadisiyah, there would be no resistance to an evening visit. If there was resistance, enemy action would speak for itself.

It was close to midnight as the first of the Little Bird MH-6s crossed the release point, noses down and heading for the town, their shooters perched and peering now through reticles in their night scopes. It was long past bedtime for the average suburban Iraqi, but a war had begun and the citizens were edgy. The thin whipping of sharp rotors called them from their homes and they peeked out, squinting skyward, but the pod-straddling customers were only interested in those with weapons. For the moment, nothing and no one opposed them, but the element of surprise was gone as more and more lights flicked on in the streets embracing the research compound. The powerful hums grew louder as the AH-6s arrived, darting, swooping and searching like peregrines, their pilots' fingers hovering over their weapons selectors.

For the Blackhawk Kilos there were four blocking positions, carefully selected to infil the Rangers into the most strategic intersections. They would defend the coming assaulters from as many compass points as possible, occluding every access road and alleyway with a cordon of firepower. At the southwest corner of the research compound, Chalk One set down amid a cloud of choking dust, yet even before the

Rangers had bolted from the open doors the bird suddenly came under heavy fire. Sparks hissed off its skin as AK-47 rounds spat out from a government building across the street from the compound.

"Chalk One, taking fire," the warrant at the controls announced coolly over his comms. As flight lead, he had planned each detail of the mission, and because the lives of so many men were in his hands, he had never assumed that it would be a quiet night. Now, there was no doubt.

"Roger," the pilot of the lead AH-6 responded. "Got it." He rolled the Little Bird over from its holding pattern above and fired a 2.75-inch rocket, whipping it in a long, low arc like a swinging golf club head, directly into the window of the offending building. Glass, flames and splintered AK-47s erupted into the street.

Scant minutes had passed since the first of the Night Stalker birds had appeared, yet already Iraqi regulars were streaming toward the objective. As Chalk Two roared into its blocking position north of the compound, bullets hammered at its body like spews of buckshot, the crew chiefs swiveling their miniguns and hammering back at every muzzle flash. The Rangers leaped from the doors, already firing their M-4s and SAWs, and then the sky above Al Qadisiyah seemed to ignite in a nuclear flash.

To the west of town was a pair of massive power transformers. In the event of a fight, two Air Force A-10 Thunderbolts had been tasked to shut the lights off, but had been delayed at an aerial refueling track. It was up to the DAPs now to keep their comrades from being silhouetted by searchlights, but the effects of their rockets and chain guns had shocked them. Instead of crumbling the power towers and sinking the town into darkness, their cannon had detonated the transformers like oil derricks, their leaping flames throwing the entire target area into ballooning light. The battle would now be close quarters, face-to-face and bright as daylight, with all anonymity gone.

For a moment, the unexpected sheen from horizon to horizon was a blessing. As Chalk Three set down at the target's southeast corner, the licking flames shimmered off a light pole and the pilot skewed his tail just in time to miss the metal. Yet as Chalk Four thundered onto a dusty lot at the final blocking position, the Blackhawk's body was clearly outlined, taking fire from multiple positions as the Rangers sprinted away, slammed onto their bellies and opened up. One of them never made it off the bird as a round entered his back, coursed through his chest and embedded itself in the rear of his front plate. The Night Stalker crew chief leaped from his gun to help the wounded Ranger, and another Special Forces operator stayed behind to assist as the pilot pulled pitch and hauled the bird away. Both men were combat lifesaver–qualified, and they would rescue the Ranger's life in the next few crucial minutes.

Having infilled all their Rangers, the four Kilos quickly regrouped outside the town and sped toward a preselected desert landing strip, where a C-130 equipped with surgical facilities had set down to receive potential casualties. As soon as Chalk Four's wheels touched earth, the wounded Ranger was carefully extracted from the helo and litter-borne to the waiting medical team. The Blackhawks then assembled and held, rotors spinning, their pilots and crews listening intently to the comms crackling from the objective above the background spatters of gunfire.

With the Rangers firmly entrenched in their blocking positions, the Chinooks and the main assault force were inbound fast now, and the Little Bird guns and MH-6s scooted out of the way to seek out targets and protect the incoming teams. Iraqi gunmen were appearing on foot below, sprinting for the research center, and the MH-6 shooters were dropping them one by one with their long-range rifles. Chalk One of the MH-47s pounded down onto his LZ near Blocking Position Three, even as a salvo of enemy gunfire raked the Chinook and pierced a utility hydraulics line. The "door kickers" raced off the ramp and the pilots wrestled the shot-up bird back into the air. Almost immediately,

Chalk Two landed in his lead's wheel ruts, just as a fusillade of fire pierced his fuselage as well. The ramp dropped and the assaulters charged from the bird, but a Night Stalker crew chief collapsed to the steel deck like a rag doll as a bullet lanced through his jaw. As the helo lifted off, the ramp man fell to his knees to aid his wounded chief. The Chinook's interior was pitch dark, and the air mission commander sprang to the rear with a red lens flashlight, as another crew member joined in to try to resuscitate the chief. He fell into unconsciousness and stopped breathing. The three desperate men applied CPR, pumping his chest until at last he opened his eyes, spit some blood and began to breathe again. Minutes later at the desert landing strip, he, too, was quickly hustled aboard the surgery bird.

Back at the target area, a seemingly endless wait ensued while the assaulters scoured the objective: searching the laboratories, offices and secret caches in the basements. Outside, the Rangers held their positions, fending off repeated attacks by groups of gunmen and vehicles. Above, the Little Birds circled—the MH-6s lower with their customers engaging, the AH-6s higher to lend heavier support. One of the snipers spotted two Iraqi gunmen maneuvering through the streets on foot, each dragging a screaming woman along. The gunmen clearly assumed the Americans wouldn't risk killing an innocent, which was true enough, but as soon as one of the hostages wrenched herself from her captor's grip, he was instantly dropped by a single bullet. Closer to the objective, a vehicle raced toward the Rangers, who released a fusillade fire yet failed to stop it, until at last a SAW gunner brought the careening truck to a halt. Two gunmen tried to flee the smoking hulk; one was killed by a Ranger rifleman, the other felled by a bullet from the sky.

The pair of DAPs had selected a long, banking track, the outermost ring of the security cordon, making sure to prevent any reinforcements from reaching the objective via the main north-south road through town. Their rules of engagement were clear—they would fire a warning shot to dissuade a vehicle from continuing on, but if it failed to heed the message, hostile intent would be assumed. Chalk One spotted a Toyota truck moving swiftly toward the Ranger positions. The pilot fired a short burst from his chain gun, and the vehicle's driver stopped and doused his lights. Yet as the DAPs turned outbound, the truck came to life and raced forward again. Both of the Hawks hammered it with 30mm rounds. Only minutes later, the same maneuver was attempted by a second vehicle of gunmen, and again they were offered a burst of discouragement. Two Iraqis abandoned the vehicle, dove into a ditch and opened fire skyward with their AKs, sending tracers zipping past the Blackhawks' cockpits. Chalk Two rolled in and finished the encounter with his chain gun.

At last, the assault force called for extraction, but the Chinooks that had infilled them had multiple mechanical wounds and were out of action. Immediately, the contingency plan went into effect and the pair of QRF birds that had been holding above the release point now turned and raced for the objective. Even though they already had the considerable weight of their Rangers and CSAR personnel aboard, careful pre-mission calculations ensured this final and most critical leg of the mission. In minutes, the MH-47s were loading the assault elements and roaring away for the desert landing strip.

Soon after, the Blackhawk Kilos arrived again on target to exfil the Rangers from their posts. The entire area surrounding the blocking positions was littered with fallen Iraqis and burning vehicles, and the pilots squinted hard as they repositioned to avoid setting their wheels down on corpses. With their Rangers aboard, they were soon rising up and banking away, their tails watched over by the following DAPs and Little Birds.

Al Qadisiyah was dark again, but for the licking of oil flames on the horizon. It was silent again, but for the moans of wounded and dying enemy soldiers. From the moment the first Ranger boot stamped the earth, until the last was aboard a Kilo, the entire mission had lasted forty-five minutes. What they had found at Qadisiyah would be decided by other men. What they had done there to complete their mission, they would all remember with pride. . . .

IN MANY WAYS, the Global War on Terror has been a special operations conflict, and in every significant operation to suppress the enemy's most elite combatants, root out Islamic militants and hunt down the most notorious terrorists, the Night Stalkers have been at the fore. The 160th SOAR(A) opened Operation Iraqi Freedom with raids on more than sixty Iraqi Visual Observation Sites, effectively blinding the enemy to the intentions of assaulting Coalition Forces. Thereafter, the unit formed the spearhead for hundreds of special tactics missions, which continue to this day. Many times they braved the Triple-A's of Baghdad, flew in the Battle of Haditha Dam, spun low and fast above Fallujah. They were there for the rescue of Private Jessica Lynch and the hunt for Saddam Hussein. It was a Night Stalker helo that flew the manacled Iraqi dictator from his spider hole to his prison cell, and the 160th's pilots and crews have been crucial to many missions that will forever remain "below the radar." The Night Stalkers were first across the borders for the war in Iraq, and they will no doubt be among the very last to leave.

There are many more tales to be told of the 160th pilots and crews, flying and fighting in this current conflict, yet events such as the assault on Al Qadisiyah must remain, for now, as sketches. The personal perspectives of the crews and revelations of the details will have to wait, for the nature of special operations is that such men must embrace anonymity where appropriate, being able to appear in distant places on the precipice of danger, yet remain unmarked for who they really are. While war still rages, it would be unwise to allow the enemy to glean more than he should.

The Night Stalkers themselves would never claim that they are the most elite in the U.S. Armed Forces order of battle. They would say that they are equal only to the best of their customers—in dedication to a difficult profession, determination to protect their country and the willingness to reach out far beyond the limits of physical stamina and normal human fears. They train no harder than the army's Special Forces, are no more courageous than the navy's SEALs, nor have more will than Force Recon Marines to pursue an enemy into the bowels of his own fortress. Yet perhaps nowhere else in America's military inventory, nor for that matter in any similar aviation element on the globe, has any organization so uniquely melded the very best of its men to its penultimate flying machines. Those Night Stalker chariots have been tuned into the finest battle craft imaginable, yet without their pilots, they'd have no hearts or eyes, and without their crews, no wings to fly. It is this band of brothers, taking to the air when few would dare to fly, that make up a unit like no other.

Since the unfurling of that first Night Stalker flag at Fort Campbell many years ago, thousands of pilots and soldiers have volunteered to take up that standard, and hundreds have succeeded in that rarefied atmosphere where only the best of the best can breathe. Across that breadth of years, the Night Stalkers have lost more than a few good men, and while each sacrifice has been grieved in a tradition of honor that took root long ago at the compound, those losses have also served as inspiration for lessons to be learned. These heroes who gave all are ever present in the minds of the Night Stalker pilots and crews. Their histories and their missions are carefully taught to the volunteers who take their reins. Their names continue to be etched in granite and grace the porticoes of hangars and headquarters, yet they are not simply memories to be mourned. The things they did and passed on to their surviving brothers are the tools that have tuned the regiment to the most precise special operations aviation machine in existence.

It is a fact of special operations life that the tip of the spear is often that most scarred by war, and so it is with the 160th. For an aviation regiment of modest size, the unit has suffered a disproportionate loss of machines and men, yet as so often with broken bones, the mending places have grown stronger. The unit looks with pride on its Night Stalker Association, which always ensures that no widow, child, sibling or bereaved parent is ever neglected or forgotten. Although a pilot or crewman may have left a toddler when he fell, that child has not been neglected two decades later, when the Special Operations Warrior Foundation steps in to aid with college funds. With regularity, and careful and efficient organization, the Night Stalker families gather at many memorial and celebratory functions, where considerably more laughter is heard than tears shed. Each year in the autumn, the birth of the 160th is heralded. Each spring, hundreds of unit members and families gather at the compound before the memorial wall, as those who gave all are recalled aloud to the background wind of rotors whirling.

"Lieutenant Colonel Michael C. Grimm . . . Captain Keith J. Lucas . . . Chief Warrant Officer 4 Clifton P. Wolcott . . . Staff Sergeant Phillip J. Svitak . . . Major Stephen C. Reich . . . Chief Warrant Officer 5 Jamie D. Weeks . . ."

And so it rolls, to the sounds of helos, yet every name means much to all, and even more to some.

There is melancholy in the echo of Mike Grimm's name, for the missions he missed, for the things he would have swelled with pride to see. Yet no doubt without him, and the men who quickly embraced his convictions, there would have been no flag at all to unfurl. Keith Lucas was the first to fall in action, yet every Blackhawk pilot knows the meaning of his name, and swears to mirror his courage, despite the odds or enemy gunfire. Cliff Wolcott—well, his echo brings a smile, for no one ever was more the Night Stalker model of courage as grace under pressure. Crew chiefs proudly raise their chins at the unanswered call for Phillip Svitak, a man who embodied their loyalty and proved it with his life. Steve Reich, whose letters are still fresh and crisp in granite, reminds all that the unit today, no less than decades past, attracts the most brilliant and brave of the ranks. And Jamie Weeks, so recently fallen at the controls of his Little Bird in Iraq, and who spent his entire career as a Night Stalker, elicits a whispered promise to always take the fight to the enemy.

The traditions begun so long ago on that parade ground at Fort Campbell are infrangible now. The unit trains exactly as it will fight. The operational tempo is merely an invitation to excel. Pilots and commanders and crew chiefs retire, as sons and nephews and young men with dreams of helicopter flight fill their flying boots. And when Night Stalkers take to the air, the ghosts of their heroes are always there, looking over their shoulders; not to chastise, but to encourage. They are gone forever yet never forgotten. Their lessons echo in attentive ears, and as each pilot or crewman returns to earth, he will again inevitably pass beneath a portico, where the muted voice of a fallen brother reaches out to him.

Those voices never say, *Do not follow in my path, because you may sacrifice everything.*

Instead, they whisper proudly from the past.

Do what I have done. Risk all, press on. . . .

Night Stalkers Don't Quit!

NIGHT STALKER
TERMINOLOGY

AMC Air Mission Commander; controls the mission from a position within the flight, though not always at the controls.

AO Area of Operation; where a particular military element generally works, such as Europe or Central America.

APU Auxiliary Power Unit; a small turbine engine that provides power when the main engines are not running and is used to start the engines on a Blackhawk or Chinook. Little Birds don't have them.

ARSOTF Army Special Operations Task Force.

Back Enders A slang term for the men who crew the cabins of Blackhawks and Chinooks.

Black SOF Classified Special Operations Forces, such as Delta, the SEALs and others.

CAOC (Kay-Okk) Combined Air Operations Center; forward operating center where all air elements work together.

CASEVAC Casualty Evacuation; an aircraft of opportunity with a medic on board that can extract casualties from a target area.

CONUS The Continental United States.

CSAR Combat Search and Rescue; an aircraft with a built-in team of rescue and extraction personnel, dedicated to responding to downed pilots and crews.

Customers A slang term for the combatants being transported via helicopter.

CWO Chief Warrant Officer; the highest such rank is a CW5.

DAP Direct Action Penetrator; a gunship configuration of the UH-60 Blackhawk (also known as Defensive Armed Penetrator).

DART Downed Aircraft Recovery Team.

ECLs Engine Condition Levers; what the engine throttles are called in a Chinook.

EDRE Emergency Deployment Readiness Exercise.

FARP Forward Area Rearm/Refuel Point.

FAST Flight Aptitude Selection Test; the basic exam taken when applying to flight school.

Flight Lead A senior pilot commanding a flight of helicopters.

FLIR Forward Looking Infrared; a thermal imaging system mounted on the nose of a helicopter. Allows pilots to view objects generating heat on a screen display.

FLOT Forward Line of Troops; the last line of friendly positions before entering enemy territory.

FMQ Fully Mission Qualified; a designation given to a pilot capable of executing all missions.

Front Enders A slang term for the pilots.

Hot LZ A landing zone where you are bound to take enemy fire.

ICS Inter Communications System; the intercom inside an aircraft.

IMC Instrument Meteorological Conditions; flying in such bad weather that you can't see a thing and are using only instruments.

IP Instructor Pilot; a senior aviator tasked with teaching other pilots.

JSOC Joint Special Operations Command; the commanding authority at Fort Bragg/Pope Air Force Base that oversees coordinated special operations efforts.

LZ Landing Zone; an open area large enough to set a helicopter down.

NOE Nap of the Earth; flying fast, low and following the contour lines of geography. A very dangerous enterprise.

NSDQ Night Stalkers Don't Quit.

OCONUS Outside the Continental United States.

PCLs Power Control Levers; the engine controls in a Blackhawk.

PCS Permanent Change of Station; when a soldier transfers to another home base.

PIC Pilot-In-Command; the primary pilot and commander in a helicopter, partnered with a copilot.

QRF Quick Reaction Force; an element of elite soldiers deployable to an emergency on short notice.

RP Release Point (Inbound); the last navigation point en route to the target and the point after which enemy action can be expected.

SAW Squad Automatic Weapon.

SIP Standardization Instructor Pilot; the pilot who trains the Instructor Pilots.

Slick The nickname for the ubiquitous UH-1 Huey helicopter.

SOAR(A) Special Operations Aviation Regiment (Airborne); the 160th, also known as the Night Stalkers.

SOATC Special Operations Aviation Training Company; the in-house training element of the 160th.

SOLE Special Operations Liaison Element; personnel who go downrange to prepare for upcoming special operations.

SR Team Surveillance and Reconnaissance Team; a small unit of customers inserted deep into enemy territory.

TFR Terrain Following Radar; allows the pilots to fly low level in zero-visibility weather conditions.

TOC Tactical Operations Center; usually a field headquarters.

Uncasing the Colors The unfurling of a new military unit's flag when it officially comes into existence.

USASOC U.S. Army Special Operations Command; the command element at Fort Bragg that is the higher headquarters of Army special ops units.

USSOCOM U.S. Special Operations Command; the command element at MacDill Air Force Base that coordinates all U.S. special ops units.

White SOF Unclassified Special Operations Forces, such the U.S. Army Rangers and others that the Department of Defense openly acknowledges.

WO Warrant Officer; a separate military professional career track usually encompassing a particular technical skill, such as piloting a helicopter.

THE NIGHT STALKER
MEMORIAL WALL

Among the many tributes to the members of the special operations aviation community, there is one monument that stands alone. The Night Stalker Memorial Wall, an arrangement of three simple stones, is inscribed with the names of all members of the 160th Special Operations Aviation Regiment (Airborne) who have given their lives in service to our nation. The memorial is located in front of the regimental headquarters on the 160th compound at Fort Campbell, Kentucky, a short distance from the flight line and the mission that these men lived and died for.

Then I heard the voice of the Lord saying,
"Whom shall I send? And who will go for us?"
And I said, "Here am I. Send me!"

—Isaiah 6:8

Names Inscribed on the
Night Stalker Memorial Wall

1980

CW2 Bobby M. Crumley
SP4 Timothy Hensley

1981

CW3 John W. Williams
LTC Michael C. Grimm

1982

SGT Ricky D. Zizelman

1983

CW4 Ralph L. Thompson
CW2 Donald R. Alvey
SGT Claude J. Dunn
SP4 Jerry L. Wilder
PFC Gregory D. Eichner
CW4 Larry K. Jones
CW3 Thomas B. Crossan III
CW2 James N. Jansen
SSG Mark J. Rielly
SSG Luis A. Sanchez
SSG Mark D. Cornwell
CPT Robert E. Brannum
WO1 Allen E. Jennings
CW2 David W. Jordan
CW3 William H. Tuttle
SP4 Richard J. Thompson
CPT Keith J. Lucas

1985

ISG Ronnie R. Orebo

1987

CPT Frederick M. Maddock II

1988

CW3 Stephen A. Hansen
CW3 Jerry H. Landgraf

1989

ILT John R. Hunter
CW2 Wilson B. Owens

1991

CPT Charles W. Cooper
CW3 Michael F. Anderson
SSG Mario Vega-Velazquez
SSG Christopher J. Chapman

1993

MAJ Robert P. Mallory
CW4 Clifton P. Wolcott
CW3 Donovan L. Briley
CW4 Raymond A. Frank
SSG Thomas J. Field
SSG William D. Cleveland, Jr.

1994

CW3 Carlos P. Guerrero

1995

SSG Edwidge Pierre
SGT Jeffrey D. Tarbox

1996

CW5 Walter M. Fox
CW3 Pierre R. desRoches
CW3 William R. Monty, Jr.

SSG Tracy A. Tidwell
SSG Bradley C. Beem

1997

SGT Edward G. Palacio

2002

MAJ Curtis D. Feistner
CPT Bartt D. Owens
CW2 Jody L. Egnor
SSG James Paul Dorrity
SSG Kerry W. Frith
SSG Bruce A. Rushforth, Jr.
SGT Jeremy D. Foshee
SGT Thomas F. Allison
SGT Philip J. Svitak

2003

CW3 Mark S. O'Steen
CW2 Thomas J. Gibbons
SSG Daniel L. Kisling
SGT Gregory M. Frampton

2004

SPC Robert D. Lund

2005

MAJ Stephen C. Reich
MSG James W. Ponder, III
CW4 Chris Scherkenbach
CW3 Corey J. Goodnature
SFC Marcus V. Muralles
SGT Kip A. Jacoby
SFC Michael L. Russell
SSG Shamus O. Goare

2006

CW5 Jamie D. Weeks
MAJ Mathew W. Worrell
SGT Christopher M. Erberich
SGT Michael D. Hall
SGT Rhonald E. Meeks
CW4 Michael L. Wright

INDEX

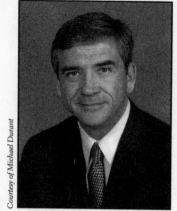

Michael J. Durant   Steven Hartov

Michael J. Durant retired from the Army as a Chief Warrant Officer 4, and is a master aviator. His awards include the Purple Heart, the Distinguished Service Medal, and the POW/MIA ribbon. **Steven Hartov** is an Airborne veteran and author of the international thrillers *The Heat of Ramadan, The Nylon Hand of God,* and *The Devil's Shepherd.* **Robert L. Johnson** served as a Night Stalker for much of his career, then went on to instruct the regiment's volunteers in the history of the unit.